D1596108

WITHDRAWN

# THE AGE OF SUSPICION

". . . I believe that that community is already in process of dissolution where each man begins to eye his neighbor as a possible enemy, where nonconformity with the accepted creed, political as well as religious, is a mark of disaffection; where denunciation, without specification or backing, takes the place of evidence; where orthodoxy chokes freedom of dissent; where faith in the eventual supremacy of reason has become so timid that we dare not enter our convictions in the open lists to win or lose . . ."

JUDGE LEARNED HAND

of

# The AGE SUSPICION

## JAMES A. WECHSLER

GREENWOOD PRESS, PUBLISHERS
WESTPORT, CONNECTICUT

46618

Grateful acknowledgment is made to *Punch* magazine for permission to reprint the material on pages 321-323.

FOR NANCY

# Acknowledgments

Many who helped in the preparation of this book are identified in the story, but others, I am sure, have been forgotten in haste, and to them I apologize. I am sure the following list should be longer:

Nancy Wechsler, who is really co-author; Herbert Wechsler, whose wise and generous companionship is inadequately indicated herein; Dorothy Schiff, whose courage and friendship were invaluable, especially in the rough days of Part Three; my colleagues in ADA—Joseph Rauh, Arthur Schlesinger, Jr., and James Loeb; my *Post* associates, especially Richard Manson, Paul Sann, Max Lerner, William Dufty and Joseph Lash; and many others who helped in the preparation of various sections, including Kenneth Crawford, Paul Hagen, Elzie Wechsler, David Ginsburg, Harold Lavine, Reed Harris, Arthur Lelyveld, Jr., William Golub, Robert Bendiner, Ruth Wechsler, Stanley Colbert and Sterling Lord. Several passages in chapters VII and X are republished here with the permission of Morris Rubin, editor of *The Progressive* (Madison, Wisconsin) in which they first appeared.

From the start I had the benefit of the thoughtful counsel and warm encouragement of Saxe Commins of Random House, and his assistant Naomi Bliven, and the tireless research and technical help of Cecile Eddy.

I, of course, am solely responsible for the words, as for the deeds.

J.A.W.

# Contents

# Prologue

In a way this story begins at a few minutes before 7 o'clock on the evening of April 23, 1953. It had been a relatively uneventful day and it seemed to be just about over. The editorials for the next day's *Post* were nearly finished; one of them, commenting on reductions in the Voice of America personnel, observed: "For many months the Kremlin has been trying to drive us from the air waves of the world. It probably never dreamed that we would so recklessly silence ourselves."

I had made my usual optimistic telephone call to Nancy, telling her I would be home for dinner shortly; I had assured Michael (aged ten) and Holly (aged six) that I would see them before their bedtimes. My desk was uncommonly clean; that afternoon I had gone through the fortnightly exercise of answering the unanswered and filing the unanswerable. This clearing of the decks is always accompanied by fatalistic jokes because it invariably precedes some new crisis that results in the reappearance of the debris.

The press-association wires next door to my office carried no portents of any big news. The city room outside was deserted, as though confident the world had paused until tomorrow's Night Extra. It really looked as if I would be home on time for dinner.

Then my secretary walked in and said Don Surine of the McCarthy committee was calling me from Washington.

The name was familiar. Although I had never met the man, I

knew he was a professional investigator who had been dismissed by the FBI in 1950 and had subsequently achieved renown in Senator McCarthy's service. This was the second time in about a month that I had heard from him. Several weeks earlier he had telephoned me in connection with the committee's attack on Reed Harris, then deputy chief of the Voice of America. Harris's name had been found among the sponsors of a dinner given by the American Student Union in 1937, my last year as an officer of the ASU. This letterhead had become a key document in the effort to prove that Harris was a dangerous man. It was the prize exhibit because it was, I think, the only one.

I had explained to Surine during the earlier phone call that Harris's presence on the list of sponsors for that event could hardly be considered significant. Many eminent anti-communists had loaned us their names; Surine himself volunteered the admission that such men as Norman Thomas and the late Benjamin Stolberg were also on the letterhead. I explained that sponsorship of this dinner in no way suggested any continuing link with the organization. When it became apparent that my testimony could hardly help destroy Harris, Surine made plain that my services as a witness would not be required.

I thought about that conversation for many days afterward. Once upon a time, in a different setting, the name of Reed Harris meant a great deal to me; that was in 1932 when I was a freshman at Columbia and he was a senior, editing the Columbia *Spectator*. Only a few days before Surine first telephoned me, I had watched McCarthy's interrogation of Harris on television. It was a badgering, angry review of a tumultuous time on Morningside Heights more than twenty years ago. In this mirthless TV show all those intervening years seemed to fall away. If it had not been for Harris's gray hairs, one might have imagined he was a college senior being grilled by a university board of trustees in the spring of 1932. Now, though he was a man in his middle years, all he had said and done in his postgraduate lifetime was being treated as inconsequential; the often ill-chosen words he had published in a volume called *King Football* more than two decades ago were

being hurled at him as if they were the text of a subversive direc-
tive he had just issued from a strategic Government post.

Sometimes wearily, sometimes heatedly, always with dignity,
Harris endeavored to convince this group of grown-up Senators,
led by the junior Senator from Wisconsin, that there were
sounder standards by which to judge his life than the purple
prose he had composed in 1932. But the chief interrogator always
came back to that. So did the chief counsel, a petulant young man
who was now just a little older than Harris had been in the days
that were being recalled to him. Vainly Harris pleaded that a
man's life is a whole thing, not to be finally measured by any of
its fragments.

For me the spectacle seemed a prelude as well as a post-mortem
because I had long assumed I would one day find myself in the
same witness chair. Under my editorship the *Post* had repeatedly
clashed with Senator McCarthy. In September, 1951, we had published the first comprehensive newspaper account of his curious
public career. It was an unflattering portrait, containing many
hints of the more devastating disclosures that were to come in the
official report of the Senate subcommittee that explored Mc-
Carthy's record. On a number of occasions McCarthy had publicly
taken notice of me and it seemed only a matter of time before
he would arrange, on some pretext or other, a personal audience
like the one he had granted Harris.

Nor was it too difficult to project the pattern of such a hearing.
I was certainly more vulnerable than Harris. In the language that
now sounds like a refrain, Harris was not now and never had been
a communist; I had been a member of the Young Communist
League from April, 1934, through 1937; I was a member of the
YCL Executive Committee for several months during that period.
On the other hand, I had—or thought I had—certain advantages
over Harris if and when such a confrontation took place. For he
had spent most of his adult life as a Government employee. He
had worked as an administrator, rather than as a writer, most of
that time. When the day of senatorial judgment came, he could
point only to his quiet record of Government activity as proof of

honorable citizenship; but what, after all, did service to the governments of Franklin D. Roosevelt and Harry Truman mean in the
American debating society of 1953? Such a man now found himself
regarded as guilty until he had produced incontrovertible evidence
of innocence, whatever that may be. Harris's problem was to produce "affirmative evidence"; unless one has written and spoken
publicly, such documentation is hard to find. Unlike Harris, I did
have such a record; I have written and spoken throughout the years
since I left the Young Communist League. On innumerable occasions I have been assailed in the official communist press as a
terrible species of red-baiter, and the newspaper I have edited for
more than four years has been described in the same journals as an
unconscionable organ of warmongering American imperialism.

Watching the Harris examination with a plausible premonition
that my turn would come soon, I had begun mentally assorting
the kind of "affirmative evidence" I would offer and even anticipating with some delight the impact such documentation must
surely have upon the committee chairman. I hasten to say that I
underestimated his resilience under fire; let it never be said of this
Wisconsin ex-judge that he is a man who lets evidence influence
his verdicts.

Now, on the evening of April 23rd, Surine was saying that the
committee wanted me to appear at an executive session the following day. He was unable, he insisted, to tell me exactly what the
session was to be about.

"Somebody else has been handling the investigation, but I think
they want to ask you about some names and places," he said. The
impression he gave was that the committee merely wanted the
benefit of my guidance in connection with some inquiry into somebody other than myself.

My first guess was that they were still trying to unearth some
desperate disclosure about Reed Harris and that I was being summoned to testify as to who said what to whom on some afternoon
in the offices of the Columbia *Spectator* twenty-two years ago.

I was wrong. Fortunately, I was sufficiently alive to the alternative possibility to make some preparation for the encounter. I spent

several hours that evening assembling some of the material I had
written and some that had been written about me.

The excuse later given for the hearing, called on this brief notice
and without advance intimation as to its substance, was that a book
I had written had been found on the shelves of a United States
Information Service library somewhere overseas. Through two
hearings and the months that have elapsed since then the committee has never indicated which book it was or where it was found
—a point of some relevance, since two of the four books I had
written were emphatically anti-communist in content and viewpoint. Neither Roy Cohn nor G. David Schine, the intrepid
young investigators who had just returned from a European tour,
was able to resolve this simple issue of fact.

But the hearing was not about my books. It was about the newspaper I edit, and about me. In another sense it was about a period
in American history in which I played a minor but not untypical
part; it was about an era whose history has, one might say, been
rewritten by ghosts even before it has been written by scholars.

It was Senator McCarthy's thesis, bulwarked by the essays of
a sociologist named Walter Winchell, that I not only was but still
am an agent of the communist conspiracy; that the numberless
anti-communist words I have written and spoken in the last fifteen
years—from the age of twenty-two to thirty-seven—have been elab-
orately designed to conceal my true allegiance; and that the proof
of my continuing sin is that I have shown no reverence for committees such as his and offered no testimony that has resulted in
anyone's indictment.

In another time an editor might properly have challenged the
basis of the proceeding and refused to respond to many of the
questions. There was not the slightest suggestion that I had concealed information vital to any authorized inquiry; my former associations were well known and acknowledged. The hearing was
manifestly intended as a harassment to me and as a warning to
other editors who have displayed inadequate respect for the committee chairman.

But ours is an age of suspicion—suspicion rooted partly in our legitimate anxiety about the Soviet threat to free society and heightened by the awesome dread of atomic annihilation. In such an age silence is no answer. Its misuse by the communists has deprived it of any eloquence it ever had. Indeed it might be said that our republic is haunted by two kinds of silence—the calculated reticence of those who have something to hide and the deepening timidity of others who have nervously concluded that it is safer to have nothing to say.

It was easy to reject silence; but what remains worth saying now that I have testified? From the time I left the Young Communist League in 1937 I have tried neither to grovel nor to revel in the memories of that experience.

That is why I have heretofore hesitated to write such detailed reminiscences as these. The libraries are crowded with the retrospections of those to whom a communist past seems the only meaningful period of their lives. I still prefer to believe that what has happened to me since 1937—and what I may still do—will eventually be deemed more memorable than my three and one-half years as a youthful communist. If I live to a reasonable old age, that will have been a small fraction of my total existence. I should like my epitaph to indicate that here rests something more than one more ex-communist, a species with which the graveyards of the world are already crowded.

There was another ground for reluctance. To those of us who served neither as international operatives nor as members of espionage cells, the communist interlude in our lives has steadily assumed an aspect of grotesque unreality. It has become hard to remember the intensities of feeling that endured even amid gross absurdities; it is even harder to relate them to the modern crisis.

There was also the haunting horror of seeming to exhibit oneself as a "case." The most depressing moments in the aftermath of the McCarthy hearings were those when I heard the episode being described as "the Wechsler case." I have known quite a few cases and only in rare instances do they recover. Once a man begins to feel that his own argument with some segment of society transcends all other business before the house, he is approaching the stage at which he is likely to start speaking of himself in the third person, a tendency, incidentally, to which the Senator from Wisconsin succumbed early in his career.

There was the final inhibition that such a recital would mean the almost continuous use of the first-person pronoun; an editor should be thinking about the country's present rather than his own past.

All those considerations would, I think, have been decisive if it had not been for my encounter with McCarthy. His distortion of my unexciting testimony about a fragment of the thirties finally seemed to make the whole story worth telling. It is to him that many of these words are dedicated; for it can be truthfully said that without his expression of interest in my political travels, this chronicle would not have been recorded.

So, approaching my thirty-eighth birthday, I find myself engaged in this somewhat premature exploration of my own past. If thereby we gain any understanding of what once made a number of young men and women turn to communism—and away from it—we may be somewhat more capable of talking intelligibly and even intelligently to the growing children of this era.

At least this story may underline the nightmare quality of some of the inquiries to which the country is now being subjected. Once upon a time what a man did or thought fifteen or eighteen years earlier was not the crucially important thing about him, if everything he had done in the ensuing years was a repudiation of original sin. That no longer seems to be true; the obsession with the thirties has deepened. Investigators yet unborn may one day inherit today's dubious archives and proceed to re-examination of the survivors of the period. It could go on almost indefinitely.

Where were you on the night of, say, April 23, 1934? You probably haven't the faintest idea. Perhaps some of you were in your perambulators and others of you had not yet been conceived. But some thousands of us will face the question interminably because we grew up in the decade to which all the world's current woes are indiscriminately assigned.

Most of us disengaged ourselves from communism before the involvement was fatal. Most of us were spared entrapment in the underground. Yet though we escaped in time, we shall obviously not be permitted to forget that we paused there at all. We could not have quite forgotten anyway, for communism has become the great issue of our time, and each of us must meet it in terms of his own conscience and experience.

Mine was a less lurid journey than those described by some more celebrated former communists whose adventures were more dramatic and prolonged than my own. It was the axiom of our elders that young radicals become old conservatives, as if this were an inevitable life pattern; but if it is true that some former communists have become more dogmatically rightist than the reactionaries they once spurned, if some have even become sympathizers of a domestic neo-fascism almost as intolerant, inhumane and irrational as Stalinism, there are countless former communists who have unostentatiously embraced the calmer credo of democratic liberalism. They have tried to retain a sense of identification with the oppressed and the unfortunate; they have refused to abandon hope in man's ability to create a good society. And they have cherished the one piece of wisdom which the communist experience inadvertently imparts—an appreciation of the grandeur of the free mind and the wretchedness of the man who has abdicated his own reason.

# I

# The Age of Rebellion

# 1

We who belonged to the class of '35 were the youngest participants in the all-university exercises which inaugurated Columbia
University's 178th academic year. The date of the ceremony was
September 23, 1931, and, in accordance with custom, the speaker
was President Nicholas Murray Butler. His theme that day was the
phenomenon of mediocre world statesmanship. "Why are midgets
so often found in the seats of the mighty?" he asked.

From many viewpoints the day seemed an appropriate one on
which to ask the question. If we may judge the predicament in
which men found themselves by the variety of dark tidings that
occupied most of next day's New York *Times*, this day, like so
many before and after, contained no hint that our class was favored
with any bright omens. Almost everywhere humanity was seemingly sick and adrift.

Although stocks were rising on the Exchange even as we listened
to Dr. Butler, the flurry was itself attributed to grim news: the
United States Steel Corporation's announcement of a 10 per cent
wage cut, followed at once by similar action by other major corporations. The development evoked angry protest from William
Green, the AFL's usually mild-mannered president. It was, he
charged, a violation of an earlier pledge to maintain wages "during
this distressing period of unemployment"; it proved anew that
"employers of labor know only one thing and that is to reduce

wages when economic depressions come upon us." Senator David Walsh pointedly contrasted the cuts with an earlier disclosure that the president of one of the large steel firms was drawing an annual income of $1,600,000.

The news from all over had a somber tone. A dispatch from Shanghai disclosed that China's major cities had observed "National Humiliation Day" to lament the Japanese occupation of Manchuria; "All China Mourns Japan's Aggression," the headline said. In Washington Henry L. Stimson had sent urgent notes to both powers imploring a cessation of hostilities; Moscow warned Tokyo that it was sending troops to "protect the Soviet's half-interest in the Chinese Eastern Railway" and War Commissar Voroshilov was reported flying from Moscow to Manchuria. In Geneva Clarence K. Streit was prophetically cabling the *Times*: "League officials believe that in the Sino-Japanese issue in Manchuria the existence of the Briand-Kellogg Pact and the League itself are at stake."

In Berlin twenty-three youthful followers of a man named Adolf Hitler were sentenced to jail terms ranging from six months to a year for staging violent anti-Semitic demonstrations on the Jewish New Year's Day. In handing down the sentences the presiding judge said: "If one party tries to open the winter as the season for riots, the courts of the state must open the season with sentences which are not child's play." The same dispatch, however, quoted Carl Severing, the Prussian Minister of Finance, as calling for a halt to all talk of "forthcoming coups d'état or disturbances"; such excited language, he said, could have a damaging effect on German credit abroad.

This day of Columbia's opening exercises was full of peril and panacea. The American Legion convention was preparing to ask President Hoover to appoint a nonpartisan council of national defense equipped with "wartime powers" and authorized to take steps to end "the unrest, indecision and dissatisfaction of the present economic crisis." Charles F. Abbott, executive director of the American Institute of Steel Construction, contended that much of the tension could be relieved if the Government suspended the antitrust law and permitted combinations in quest of "reasonable profits." In a statement released after a conference with Mr. Hoover, Abbott conceded that "it is highly desirable to alleviate human distress and to effect a more equable distribution of material goods," but added this note of caution: "We can do much more in this direction with the agencies we now have, and without upsetting the capitalistic principle upon which our business is based. But we must not forget our fundamentals."

On Broadway *Shoot the Works*, Heywood Broun's co-operative revue combining the talent of numerous unemployed actors, was continuing at the George M. Cohan Theatre. In Boston, 20,000 people attended a baseball game conducted for the benefit of the local unemployment fund; a similar event was scheduled for the following day in New York City. In New York, too, Charles Burlingham, president of the Welfare Council, voiced hope that bread lines might be eliminated from the city's landscape in the coming winter through the creation of a Central Registration Bureau for Homeless Men.

"The experience of the past winter, when public-spirited generous citizens, impressed by the problem of the destitute homeless, caused the creation of over eighty bread lines throughout the city, serving more than 80,000 meals, is a warning of what may be expected in the future unless steps are taken now to prevent repetition," said Mr. Burlingham.

Senator Burton K. Wheeler, passing through New York that day after a trip through several western states, said the plight of the farmers was growing steadily worse. In some northwest areas, he reported, "many farmers are unable to pay their taxes, owing to low prices."

The day was cool and pleasant. Dr. Butler, who was about to begin his thirtieth year as university president, was neither a mirthful nor fiery orator and he did not choose on this occasion to address himself too directly to what might have been called the burning issues. Most of us rarely, if ever, saw him again in the course of our undergraduate careers, which is probably a pity; our lingering vision of him tended to be that of an ageing, pontifical man who had assumed the dimensions of a myth and whose pronouncements usually seemed an invitation to irreverent burlesque. He deplored lack of leadership, but it cannot be said, even in retrospect, that he offered any strikingly fresh insights. If the *Times* had not thoughtfully published the text of his remarks, I should have been unable to reproduce any of them here. His point was that democracy seemed incapable of choosing wise men for high posts. Noting that the world had experimented with many methods for selecting leaders, he recited this extraordinary passage:

> Taking the civilized peoples of the world as a whole, it may be said that all these methods have now disappeared with the exception of two, namely, election and the assumption of power by a virtual dictator whose authority rests upon a powerful and well-organized body of opinion. It is rather startling for convinced believers in democracy to observe that this latter system of choosing rulers, if it be a system, appears to bring into authority and power men of far greater intelligence, far stronger character and far more courage than does the system of election.

On this note of democratic despair we were officially welcomed to Columbia. Dr. Butler's intimation that the people of despotisms had been more fortunate in selecting their tyrants than were the citizens of democracy in choosing their leaders was delivered some months before the advent of Adolf Hitler and the departure of Herbert Hoover. But Mussolini and Stalin were very much in business, and it was, the knowing ones said at the time, the Italian dictator who had conspicuously impressed our university president.

What now seems most memorable about Dr. Butler's melancholy greeting to young men and women in that autumn of 1931 is not what it said but what it did not say: its emptiness of spirit, its querulous pessimism about the democratic future, its impatience with the foibles of freedom.

Neither those introductory words from on high nor the bleak front pages cast too depressing a shadow over the class of '35 in that initial autumn.

The record should show at this point that I was approaching my sixteenth birthday when I entered college.

I was a year or two younger than most of my classmates, an asset or liability acquired by attending Townsend Harris High School, where the usual four-year curriculum was compressed into three years. This now defunct institution was a lively public school which had severe entrance examinations. As a result it boasted championship chess teams, and suffered almost uninterrupted athletic disaster. Derisively known as a "school for bright boys," Harris developed in us a certain self-conscious arrogance; this was our answer to the contemptuous parodies of those who, in our view, were vulgarly seeking to establish the supremacy of brawn over brain.

My entrance into Columbia was almost thwarted at the last moment by my inability to achieve a qualifying mark in the Regents' examination in physics. I had to spend the pre-college summer taking a special course in that incomprehensible subject and then, finally, another pre-admission exam. My bewilderment in the sciences has never left me. I am still fighting the fuse box in the atomic age.

The only certainty I brought to college was that in the long run I was going to be some sort of journalist and that everything else was largely preparatory. As far back as I can remember that was perfectly clear; at a boys' camp preposterously known as Camp Chicopee, I became editor of *The Chicopee Chirps* at the age of eleven; I was the only aspirant for the post and the renown associated with it was a sublimation for my deficiencies at bat. (Although I loved baseball and studied the archives of the game harder than most boys, it was to be said of me early in life: "Good field, no hit." I was gradually relegated to the post of third-base coach and I recall the misery of the afternoon when my failure to send a runner home from third cost Chicopee's Intermediates a game with our bitter rivals at Equinunk. So I buried myself deeper in *The Chirps*.)

At Townsend Harris I quickly volunteered for the *Stadium*, the school's weekly newspaper, and there, as at college, I spent an inordinate number of hours pretending to be a full-time newspaperman. My gods then were H. L. Mencken and Heywood Broun; I somehow mated the cynicism of one and the passion of the other into a single image of virtuous valor.

Under the spell of such rebellious spirits I began brooding about faculty "domination" of student affairs and finally, when I became editor of the *Stadium*, our little staff decided that the time for revolt was at hand. We published a front-page editorial deploring the faculty's greediness for power. To avoid any suppression of this manifesto, we neglected to send it through the usual channels of faculty censorship and, immediately upon publication of the document, I was relieved of my duties as editor. But this clash with autocracy had a sentimental ending which rather removed the sting. Although my name was removed from the masthead, I continued to work on the *Stadium* and, to my astonishment, was given a medal for this underground labor at our graduation exercises; that is the kind of school Townsend Harris was.

All newspapermen like to believe they were born with the scent of printer's ink about them. To make such a claim I must skip a generation; my father started out as a schoolteacher, earned his way through law school and has found his greatest joy in painting; my brother, six years older than I, always seemed destined to be a lawyer, and became a professor of law at an implausibly early age.

My father's father, on the other hand, had a long and stormy career as a rabbi and as an editor. According to a volume called *Israel's Scholars in America*, edited by Dr. Ben-Zion Eisenstadt and published at the turn of the century, Rabbi Dr. Moshe Wechsler, born in 1851 in the Hungarian town of Mihaly, was in his early years editor of *The Jewish Press* in the Hungarian town of Miscolz. The paper's existence was abruptly ended by a fire which swept its plant; my grandfather then migrated to America. He arrived in New York City in 1882 and shortly thereafter went to work for *The Jewish Daily News*, the first Jewish daily in the United States. Then he started a daily of his own, known as *The Jewish*

*Times*, and Dr. Eisenstadt summarizes my grandfather's editorship this way:

> He [Dr. Wechsler] was taking positions requiring some understanding of political, moral and religious views. . . . He spoke out on controversial issues . . . and he never hesitated to handle currently unpopular issues; he had no fears of social disapproval or possible restrictions on dissenting opinions.

He was an editorial writer and an orator, a Talmudic scholar and crusader.

Possibly, then, that is how the fragrance of the print shop was transmitted to me.

It is hard to reconstruct, at thirty-seven, how young it was to be just under sixteen when the class of '35 reached Columbia in September, 1931.

I was a Columbia man, wearing my freshman cap. Columbia's attempt to conform with many of the rituals of collegiate existence was half-hearted and awkward. It seemed to be increasingly difficult to sustain any degree of enthusiasm for the enforcement of "freshman rules" which dictated, among other things, that no first-year man should leave a football game until the final whistle or stand beside the fence at Hamilton Hall. In times past there had been a band known as "The Black Avengers" which rigorously imposed these regulations; but each year it had apparently become harder to recruit members for that punitive patrol.

Columbia suffered from a split personality. It was a great educational plant located in the heart of a huge metropolis; it had no vast expanse of green terrain which was the orthodox conception of a campus; many students lived at their homes in the city rather than in the college dormitories. This was no college town; the college widow was the unsmiling statuesque lady known as Alma Mater who sat impassively on the steps of the Seth Low Library through all the stormy scenes of the ensuing years.

But Columbia had a pride and prejudice of its own. It wanted its students to achieve equality of social status with the sons of the Ivy League. It also had large intellectual pretensions, and was torn between a desire to imitate the prevailing collegiate capers and an impulse to ridicule such juvenile exhibitionism. When the victory seemed to warrant it, Columbia men could tear down the goal posts as energetically as Pennsylvania men, but many undergraduates always stood around in embarrassment when it happened.

We did not enter Columbia in that autumn of 1931 as a band of socially conscious freshmen eager to plunge into our Marx or to herald a new undergraduate age. If, on the word of some of our elders, the world seemed to be cracking up, we nevertheless harbored dreams and schemes that were all predicated on the assumption that life would go on.

Whatever our private musings, we were at Columbia to prepare for conventional success in life; we felt we were lucky to be there because, according to legend, a college degree would give us a big advantage over our contemporaries in the ultimate pursuit of success. Many depression-struck middle-class families were making real sacrifices to finance the education of the family prodigy; surely the investment could not be a delusion. To them and to us a university did not exist for the end of learning itself; to be a Columbia man meant to have a certain running start in the great competition ahead. We really assumed that the story of civilization had to turn out all right in the end.

"The well-loved child of the middle class is taught about the future by means of the promises made to him—the birthday gifts will come and the Christmas gifts will come, and the performance at the Hippodrome, and camp and college and the trip to Europe," Lionel Trilling has written.* "How the mind of the fortunate young man of the middle class is presided over by the future! It is his mark, his Muse—for it is feminine in its seductiveness—and sets him apart from the young men of the truly lower class and from the young men of the truly upper class."

At Baker Field, Ralph Hewitt, one of the greatest quarterbacks in Columbia history, drilled with what coach Lou Little described as a "promising, fighting team." The campus observed its usual

* *The Middle of the Journey.* The Viking Press: 1947.

autumn ceremonies, dominated by athletic rallies and the beginning of fraternity pledging. Most of us tried hard to get into the spirit of these gatherings.

I had become a candidate for *Spectator*; on the second day of college the call for freshmen applicants was issued and I responded promptly, along with forty or fifty others. That was when I first saw Reed Harris. He spoke to us briefly but my recollection is unusually sharp. He was a tall, reserved, soft-spoken young man and he seemed terrifyingly mature. His chief associates were Emanuel Freedman, now the foreign editor of the *Times*, Don Ross, now a member of the staff of the *Herald Tribune*, and Lamoyne Jones, who served as Wendell Willkie's key publicity aide during Willkie's last sad days. They were an impressive, formidable quartet; they all seemed incredibly old and wise.

The functions of a freshman candidate for *Spectator* were limited; my principal assignment in those early months was to cover hockey games played by Columbia's unofficial team before empty galleries at Madison Square Garden on Sunday afternoons. On other days of the week I performed a variety of humble chores, perhaps the most responsible of which was to carry Manny Freedman's copy to the city desk of the *World-Telegram*. He was its Columbia correspondent and therefore the closest approach to a live professional newspaperman I had known.

That opening semester was comparatively tranquil; it was, indeed, almost the last continuous interval of peace Dean Herbert Hawkes enjoyed during the four-year sojourn of the class of '35. We were intermittently aware that the world showed no significant sign of improvement but we were absorbed with other things, not excluding girls. The only historic hour of decision we faced was the choice of a fraternity. Mine turned out to be Zeta Beta Tau.

Those months as a "Zebe" undoubtedly played an unforeseen part in my evolution as a campus radical. If anything pointed up the ambiguity and aimlessness of undergraduate customs, it was the life of an earnest fraternity man whose commitment to "the house" transcended all other earthly loyalties.

What I recall most about my rather brief identification with the clan was the total absence of any serious conversation, beyond, of course, the very serious speculation about who had done what to whom after the Saturday-night dance. This was the winter of 1932. There was tangible evidence of human distress everywhere in the city. But the fraternity house was the last refuge of an earlier, carefree student time, when young men were expected to devote themselves to love and liquor.

Through the portals of the ZBT house passed some of the nicest girls I've ever met, and remarkably few of them went upstairs. Many of the brethren were bright, witty and generous, and many of them have become useful citizens. But the infantilism of fraternity life was embarrassing.

While other matters triumphed over mind along Fraternity Row, a dissenting voice was beginning to jangle Columbia's nerves. It belonged to *Spectator*, where Reed Harris and his associate Don Ross were using the editorial page to offend campus complacency. This all started in the first issues of *Spectator* in my freshman year; before it was over, many of us were never to be quite the same again.

Earlier that year Harold Laski had written his celebrated *Harper's* article entitled: "Why Don't Your Young Men Care?" "He [the student] studies politics as he studies biology or the fine arts," Laski wrote. "It is a unit in the taking of a degree. It has no connection with the prospect of citizenship. . . . To improve the student's economic or social position has been the purpose of university life rather than a desire to enrich the community by disinterested service."

Harris and Ross were two young men who cared. What I found most intriguing about these rebellious characters was that they bore no resemblance to the stereotype of a radical. They were both fraternity men. They looked like their orthodox brethren; they dressed like them; they just didn't talk like them. Harris had prepared for Columbia at the Staunton Military Academy, never hitherto regarded as a training school for subversion.

Overnight, this duo began to inflict a series of shocks on the university community. They preached no doctrinaire radicalism. They merely questioned everything that was sacred. On the first day of the year, just twenty-four hours after Dr. Butler's inaugural address, *Spectator* greeted us gaily: "New students and old, you are at the high altar of education in the American manner. This is the home of N. M. Butler and myriads of professors who are planning to write a book this year if they ever get around to it."

They lampooned the fraternity system; they suggested that Norman Thomas was the best qualified candidate for mayor in the special city election that November; and—perhaps most explosive of all—they laughed at "king football" at a time when Columbia was at last showing promise of achieving the gridiron glory for which so many alumni longed.

"Personally we'd exchange the whole Columbia football team for a place in the country with cows, chickens and eight hours' sleep each night," *Spectator* gibed one day.

There was a deafening uproar.

When *Spectator* reiterated its view that "college football had become a professional racket," the alumni secretary remarked, "The editor of the *Spectator* is too serious-minded. He should be more collegiate." There were rumors and reports that the university officialdom was irate; on Fraternity Row there were sounds of increasing impatience over Harris's "troublemaking"; and several members of the football team were reported eager to tackle him on a side street.

While the controversy over the care and feeding of football players was stirring the loudest noises, what *Spectator* was saying about the state of the nation was a good deal more provocative. Although most of us still led reasonably sheltered lives, the depression shadowed the college's editorial page. *Spectator* dourly reminded us each morning that many of our fellow men were in bad shape. On Thanksgiving eve these thoughts appeared:

> We have been stimulated to do a bit of thinking about what we are to be thankful for this year . . . an inspection of the soup lines of the town was very productive. Here, shivering

miserably, threadbare coats drawn ineffectively about chilled necks, waiting patiently for the long line in which they were standing to move forward, so that they might acquire their meager portion of free soup, we found graduates of the leading universities—some members of the class of 1931, and others of classes not much older. Wearily these men, we discovered, have been dragging themselves from office to office in search of a job—regardless of its nature. . . . Yet these men a short while ago left college filled with ambitions of a type so high that only a newly graduated and naïve senior could conceive of them. . . .

Just what can these unfortunate standees in the city's soup lines be thinking?

These came under the heading of dangerous thoughts, especially since they were being voiced by young men who could not be classified as hopeless neurotics or alien crackpots. Yet perhaps the wonder is that such opinions made no sweeping headway on the campus in that winter of national discontent. Infinitely more distress was created by Harris's war on football than by his visit to the bread lines.

"Lord, give us a leader out of this wilderness," pleaded *Spectator* in February, 1932, after critically appraising and rejecting all the prospective presidential candidates of the major parties. But the radical contingents on the campus remained small and scattered. There was a Socialist Club and there was also a Social Problems Club which the handful of campus communists ran. Neither group seriously made its presence felt until the sudden announcement on the afternoon of Friday, April 1st, that Reed Harris had been expelled from Columbia.

For most of the ensuing three weeks the campus was swept by turmoil. It was an interlude which probably had as much impact on a segment of that undergraduate generation as anything that happened to us during our four years at Columbia.

The situation was tinged with a ridiculous irony; Dean Hawkes, a friendly, pleasant man of the old academic school, had not realized that the day he expelled Harris was the last day of Harris's term as editor of *Spectator*. If he had known that, he would hardly have taken so drastic an action and all the ensuing tumult would have been avoided. Thus is history shaped by absent-mindedness.

The issue that nominally brought matters to a head was a series of articles published by *Spectator* criticizing the management of the main university dining hall. In explaining the expulsion, the Dean said: "Material published in the *Spectator* during the last few days is a climax to a long series of discourtesies, innuendoes and misrepresentations which have appeared in this paper during the current academic year and calls for disciplinary action."

The Dean undoubtedly believed he had been subjected to unbearable provocation by young men who persisted in rocking the academic boat. With equal certainty many of us viewed the event as a shattering episode in what we came to describe rather grandly as our "disillusionment" with the professed liberalism of Columbia. Our sour verdict was sustained by many eminent essayists of the time.

The campus quickly divided. For the large number of students who sympathized with Harris, this was a first glimpse of communists in action and, as was to occur so often, they simply seemed to be the most dedicated and energetic champions of a great cause. Few of us paused then, or for a long time afterward, to examine their motives or to reflect on the paradox of their espousal of free speech for everyone except those with whom they disagreed. They resolutely took command of the proceedings and, since no college course had tutored the rest of us in such arts as the preparation of picket signs, the communists swiftly dominated the machinery of protest. They were a small but busy handful; there could not have been more than thirty of them on the Columbia campus at the time. But they were tireless. They had discovered an issue which had shaken even the most staid sectors of the university; and, with the exception of an even smaller group of university socialists, there was no one else around to assume leadership of the indignant throng.

Technically, the instrument through which the communists operated was the Social Problems Club, which later officially became the Columbia affiliate of the National Student League. The NSL was, in turn, the front organization established by the Communist Party in 1931 for the purpose of winning the "broad student masses" to the communist banner. There was nothing very deceptive about this elaborate structure. Nearly everybody knew the SPC was in some way or other run by communists but, at that juncture, not too many cared. After all, they did paint the picket signs.

There was one point of friction. Soon after the protest rallies began, the communists started to import their adherents from other metropolitan colleges to augment the ranks of rebellion and, incidentally, to give the event the international significance which they believed it deserved. This mingling of non-Columbia stock with the pure breed caused resentment among some of Harris's moderate supporters who felt it was asking a little too much to require Columbia men to share their campus with City College and NYU radicals, even in the interests of a lofty principle. But the communists patiently explained that such reactions were chiefly symptoms of bourgeois prejudice.

The expulsion had occurred on Friday. There was an inevitable week-end lull in which the communist group caucused and painted signs and feverishly mobilized while the rest of the university drank, danced or aimlessly debated what to do about the injustice that had befallen Harris. On Sunday night, about a thousand members of the National Student League, drawn from schools all over the city, met in a downtown theatre. There Donald Henderson, an instructor in economics at Columbia and one of the earliest campus radicals, announced: "The National Student League has accepted leadership of the fight to reinstate Reed Harris."

On Monday, there was a slight change of plans. While it had been announced previously that the Social Problems Club would stage a rally that day, *Spectator* carried the news that a group of "anonymous conservative students" sympathetic to Harris planned to stage a meeting on the steps of the Columbia Library. This was an obvious effort to conduct the protest in a manner befitting Columbia's traditions and to remove any hint of radicalism from the venture. The Social Problems Club adroitly canceled its own meeting, pledged its full support to the "conservative" gathering and managed to provide most of the speakers for the "conservative" rally.

It was one of the communist speakers who proposed to the assemblage that a student strike be held on Wednesday and most of the fifteen hundred students in the audience cheered the recommendation. That made it official.

What probably contributed as much as anything else to the intensity of feeling in the pro-Harris campaign was the behavior of those who had appointed themselves to defend the university's good name against the combined menace of Harris, the Social Problems Club and the non-Columbia forces of insurrection. They called themselves "The Spartans." On the day of the initial mass meeting they arrived to heckle; when one of their number was invited to speak his mind, he strode to the statue of Alma Mater, declared, "It's a lot of bull," and retreated. Another Spartan then stepped forward to elaborate. Referring to Harris's exposure of varied abuses at the university, he shouted: "Everyone knows these things were going on but Harris had no right to bring them up." Such nonsense inevitably strengthened the belief of the Harris legions that witlessness was arrayed with oppression on the other side of the campus barricades.

Our faith in the virtue of our cause was enhanced by the violence which reached its peak on the day of the student strike. The first big scene occurred outside of Hamilton Hall that morning. There, along with many others who were picketing the building, Rob Hall was distributing leaflets imploring students to shun their classes in behalf of Harris and academic freedom. Hall was an affable, quiet Alabaman. A college senior, he was one of the leaders of the communist group; despite this unconcealed quirk, he was generally well liked. He is one of the few Columbia communists of that era who remained a communist in good standing throughout all the subsequent debacles of world communism, later rising to the managing editorship of the *Daily Worker*, then becoming its Washington correspondent. Outwardly he always seemed to remain untroubled by the news that his mind had been changed again.

On that morning he was, as usual, smoking a pipe. Suddenly he was approached by one of the star ends of the football team who announced that he was planning to shove the pipe down Hall's throat. They were separated before any serious blows for liberty or tyranny were struck; despite the unspectacular ending of the encounter, it is one of the undergraduate scenes I recall most clearly, and I have a detailed recollection of my sensation of anger when it looked as though Hall was about to get a beating, and that I wasn't big enough to intervene.

What the Marxists regarded as the campus counterpart of the class struggle was, it must be conceded, somewhat inconsistent with their version of the real thing. Then, and for some years afterward, Columbia's athletic battalions tended to produce the most violent opponents of radicalism; frequently they manifested their conclusions in the manner attempted by Columbia's left end that morning. Yet it was indisputably true that the most "proletarian elements" at Columbia were almost exactly the same wage-slave warriors of the gridiron. Through the system of benign recruiting conducted by Dr. Little and his associates, boys from mining towns and other industrial areas were brought to Columbia to fortify the limited and fragile manpower usually available to Columbia coaches. In general these young men did not consider themselves intellectuals; they also felt, perhaps, a special obligation to protect the honor of the university since they were the beneficiaries of varied forms of subsidy, ranging from scholarships to campus employment. They were frankly impatient with those who seemed to be inflicting a reputation for radicalism on Alma Mater at the very time our football prestige was being valiantly retrieved by their labors.

Whatever the complexity of the instincts that drove them into periodic political battle, the athletic proletarians were always warring against the champions of Marxism and any symptom thereof.

In the Reed Harris episode they had, of course, special reason to be aggrieved, for Harris, with his constant denunciations of professionalism in football, was striking at the heart of their existence. He did, it is true, occasionally urge that gridiron wages be increased and the whole spectacle placed on a frankly professional plane but most people deemed this a thoroughly frivolous proposal.

Although I was hardly conscious of the point at the time, Harris's unsympathetic attitude toward football undoubtedly distressed the communist analysts; they had to visualize the imported football heroes as underpaid proletarians. During the controversy one of the leading campus Marxists ghosted a letter for several football heroes protesting *Spectator's* stand on football financing. This document no doubt represented the high point of communist infiltration on the gridiron; it was probably the first and last time that so many football luminaries permitted their thoughts to be phrased for them by an avowed red.

For some freshmen Columbia's upset triumph over Dartmouth was the unforgettable day of that academic year. I remember it well; but for myself and surely for some others the day of the strike in support of Reed Harris was the event that mattered. I can recall the quality of the soft spring air, the crispness of the blue sky, and the succession of alternately violent, heroic, intense and bitter scenes. My assignment for *Spectator* that day was to write a "color story," the parenthetical words and the entertaining sidelights incidental to the major developments. I didn't write much of a story; I kept forgetting to take notes. There seemed to be nothing funny about the way the defenders of free speech were being attacked and heckled and pelted with water-bags and pushed around by those who refused to understand the solemnity of the occasion. And surely not even a newspaperman could strive to be "neutral" in such a struggle.

The most exciting figure of the day, I was sure, was Howard Westwood, a blonde, slender law student, a passionate orator and a target of the bellicose youths on the anti-Harris side. Almost from the first he was in the thick of the battle and I was certain that everything he did was a conspicuous example of gallantry under fire.

The fighting had begun almost as soon as the meeting started. When the crowd assembled at the base of the Alma Mater statue, Arthur Goldschmidt, the chairman of the strike committee, announced that a black crepe gag would be placed over Alma Mater's mouth in observance of the dark night of oppression that had descended on Columbia. There were immediate murmurs of outrage from the athletic band and its sympathizers; a crew man led the counter-charge and a fierce struggle ensued. The melee reached its climax when Westwood was dragged across the harsh pavement on One Hundred and Sixteenth Street, his shirt torn, his face pale and angry and, I think, slightly bloody. I have forgotten now whether he was finally rescued by his supporters or simply abandoned by his assailants. Anyway, when he returned to the library steps to deliver another of his many impassioned orations of the week, he seemed the personification of the invincible cause of freedom, and I could only pity those who failed to appreciate the magnificence of the moment. It seemed beyond dispute that this had to be one of the great turning points in the affairs of men, even if the undiscerning press aloofly dismissed it as "Students Riot at Columbia."

No one, of course, ever knew exactly how many students went on strike that day because they felt deeply about the matter and how many stayed away from the classes simply because it was a fine April day with excitement in the air. The radicals probably told themselves that this was a clear omen of the coming American upheaval; to many of us it was a stirring demonstration of love for liberty, and a mark of our own maturity that we were at last engaged in the resolution of crucial issues.

One consequence of the great day was a vague but inescapable student resentment over what we considered to be the unconscionable timidity of the faculty. On the eve of the demonstration a faculty petition protesting Harris's dismissal was released; in all of Columbia University, only sixteen men had been willing to affix their names. In Columbia College itself there were just nine signatories; eight of them held the lowly rank of instructor and Mark Van Doren was the only man of professorial status to join the group. That was another episode in the cycle known as "disillusionment." It was generally believed that anyone signing such a statement was risking his academic neck; for precisely that reason the petition seemed at that moment of our lives to be a clear test of any professor's manhood, and the widespread failure to respond new proof that Columbia's liberalism was a fraud. This conclusion was slightly tempered by the news that a number of men of higher academic rank had dismissed their classes when the strike began. But it was nevertheless noted that Henderson was the only faculty member to address the strike. The significance of his presence was in no way reduced by our belief that he was a practicing communist; we tended instead to ask ourselves why there were so many non-practicing liberals.

Two weeks after the strike the university abruptly announced that Reed Harris had been reinstated. In return for what was generally interpreted as vindication, Harris withdrew from college voluntarily and agreed to send a note to the Dean regretting any personal discourtesies to which the Dean felt he had been subjected. These were viewed on and off the campus as face-saving gestures for the administration and as in no way detracting from the magnitude of the student triumph.

Throughout the tumult preceding and following the strike Harris himself remained away from the campus. Except for a few statements to the press, he remained completely aloof from the protest in his behalf. I do not believe I ever saw him again until his image appeared on the television screen, twenty-one years after his departure from college and eighteen after mine. In the ensuing years he had become a Columbia legend, largely because the Dean forgot that the editorship of *Spectator* changes hands in the first week of April.

Harris wasn't a communist when he was at Columbia and he never became one. The *Spectator* that Harris edited reads remarkably well two decades later. It was unquestionably the liveliest undergraduate journal of its day and even its more strident sermons were mingled with warmth and wit. What Harris had actually done was to awaken some of us to the bleakness and barrenness of that year in American history; what happened after we opened our eyes is another matter. It still seems curious that Harris was designated "abnormal" and "too old for his age" because he thought about such things while those who didn't give a damn are still being hailed as the robust, well-adjusted products of the educational system.

But all that was very long ago. It was the year after a young man named Joseph McCarthy had entered Marquette University, where he was to earn part of his tuition by serving as boxing coach and another part at the poker table.

Twenty-two years later, a Senator named Joseph McCarthy was to summon an official of the State Department named Reed Harris before him for an accounting of his undergraduate years. Was he not the same Reed Harris who had written a book called *King Football?*

He was.

# 2

During my Columbia days campus radicals were considered to be the young men and women who spent more time than anyone else brooding about our century's melancholy destiny. They probably were. They also probably did less thinking than some of our incorrigibly non-Marxist contemporaries whom we visualized as tender escapists. One of the worst effects of communism on the campus, 1930's variety, was that it retarded education. Once one had glimpsed the simplicity of the Marxist answers to the cruel questions of the time, the impulse to search out other varieties of knowledge was obviously reduced. The convert was too busy enjoying his conversion to re-examine the source of his bliss.

Once upon a time there were men who actually believed that the university was the place for serene contemplation; their undergraduate recollections are crowded with memories of intellectual quest and discovery. For some of us in the class of '35 the true high points are the mass meetings, the pitched battles, the organized discord. We are somewhat akin to those who had the misfortune to be arrested during the celebration that heralded Columbia's first and only football triumph in the Rose Bowl, and who remember that episode above all else. The landmarks of our college years are the consecutive strikes that occurred each April we were there: the Harris strike of 1932, the strike in protest against the dismissal of Donald Henderson in 1933, the anti-war strike of 1934 (repeated in 1935), the *Spectator* staff strike of 1935. The springtimes of our college careers were symbolized by picket signs.

I came to Columbia with only the haziest kind of political background. Although I thought Broun and Mencken were great, my attachment for them hardly represented any systematic world view; they were primarily bold journalistic spirits who despised stuffed shirts, and it surely did not occur to me that there was any serious conflict between Broun's sentimental equalitarianism and Mencken's contempt for *homo sapiens*. A couple of times, as a senior in high school, I did go down to meetings at the Rand School, where the socialists held forth, and even then I found something fundamentally right and just about the view that no man should exploit his brother.

As for the communists, I do not believe I had ever met any until I got to college and I was quite certain that, unlike the friendly socialists at the Rand School, they were monstrous men who probably did carry bombs, were forever plotting random violence and simply did not belong to the ordinary community of men.

I didn't join the Young Communist League until April, 1934, a little more than a year before Commencement. But the process of getting there absorbed a disproportionately large part of the preceding semesters. My undergraduate career seems to have been almost equally divided between the time spent working on *Spectator* and involvements in left-wing politics, with the remaining hours vaguely allotted to the classroom and to extracurricular diversions that ranged from fraternity frolics to the *New Masses* ball.

In terms of the classroom pursuit of knowledge I was less than a diligent student; I learned a lot about journalism working on *Spectator* and that knowledge has probably proved more useful than anything I acquired in the classroom. I got fair grades, after a minor academic disaster in the first half of my sophomore year when I flunked two courses.

By the time of my graduation I was not quite twenty and a believing young communist. I bore little resemblance to an educated man but was fairly convinced that what I hadn't learned was irrelevant or obsolete bourgeois matter.

But now the Senator says he wants to know why I and some others became communists in the first place. It is perfectly true that some did and many didn't; so one tries to go back and piece the clues together.

It is possible, Silone has said, to write of oneself with sincerity but not with objectivity. Moreover, the inquiry is complicated in this instance by the age of the subject during the years in question. Whether that is an extenuating fact is for others to judge; but it enormously clouds any attempt at honest recollection. To what extent were ideas consciously and thoughtfully embraced and to what degree were they shaped by accidental encounter?

In some places now the only question considered relevant to any inquiry into the origins of radicalism is: How did you get along with your father? The assumption is that any unconventional social protest must reflect a childhood insurrection against the head of the family. But to the best of my knowledge and belief, I have always been fond of my parents and my brother, who were the only immediate members of my childhood family. I was unquestionably overprotected as a child, if that clarifies anything. To this day my mother affectionately showers me with admonitions about the ordinary perils of existence, such as the danger of smoking in bed; if I had become a full-fledged revolutionary, I am sure she would have anxiously cautioned me to be careful crossing the streets on the way to the barricades.

No one, however, is well equipped to probe the psychic depths of his own motivations. It is a fact that from the age of eleven to fourteen I rooted passionately for the Boston Red Sox, although I was born and brought up in New York City. That was the period when the Red Sox almost invariably finished last and the Yankees were trampling all opposition. Make what you will of that.

In the long run, I assume, all our ideas and actions and passions are influenced by a complex of obscure physical and psychological accidents. The notion that radicalism in the 1930's was merely a vast symptom of internal disorder is as insubstantial, however, as the equally simple-minded view that reformers are a peculiar breed of gentle people, unafflicted by those darker instincts common to ordinary humanity.

If we are to say that American radicalism can invariably be traced to the dropping of some babies on their heads by careless handlers, we are on the road to a psychological determinism as rigid as the Marxist "inevitabilities." By this dogma, ideas and ethics are deprived of any independent validity. Then there is no longer any such thing as a virtuous man; anyone who seems to be is just a lucky devil.

What is interesting about the sound and fury of those distant days is not the emotional state of the participants. Generally overlooked or forgotten now is the sense of breakdown which for several years swept large areas of American life. Forgotten too is the absence of clear, affirmative and plausible alternatives to Marxism, the hesitancy of scholars and statesmen in the face of the Marxist critique. It was not merely what the communists said that enthralled us; it was what other men failed to say. The self-assurance of the communists proved contagious; the liberal loss of nerve repelled us.

From the time Reed Harris started asking questions out loud, the world was very much with us. We were sure we were living on the edge of catastrophe. Perhaps we have since grown more accustomed to suspense as a condition of life.

Frustration and emptiness were expressed on all sides; the Marxists came breathing certitude and salvation. Contrast, for example, two books many of us read as sophomores. One was Walter Lippmann's *A Preface to Morals*, the other John Strachey's *The Coming Struggle for Power*. Lippmann's book had been published in 1929, just as economic crisis descended on America. After nearly four years of depression, the book seemed to us a conclusive acknowledgment of the hopelessnesses of non-Marxist thought. Its author could read it now with far more equanimity than Strachey would find in re-examining his Marxist polemic. But to those of us who placed them side by side in 1933 Lippmann's was a confession of defeat and Strachey's a ringing summons to action.

The gap seemed dramatically revealed by a comparison of the final passages of the two works. Lippmann, conceding that the old gods were dead and new ones hard to find, exhorted us to acquire a "religion of the spirit."

". . . the mature man," Lippmann urged,

> would take the world as it comes, and within himself remain quite unperturbed. . . . he would move easily through life. . . . And so whether he saw the thing as comedy, or high tragedy, or plain farce, he would affirm that it is what it is, and that the wise man can enjoy it.

Easy talk, we said derisively, for a man who had managed to obtain a seat in a press box above the human ordeal. But what of the rest of us down below? For our mortal danger, a thing of the flesh as well as the spirit, there was Strachey's simpler diagnosis and cure:

> There is literally nothing to prevent the American people from producing and distributing *from tomorrow* sufficient goods and services to secure for every single one of them an ample and secure standard of life. . . . They have only to free themselves from the net of the private profitmaking ownership of the means of production, and to organize production for use on the basis of communally owned industry, agriculture and transportation to realize their wealth. Thus, and thus alone, may they leap from the kingdom of necessity into the kingdom of freedom.

The issue was joined. It was the solitary man futilely contemplating the spectacle of the West's decline arrayed against the man of the future. One road was lonely escape; the other was valiant struggle.

Lippmann assured us that the world would "go on somehow." And it did. Yet one must also concede that the record of the last two decades has provided a certain justification for those who foresaw nothing but trouble ahead. Where the Marxist form chart dismally erred was in its failure to anticipate that the first self-proclaimed Marxist state would be a major source of mankind's ensuing agony.

With all that we know now, it may appear incomprehensible that any outwardly sane young men and women could find in the communist version of Marxism a gleaming hope of escape from the bleak impasse of war and depression. But much of what we know now is based on two decades of shattering revelation about the Soviet despotism. There were a few who had already perceived its inner decay by 1932; but they were lone voices, and too often their motives were mistrusted. Arrayed against them were journalists and scholars whose integrity was rarely challenged even by their critics; there was the solemn assurance given us by Lincoln Steffens, who seemed the most fearless journalist of all: "I have been over into the future and it works."

Moreover, the American soil in which Marxism eventually flourished had been cultivated by some of our best minds. Much of what we read and took seriously was in the nature of an orientation course for the greater illumination to come. Our prize intellectual possessions in the early thirties were the brilliant contempt for the vulgarities of American culture voiced by Mencken; the "economic interpretation" of American history so sweepingly unfolded by Charles A. Beard; the cynicism toward traditional liberalism and patchwork reform so militantly expounded by Steffens; and the sardonic examination of capitalism's leisure class conducted by Thorstein Veblen. Mencken convinced us there was little worth defending in the American Way of Life, which had, after all, produced George F. Babbitt as its monument to the middle class; Beard taught us that America was in no way immune to the decisive pressures of class conflict and that our Constitution was in fact the devious creation of selfish men of landed property disguised as representatives of the people; Steffens proclaimed the helplessness of well-intentioned men caught in the toils of an evil "system" which did violence to the Golden Rule. Mencken, Beard and Veblen indoctrinated us with a proper cynicism about the institutions which stuffy men held sacred; Steffens helped us to decide that Strachey was right about the solution, and that it applied to America as well as to the rest of the world.

The liberals had had their chance, from the time of Teddy Roosevelt through Wilson's New Freedom and the lost-cause adventure of Bob La Follette, Sr., and the feverish efforts of all the reformers in cities scattered from coast to coast. And where were we now? The trust-busters had had their day but they had never dared go far enough; the reformers had had a few big innings but invariably lost the ball game; the idealists had merchandised a war to enthrone freedom on earth and Versailles had ended all that. All the noblest strivings of the best spirits had come to naught because they couldn't beat "the system." Now "the system" was finally bringing chaos down on all our heads, and we inherited a wasteland crowded with hollow men.

This was a common verdict; few effectively disputed it. A young man named John Chamberlain came out of Yale with his merciless recital of the failure of the men of good will; in *Farewell to Reform* he described all the well-meaning attempts and all the ghastly disappointments. He agreed with Harold Stearns that "the technique of liberal failure" was "the unwillingness of the liberal to continue with analysis once the process of analysis had become uncomfortable." Thus, while a few gallant dissidents like Randolph Bourne and old Bob La Follette had resisted the slogans that sent us off to war in 1917, most of the progressives beat the drums more cheerfully than anyone else; the liberals (we were told) had been too timid to recognize that the roots of injustice and corruption were planted deep in the capitalist structure. Chamberlain, after examining the debacle of liberalism, ruefully concluded, "The situation, looked upon with intelligence and considered as a long-range proposition, can lead to but one of two personal conclusions: it can make one either a cynic or a revolutionist."

The year was 1932, the time of Hoovervilles and a Bonus Army marching on Washington and angry farm revolts and everywhere the pall of fear and frustration. While Chamberlain was writing

the obituary for liberal hopes, the conservatives were quietly bury-
ing themselves. When the Senate Finance Committee summoned
leading businessmen to get their views on what ought to be done,
John W. Davis, one-time Democratic presidential candidate, testified sadly, "I have nothing to offer, either of fact or theory." And
W. W. Atterbury of the Pennsylvania Railroad declared, "The
only way to beat the depression is to hit the bottom and then
slowly build up."

At seventeen I was a sophomore and a socialist. Life had really
begun, I was convinced, with the Reed Harris strike; when I started
my second year at Columbia in the undiminished crisis of 1932,
I was quite certain that only drastic measures could rescue the
world. There were those who said we were too young to make
decisions; but time was too brief to heed such adult counsel. One
could follow Walter Pater's admonition to live as if each moment
were one's last, or one could resolve to do something about it. By
early autumn I was calling myself a socialist.

To most of the country, the presidential election of that year
was a battle between Herbert Hoover and Franklin D. Roosevelt;
but on many campuses, and particularly Columbia's, the central
figure in the campaign was tall, tireless Norman Thomas. The
Thomas-for-President movement was the talk of Morningside
Heights; there was no comparably animated drive for either Hoover
or Roosevelt. When *Spectator* began a poll of student sentiment,
Thomas was conceded third place. He won. At Columbia College,
with about two-thirds of the student body balloting, Thomas received 421 votes to 307 for Hoover and only 221 for Roosevelt.
Almost as notable as Thomas's triumph was the weak showing of
William Z. Foster, the communist nominee, who received exactly
21 votes in the college and a total of 81 throughout the university
out of 2494 votes cast. Thomas's all-university total was 1033;
Hoover received 833 and Roosevelt 547.

The almost universal lack of undergraduate excitement over
FDR's candidacy may be an illuminating footnote to that era.
In the light of subsequent history one may wonder that he was

so unsuccessful in channeling the mixed idealism and unrest that rallied nationally behind Thomas's candidacy. In part the answer was that, as of the fall of 1932, Franklin D. Roosevelt was the candidate of the party whose last President was held responsible for the betrayal of idealism. There were few among us, faculty or students, who doubted that the war had symbolized the treachery and failure of our civilization. It is one of the extraordinary aspects of that time that Wilson's name meant little more to us than that. The "New Freedom" had a hollow sound; it was the primer of liberal failure. We were reading Dos Passos, Hemingway and Remarque. Wilson was the real villain in all the horror stories that bared the cruelty and waste of war.

That fall I worked actively with the Thomas-for-President movement. By October I was writing my brother, who was then serving as law clerk to Justice Harlan F. Stone, that I had left my fraternity; there were more important things to do. A week before election I interviewed Thomas for *Spectator* at his campaign headquarters. While I had previously felt committed to his cause, I now fell politically in love. "He's the most impressive gentleman I've ever encountered," I wrote Herb, adding that it was evidence of the utter bankruptcy of our culture that he had no apparent chance of victory.

The Socialist Party's drive was enhanced in the city by the mayoralty candidacy of Morris Hillquit. We had just lived through the revelations of the Seabury Committee; were these not just a municipal symptom of the corruption and sickness that "the system" had produced? So on election day, along with a lot of other Columbia students, I found myself working as a poll watcher for the Socialist Party in Harlem. Despite all the disclosures of the previous months, Tammany Hall conducted its business as usual. Its victorious nominee was that pathetic Throttlebottom, John P. O'Brien. Time after time during the long day we watched voters come to the polls, only to discover that their names had already been used by some Tammany early bird; it was a day of continual arguments and futile protests, and also a day of dedication.

That evening, after writing an article for *Spectator* on the evil I had seen, I returned to John Jay Hall and wrote another communiqué to my brother Herb which included a momentous announcement of political intention: "Today was one of the most exciting days I've ever had. I was a watcher for the Socialist Party; some details of my impressions will be published in *Spectator* tomorrow and forwarded to you.

"One thing is now definitely established. I am unequivocally a socialist and intend to become active in the party's work. It was inspiring to work with members of the party today; they are people who can think and do think. They aren't long-haired radicals with a wild gleam in their eyes. They are just people who find more important things in life than dances, women and football. They have their diversions but these do not supersede their intellectual interests.

"Socialism seems to me the only hope for democracy. The calibre of the voters is terribly low. They know nothing but what Tammany tells them. And Tammany tells them nothing but whom to vote for. The corruption that takes place on election day is fantastic. I'm terribly tired or I could write for hours about this. . . .

"Why did Walter Lippmann support Roosevelt?"

Thus, a week after my seventeenth birthday, I went to sleep an ardent socialist. I would have been deeply injured if anyone had tried to tell me that American socialism had just had its last big hour and that it would not again approach this peak.

In a matter of months my own vows of eternal fealty to the socialist cause began to falter. In the intellectual world the great new cleavage was taking shape between those who placed their hopes in the pragmatic undertakings of the New Deal and those who were calling for the sterner stuff of communism.

One night near the end of November two homeless men died in New York City, one of undernourishment, the other of exposure to the frigid winds of winter. *Spectator*, then under the editorship of Arthur Lelyveld and remaining faithful, if a little less rambunctiously, to the Harris heritage, wrote:

The official season of suffering and want opened Sunday night. . . . The task of unemployment relief needs the aid of the Federal Government. What can we expect of President Hoover during this interregnum, while he waits for the Smiling Lieutenant to assume the official power of dodging important issues? Can we expect both the Republican and Democratic Parties, with their reactionary elements, to meet this crisis?

There is still an army of 12,000,000 stumbling about blindly from place to place—and tomorrow for them is a thousand years too long.

It was in that mood of skeptical nonexpectancy that we awaited the advent of FDR and some of us began to read the angry mutterings of the *Daily Worker* more attentively than before. Then, later that winter and before the Roosevelt inaugural, Adolf Hitler seized power in Germany. At just about that time I came to know Addison T. "Tuffy" Cutler and Don Henderson, who were the voluntary and unofficial faculty advisers to the still small communist set on the campus.

From some of the ensuing developments it may be deduced that the downfall of those of us who became communists can be simply ascribed to the witchcraft of these men, thus proving how mortally dangerous it is for a republic to expose its young to such teachings. If that is the only inference drawn, this will have been a misleading exercise. They did influence young men, including me; to some of us they were the major faculty personalities of the era, and the bull sessions we had with them off the campus, amid beer-drinking and the singing of revolutionary anthems, had probably greater impact than anything said in the classrooms. The road to communism those days was often a sentimental journey, filled with an atmosphere of adventure and high feeling unlike anything else we experienced at college.

But why did these two thin, high-strung, likable men attract more followers than some of their abler and more erudite colleagues? Other men drank beer with other faculty members and some were unquestionably swayed in other directions by them; Thomas Merton, the poet and Trappist monk who had a momentary sojourn in the Young Communist League, attributes his escape from communism, in part, to the wise and gentle counsel of Mark Van Doren. But on the whole Cutler and Henderson met little competition in the political arena. In the academic world as elsewhere democracy was defensive and inarticulate.

While Columbia's faculty was heavily represented on the early "brain trust," the pilgrimage of Tugwell, Moley and Co. to Washington evoked no tremendous burst of local pride in the student body. When Tugwell visited the campus in 1933 to boast that NRA had met "the immediate demands of a population hungry, cold and in despair," *Spectator* impatiently disputed him: "The Administration has not dared to go to the bottom and find out what is wrong basically." Recalling that in 1932 Tugwell had written a bleak diagnosis of the decline of the profit system, the undergraduate journal chided him for his newly acquired optimism. And it took sharp issue with his plea for avoidance of any commitments to "blind doctrine."

"This is the crux of the problem," said *Spectator* sternly, "this blind stumbling in the most chaotic fashion—experimenting from day to day—without any anchor except a few idealistic phrases— is worthless. It is merely political pragmatism."

What *Spectator* did not seem to know was that pragmatism was the essence of the American political technique and tradition and conceivably there might be something to be said for it; that the minuteness of a blueprint does not establish its validity; and that, in earlier crises of our history, the use of skilful improvisation had saved us. But what restive undergraduate would have joined a "Pragmatists' Club" in the depth of the Great Depression and amid the collapse of world order?

In the face of the Strachey challenge—and many little Stracheys sprang up to echo his thesis—few academic voices rang out in clear tones offering a rival faith. There were those who challenged the dogmatism and intolerance of Marxism and exploded some of its more blatant banalities; but they offered nothing in its stead that carried with it any gleaming promise of a better day on earth.

The president of our university had forfeited our serious attention when he annually affirmed his opposition to the child-labor amendment. Moreover, we were always being reminded of his harshness toward such distinguished faculty members as Beard, Dana and Cattell when they refused to join the academic goose step in World War I.

We viewed Dr. Butler as a man whose pretensions were eternally mocked by this episode. Anyway, we had no contact with him; all we knew about what he was saying and doing was what we read in the papers, beginning with his endorsement of the expulsion of Reed Harris. And he did have an extraordinary capacity for saying things that invited derision. "Child labor does not exist in the United States. . . . This is the undoubted fact despite the quite irrelevant statistics marshaled in opposition to it," the papers quoted him as saying one day during state hearings on the child-labor amendment. On another day we woke up to read that he had said, "Much of the talk of maldistribution of wealth is sheer invention . . . mischievously devised by radicals" and on still another he observed that "capitalism is a debating term invented by Karl Marx." If he did speak for an internationalism considerably more enlightened than the attitudes prevailing among the Republicans of his time, he got little applause from us for that. To us the League of Nations was dead and his declarations of faith in it were merely a voice from the cemetery.

The scenes he encountered on the campus in the first years of the thirties must have been baffling and painful to him. The hubbub was incessant; he was forever being picketed, whether it was because of the inadequacy of wages paid employees in the Teachers College dining halls or the expulsion of a dissident. He in turn lamented the bad manners of modern youth and was promptly rebuked for suggesting that we who were about to die should lower our voices.

There were good men around, far better than I had humility or perception to recognize at the time. Irwin Edman's philosophy lectures were models of intellectual grace and, for a few moments at least, they may have lifted our eyes above the level of the day's leaflet. But he was at a fatal disadvantage; he was dealing with eternity and we were heroically tilting with immediacy, and to us it seemed unlikely there could be any connection. With some pain I recall a term paper I wrote for him in my senior year in which I pleaded the then fashionable case for proletarian literature and disposed of the problem of beauty with the dreary remark that the poor did not have sufficient leisure to watch sunsets.

There was "Tommy" Cook teaching government, valiantly arguing the proposition that freedom was the only justification democracy needed; that no blessings fascism or communism might bring could possibly compensate for the destruction of man's right to think and speak, and that no society built on oppression could be regarded as a way station to Utopia. After two decades of totalitarian self-revelation, his words have the irresistible force of a well-beloved axiom. But at the time they were spoken with defiance and despair in the face of heckling from some of us who presumed to know better. I can almost hear our raucous demands to know whether he really believed that America was a free land in the light of documented evidence that workers were penalized for trying to form a union in Weirton, West Virginia. When he suggested that we had the vital freedom to raise hell about exactly such blemishes, we retorted by wanting to know whether he considered "freedom to starve" a precious possession of Western man. With such irrelevant ripostes we greeted each of his attempts to prove that democratic society had virtues not necessarily blighted by the private ownership of the means of production.

In sociology there was a wonderful eccentric named William Casey whose daily delight was to contend that the only trouble with most young men was that, quite simply and literally, they didn't know what they were talking about. Casey had come to Columbia out of the West and the Casey cult was perhaps the most formidable opposition that the rising Marxist clan faced. In much the manner later popularized by Stuart Chase in his

*Tyranny of Words* and his other studies of semantics, Casey took
the view that most people—right, left, center or underground—
were the helpless prisoners of stereotypes whose meaning had
long ago escaped both the user and his victim. It was Casey's
contention that most modern conflict reflected nothing more
than a cosmic verbal misunderstanding; everywhere men were
quarreling with one another in defense of symbols whose original
significance had long ago been forgotten, if indeed it had ever
been known. Nations, in effect, were huge collections of Pavlovian
dogs, ready to salivate and tear at each other's throats at the
ringing of some phrase-monger's bell. Casey not only told us that
we knew virtually nothing about the subjects we discussed with
much heat; he predicted we would probably know less and less
as we grew older. He made it plain that he had no faith in the
common man, no faith in any institutions and, indeed, no faith
in anything except the obvious premise that man was one of the
sillier animals. He declined to be interviewed by newspapers on
the ground that his words would be translated inaccurately by
the press, which was a major instrument of confused communication.

His was bitter medicine for budding Marxists; it brought some
of us the pains of momentary self-consciousness but, in most cases,
it worked no miracle cure. While the "Caseyites"—and there
were those who so designated themselves—taunted us with his
warning that anything said could be used against us, we did
not lapse into speechlessness. For was he not, after all, preaching
total futility? If we could not risk believing anything we heard,
if we could not trust what we had hitherto regarded as our own
senses, what remained except submission to a horrible fate? We
did not want to be told that all fighting faiths were expressions
of man's empty-headedness; there was a world to be saved, and
precious little time.

The conviction that time was running out was ever present. In
a history classroom in that spring of '33 Walter Langsam told us
that the world was nearer war than it had been in the spring of
1914. Some measure of the day's mood may be found in this ex-

cerpt from a letter I wrote to my brother in March of that year. "Langsam's history course is a pleasure. The story of the World War, as he tells it, is a ridiculous and tragic spectacle. . . . He is convinced we are nearer war now than in 1914. In connection with that I must tell you an interesting story. As he was lecturing he came to the point at which the United States entered the war. When he said 'and then the United States entered the war,' the class hissed with beautiful spontaneity. It was a remarkable and inspiring demonstration. Whereupon Langsam said, 'If you're hissing now, wait till I tell you why we entered the war.' I'm waiting eagerly. Anyway I'm convinced that our generation is a little too close to the chaos of that war to end wars to allow itself to be dragged into another one. I think we're remembering the lesson."

In the same letter I reported that "Tuffy Cutler and I get on splendidly; he's really a fine guy, although I think Santayana's definition of a fanatic—'one who redoubles his energy when he has forgotten his aim'—may be used in describing him."

I was obviously unready to join the fanatics but I was moving along. Pacifism was a strong inhibition; one of the greatest difficulties plaguing the communists at the time was their effort to exploit the prevailing view that international war was hell and simultaneously maintain that class war was the inevitable and only road to paradise. It took many of us quite a while to become reconciled to the distinction.

There were other non-Marxist faculty members whom I remember with affection and respect, like Horace Taylor in economics and James Gutmann in philosophy. But in the decisive roll call Henderson and Cutler were the important characters. They were the "men of action"; they were committed; they knew—so it seemed —where they were going. They might not be the most distinguished scholars of the day, but they never lacked answers to the life-and-death questions. What lifted Henderson to even higher eminence was the announcement early in April, 1933, that his appointment as a member of the economics department would not be renewed for the following academic year.

His martyrdom was assured; he was enshrined with all the other immortal victims of Columbia oppression, from Cattell to Harris. In the ensuing clashes "Tuffy" Cutler assumed an equally exalted status for valor above and beyond the call of academic duty. A year earlier Henderson had been a lone faculty voice actively agitating for the reinstatement of Harris; now Cutler was a solitary faculty spokesman at the mass meetings which described the ouster of Henderson as further evidence that Columbia lived in dread of really vital ideas. Until he was dismissed Henderson was a man with a limited audience. Now he occupied the center of the university stage. His ideas were given a dignity they never could have otherwise achieved. He had been cultivating a small contingent of earnest disciples; now his name was on nearly everyone's lips and everything he said was deemed worthy of quotation.

The Reed Harris episode was unquestionably the grand climax of my freshman year; the Henderson case was the epic of my sophomore semesters. So these college years may seem to have been just a continuous mass meeting on a one-way street leading to political perdition. But although this is primarily the log of a political voyage, I would be writing a fanciful record if I indicated that there was nothing on my mind except the date of the next protest rally.

In terms of man-hours expended, my work on *Spectator* had been my paramount interest. I had not the slightest doubt that I wanted to grow up to be some miniature of that great and good bulk of humanity known as Heywood Broun. In my view he was the supreme combination of journalist and crusader; he was the large, living demonstration that a man could be both. I still think so, and I have very little patience with those who have been posthumously exhuming his ideological errors.

*Spectator* absorbed days and nights. About one night a week came the role of "assistant night editor" which meant working at the printing plant until the paper was off the presses; while there we read proof, wrote headlines and played newspaperman on every level. The next morning we cut classes to retrieve lost sleep. This was life!

Naturally, I was involved in those futile and feverish relations with a girl without which no novel about a sophomore year in college could be written. Like nearly everyone else, I encountered the stubborn fact that girls do not casually yield everything to sophomores, a disappointment augmented by the fact that the girl in question derived no stimulus whatever from my political development.

In March I was sent to Washington to cover the convention of the pacifist War Resisters League for *Spectator*. All the men and women attired in green shirts or some replica thereof were impressive in their earnestness. It was during that winter, too, that the Oxford Union adopted its historic pledge "not to fight for king or country" and the notion that such vows of abstinence could finally deter the "war makers" had a rather magnificent plausibility. Unhappily the contagion of such brotherly feeling was never allowed to spread to the youth of the dictatorships.

Then, in early April, we learned about Henderson.

The news did not create the immediate furor that followed Harris's expulsion. To some degree, at least, the ensuing protest was contrived.

In the Harris dispute the issue had seemed clear-cut; in the Henderson case it was confused. The grounds given for letting him go were that he had exhibited no academic distinction and that the university often terminated the services of men of his rank who displayed no promise. Among his former students there was an embarrassing division on the merits of the university's contention. There were indeed some who maintained that he had been a classroom bore.

But to those of us who knew him outside the classroom and who distrusted the academic overlords anyway, the charge of incompetence was unpersuasive. All of us could name boring instructors who were seemingly headed for permanent tenure. It was argued by some that the university had no obligation to retain an uninspired radical teacher simply because his boisterous radicalism had gotten his name into the papers; our rebuttal was that his classroom deficiencies, if any, would never have been noticed if he had played it safe.

My own reaction was one of instinctive loyalty to a man whom I had gotten to know and like and who was engaged in the great front-line endeavors of the day. By then Henderson was devoting a large amount of his time to the affairs of the National Student League; if the devotion he had invested in the momentous battles of the real world beyond the campus kept him from his scholarly pursuits, I was sure he deserved reward rather than punishment for such absence without leave.

Broun came to the campus to address a protest rally in Henderson's behalf. I covered the meeting and my ineradicable recollection is the huge slug of gin he zestfully downed before mounting the narrow base of the Sun Dial across the street from the library steps.

"It is a strange thing," Broun said, "that an instructor is incompetent as soon as he becomes interested in radical activities. A remote administration is not a judge of competence in this matter. The most important thing is what his classes think of Donald Henderson."

Broun further declared that it was time for a student strike to prove that "this university is ours and belongs to nobody else."

There, I told myself again, was a man.

The next evening Henderson's supporters staged a torchlight parade as the preliminary to a student strike. From the moment the meeting began—in the clear spring night on One Hundred and Sixteenth Street—the violent clashes of the previous spring were quickly repeated. The first speaker was red-haired, white-faced "Tuffy" Cutler, a shy, self-conscious man for whom public oratory was plainly a desperate trial. He was greeted with rotten eggs, tomatoes and all the usual expressions of undergraduate derision. His successors received the same greeting. The noise increased when a speaker representing the National Student League, who had no semblance of connection with Columbia College, was introduced. There were audible demands that he go back where he came from, the point of his origin being, it was strongly suggested, either Moscow, Union Square, or, worst of all, CCNY.

The sponsors of the meeting had run out of speakers who possessed any claim to legitimate association with Columbia. Then somebody turned to me and asked me whether I would talk to keep things going. I was there as a reporter for *Spectator*. I knew all the rules of journalism which presumably apply to such an occasion. But what did protocol matter now? Would Broun have stood aside while men's very right to speak was being challenged in this ugly form? I was fighting mad over the sight of the eggs that had spattered "Tuffy" Cutler. The now familiar combination of football players, crew men and fraternity dignitaries had behaved in characteristic style. Who could remain silent? Since I had spent many hours as a high-school debater and a contestant in oratorical contests, it required no great feat of will to deliver an extemporaneous address, the content of which was fortunately never recorded for posterity.

But the evening didn't end there. Fights were breaking out all over the place and, when there were no speakers left, it was decided to transform the meeting into a parade. And so I paraded, while water-bags and other missiles were hurled from dormitory windows. Those of us in the line of march were convinced that this was truly one of mankind's most fearless advances under fire.

It was nearly midnight when I returned to the *Spectator* office, where my disgrace had preceded me. What I had done was obviously illicit; Arnold Beichman, one of my closest friends, who had been elected just a few weeks earlier as editor of *Spectator*, told me sorrowfully that my story had already been written for me and that I would henceforth be barred from covering any assignments at which I might feel an irrepressible urge to get into the act. No greater humiliation can befall an apprentice newspaperman. For approximately a week, however, I didn't care. One could not remain in the press box indefinitely, I told myself solemnly. Everywhere men were being forced to take a stand and this had been as good a time as any for me to abandon a synthetic neutrality.

The circumstances of my dishonor quickly became hot campus gossip. By lunch time the next day I was being heralded by the Henderson inner circle as a man who had seen his duty and done it.

With a large section of the student body still apathetic, the strike was nevertheless held a couple of days afterward. It was certainly not as spontaneous or impressive an affair as the one that had been staged in behalf of Reed Harris, but it was a reasonably lively demonstration and, once again, the behavior of the undergraduate "loyalists" resulted in fairly favorable press notices for the strikers. Again there were eggs and tomatoes and water-bags.

Roy Howard, whose newspapers are currently active in revising the history of the thirties, should perhaps be reminded at this point that on the next day his New York *World-Telegram* bitterly denounced the "unreasoning attitude of certain of the students who attacked the pro-Henderson agitators" and added:

> The authorities at Columbia could afford to tolerate one radical instructor rather than loose upon the campus such bitterness. . . . At least the institution could have waited until it had a case against him so clear that its merits could not have been disputed.

Henderson wasn't reinstated. In communist terms the strike had been chiefly an agitational enterprise, and a fruitful one. Certainly it had agitated me.

But I was still unwilling to call myself a communist. Late that spring I was still mailing inconclusive meditations to Herb: "I am not sure what I want. I believe in the abstract principle of a socialized society but at times I lapse into a depressing subjectivity about the whole business. Then I lose my certainty and wonder whether anything is really worth fighting for that hard, whether there is a single ideal in this mixed-up universe worth pursuing."

Clearly a lot of these agonized words were merely the old outpourings of the Ancient Order of Adolescence. Confusion and drift were not unique to the class of '35. To believe on one morning that one knew the exact nature of one's mission in the world and wonder on the next whether anything is worth the effort can hardly be described as an unprecedented condition; it is perhaps the first mark of maturity to know that these emotions will compete with each other for the rest of one's life.

After my monumental journalistic indiscretion at the Henderson torchlight parade I worked harder than ever on *Spectator*. As a newspaperman I had sinned grievously; now I had to prove I was a responsible man. The test came in December, 1933, when Hans Luther, the Nazi ambassador, spoke on the campus under the auspices of Columbia's Institute of Arts and Sciences.

The advance announcement of Luther's talk touched off another left-wing explosion and illustrated the ambivalence of the communist attitude toward free speech. The Social Problems Club proclaimed that in the days remaining before his scheduled appearance every effort would be made to convince the university to cancel the meeting. In hotly worded leaflets the club, along with other National Student League units in the city, accused Columbia of giving its blessing to the despicable barbarisms of the Nazi regime by inviting its emissary to the campus. It was asserted that Dr. Butler was now showing the true color of his political sympathies and the word "pro-Nazi" was carelessly hurled across Morningside Heights. Roger Baldwin of the American Civil Liberties Union chided the opponents of the meeting; then, as always, the ACLU asserted that suppression was a futile way of combating any idea. Certainly it seemed odd for those who had been carrying the banners of freedom in all the great demonstrations of previous months to accuse the university of excessive tolerance. Even some of the communists were reported uneasy about the logic of their line. But they gradually pieced together an answer, poor as it was. They were not, they said, denying Luther's right to hire a hall; they were condemning Columbia's offer of its own facilities to him because that could only be interpreted by the world as a sign that a great university condoned book-burning, concentration camps and all the other Nazi infamies. On exactly the same ground, of course, it could have been alleged—and was by some zealots of the right— that Columbia was "approving" communism when it invited John Strachey to appear in the same lecture series. That was different, the communists mumbled, but the distinction remained invisible to most of us.

Then Dr. Butler stepped into the argument with an unfortunate parenthetical remark. Declaring that "Columbia University has been for more than a century and three-quarters a home and center of freedom," he said, "It does not ask what a man's opinions may be but only whether he is intelligent, honest and well-mannered in their presentation and discussion." He was promptly jeered on two counts. In view of the Harris and Henderson affairs, how dared he invoke the tradition of "academic freedom"? And how could he depict the chosen representative of nazism as an "intelligent, honest and well-mannered" man? Even many of those who had initially opposed the campaign to suppress the meeting were troubled by Dr. Butler's unfeeling talk.

The communists persisted in the campaign. In times of excitement the argument for suppression is always the same. There is always the intimation that each particular crisis is the last, and somehow different from all others, and that this time the rules of free society must be abruptly suspended if we are to endure. And people like Roger Baldwin who have heard the same argument a thousand times are forced to repeat that once any man's speech is silenced, every man's voice is in danger.

Anyway, on the freezing night of December 12, 1933, Hans Luther delivered his speech at the Horace Mann auditorium on Columbia's campus while about a thousand students recruited by the National Student League from colleges and schools throughout the city gathered outside in protest.

Inside Dr. Luther explained that the new Nazi state represented the true will of the German people and that only "incorrigible old timers" doubted either the good intentions or the durability of Hitler's Reich. It is unlikely that anything he said won many converts to his cause.

Outside, the police, trying to keep the demonstrators at a discreet distance from the auditorium, got into repeated battles with the students. One of the girls who was rudely interrupted while attempting to circulate anti-Nazi handbills was a blonde, hatless, quiet and, it seemed to me, imperturbably valiant freshman at New College, then the experimental unit of Teachers College. She stood her ground firmly but undemonstratively and finally she was led forcibly across the street by an officer of the law. I had seen her at meetings of the Social Problems Club which I had covered.

I knew her name was Nancy Fraenkel and that her father was a Civil Liberties Union lawyer.

I saw her much more frequently after that evening which, I learned later, was her seventeenth birthday. We were married the following October.

Beichman had reminded me in advance of the Luther protest that I was attending as a reporter and that it would be unfortunate if I ended up on a soapbox. So I diligently remained a bystander. Despite some strong feelings about what I regarded as the un-chivalrous behavior of the cops, especially in the treatment of Miss Fraenkel, I stayed out of the proceedings. The next day's *Herald Tribune* carried a picture of Nancy and her police escort during her forced march across One Hundred and Twentieth Street. Again I suffered a twinge of conscience about the passivity of my own role. I also thought Nancy Fraenkel looked like a heroic figure of a woman because she seemed to be neither acting like a martyr nor preparing to dissolve into tears of feminine helplessness.

# 3

To some, official enlistment in the communist order in the mid-thirties was a supreme act of faith. To others it was an imperatively "logical" step. Once inside, however, all of us submitted to the ragged discipline of this ill-trained but dedicated army, and to the outside world it must have seemed that ours was never to reason why. Actually, the history of United States communism in that decade was one of feverish arrivals and departures. The congestion at the exit was often as great as at the entrance. Many of us tended to slide into the communist ranks with far less ceremony and excitement than attended our initiation into a college fraternity. By the time the moment of decision arrived it seemed already to have been made. It was the climax of the associations, misgivings and flounderings of many months.

By late spring of 1933, after the Henderson episode and its attendant turmoil, I had already begun to think of myself as "a communist sympathizer." When I visited Herb in Washington one week-end, he and some of his New Deal friends quietly chided me. Their point was that my heart, rather than my head, had brought me into the Marxist circle and that I knew very little about the real content of the crusade that was beckoning me. They even advanced the extravagant view that some good might come of the Roosevelt adventure. They urged me to consider the possibility that American society as we knew it wasn't entirely hopeless. I remember Gardner Jackson arguing that the fatal flaw of Marxism was its crude materialism and its denial of the independent existence of the human spirit. It was a rough evening, and when I returned to the campus the following week I wrote Herb with mingled indignation and embarrassment: "This is about my supposedly 'red' orgy. I want to allay your fears about my trying to be 'smart.' I was merely perturbed by the calmness and imperturbability of your Washington circle and I probably overstated my case. I am, I think, a communist sympathizer—at least with their aims. I couldn't help being troubled by the calm and quiet faith that I found among your friends. I feel the same things you do about communist dogma and intolerance but I resented your virtual dismissal of the entire movement on that ground. When, as a simple fact, there are 13,000,000 still unemployed and Roosevelt promises jobs for 250,000, I can't help feeling that Washington life has made you too hopeful about how things will turn out. Consequently I was probably dogmatic and unthinking in my attitude. I had left an atmosphere of revolution and passed into your quiet realm of evolution, of 'faith in time.' I'm still too much of a newspaperman to be a good communist but I think you are thinking of the movement in terms of people you don't like rather than of ideas. I don't expect a revolution in America to parallel that of Russia's; there will be many variations of pure communist doctrine. But I hope that you recognize the need for a change. Let me repeat, I am not sure where I stand and I should probably still prefer to work for the *Times* than the *Daily Worker*."

In the autumn and through the ensuing winter of 1934, the world still seemed hell-bent for self-destruction at exactly the pace foretold by the Marxist prophets. Early in January, John T. Flynn, then an editor of the *New Republic*, came up to the campus to tell us that Roosevelt's NRA was the highway to American fascism. "We are far on the road that in Italy meant the permanent adjournment of the legislative body," he exclaimed. In Austria the socialists fought gallantly in defense of social democracy, but they lost; the guns that destroyed the workers' homes in Vienna seemed to sound a farewell salute to the dream of peaceful reform.

In New York a dismal echo of the Austrian debacle should have given us longer pause than it did on the journey to communism. The socialists had joined with the big liberal unions to stage a Madison Square Garden tribute to the victims of Dollfuss's assault. The communists, outraged because Fiorello H. La Guardia, whom they were currently describing as a "fascist," had been invited to address the rally, stormed the scene and precipitated a riot. The result was a shambles and it should have been eye-opening. But the communists had an inordinate gift for muddying such an argument. They quickly devised elaborate explanations of their conduct, insisted that the presence of La Guardia was a provocative affront to the militant working class and, moreover, the socialists were always getting mixed up with dubious characters whose hearts belonged to the bourgeoisie. For a few days up at Columbia some of the devout communist leaders were hard put to translate these explanations, but gradually the matter was written off as another, if unhappy, incident in the larger struggle.

It is, I think, partly fortuitous that I left socialism so quickly and headed for communism. Had Don Henderson and "Tuffy" Cutler been socialists, it is conceivable that some of us might have stayed with them; yet what was happening at Columbia mirrored the general trend in the radical intellectual world where Stalinism was steadily brushing the socialists aside. There were probably two chief reasons for its success in this rivalry. One was that a time of disorder breeds an attachment for extremist solutions; Charles E. Coughlin was beginning to be heard, and other demagogues of the Right were inflaming their followers. More important, however, was the communist claim to a proprietary interest in the Soviet regime. After all, there had been only one "successful" workers' revolution and the communists professed to be its local descendants. Russia was a going concern. In a world beset by unemployment the Russians (we were told) had everybody working. If there were occasional reports of trouble in paradise, they could be discounted as the evil imaginings of the "capitalist press."

At any rate, this was no time for quibbling. Admittedly I was never able to master the Theory of Surplus Value, a key tenet in the whole Marxist analysis of capitalist economy, and there were whole sections of Lenin I found insufferably dull and seemingly descriptive of a planet thousands of miles removed from America. One of my deeper humiliations as a Marxist scholar occurred at the end of my junior year. I had fairly regularly attended an economics seminar jointly conducted by Cutler and an astute classical economist named Raymond J. Saulnier. There, among other things, we read *Das Kapital* and the two instructors wrangled pleasantly through most of the semester. For more open-minded students than me their cordial encounters may have been illuminating. It was obvious even to me that Cutler wasn't scoring any knockouts but I automatically gave him the decision on long-range points. At the end of the term half of the examination consisted of oral questioning jointly conducted by the two instructors. I appeared for my grilling at the appointed hour and spent a mortifying interval trying to answer questions about the Marx I had read. When we got to the Theory of Surplus Value and the esoteric details thereof, I suffered an almost total loss of speech. I am sure Saulnier enjoyed my embarrassment as poor "Tuffy" tried frantically to rescue me, but to no avail. In the end, by some sort of compromise never divulged to me, I was given a B in the course. This grade could only have signified that Saulnier's charity had been blended with Cutler's belief that there should be some earthly reward for the author of anti-fascist *Spectator* editorials.

But these theoretical difficulties were secondary. The essential fact, stated and restated by Strachey and the other popularizers, was that America had limitless resources; that it was man's blindness and avarice, rather than any act of God or immutable law of nature, that was responsible for continuing economic crisis; and out of such crisis came suffering and war. The fault could always be traced to the ownership of the means of production.

Lenin's diatribes against Kautsky might be academic, but there was nothing complicated about the unemployment statistics issued annually by the International Labor Office. In the spring of '34 the ILO offered what was supposed to be a hopeful note. In the year in which Franklin D. Roosevelt had occupied the

White House, unemployment in the United States had declined from 13,294,000 to 11,374,000. We made wry jokes about this modest "progress." It was, we thought, adequate commentary on the period when Chester McCall, the Assistant Secretary of Commerce, publicly implored business organizations to hire college graduates as "apprentices," paying them nominal salaries but "preparing them for future economic leadership."

As the months of my junior year went by I increasingly felt that my failure to join the communists was simply proof of my own timidities and prejudices rather than the product of any reasonable objection. I was middle class, a disability of which the communists never hesitated to remind me. Being middle class, I was afflicted, I told myself, by obsolete notions of making my way in the world. In the same self-accusatory tone I charged myself with an attitude of superiority toward the working class. I feared I might even be furtively guilty of some type of Columbia snobbishness toward the boys and girls from other local colleges. I was being too sensitive to the widely voiced assertion that neurotics dominated the local communist hierarchy.

There were, indeed, many communist eccentrics. But in any discussion of the deficiencies of communists as human beings, my classmate Dave Cook was the answer. He was, I was sure, destined to be the John Reed of our generation. Born and raised in Britain, he had come to the United States to work his way through Columbia. He was thoughtful, witty, tolerant and articulate; he was also very handsome, dark-haired with flashing brown eyes and a countenance that hovered between gaiety and gravity. He looked like a matinée idol with character. Unlike many of us, he took his studies as seriously as his communism. He was an extremely able student, well liked by classmates of all political hues and respected by his professors. In another time he would almost certainly have been voted the member of his class most likely to succeed. Instead he had chosen to be a communist. This had not deprived him of his humor, his flexibility and his kindness; he was the most persuasive communist I ever knew, and I have met few human beings as decent and generous as he seemed to be.

Cook was the answer, it seemed to me, to those who cried that communists were disorderly malcontents incapable of achieving stability in any society. He had all the attributes usually regarded as the requisites of success in the competitive system; but he had— so I believed—the sense to recognize that such worldly prizes were meaningless on a planet facing doom.

As the *Spectator* elections approached, I began to wonder whether I hesitated to become a communist only because I feared that doing so might impair my chance to become editor. I agreed with the communists that the world was in dreadful shape and that any possibility of achieving tranquillity hinged on men's capacity to change the system. If I firmly believed that, how could I remain apart from those who were really laboring day and night to accomplish the change? Wasn't I simply trying to keep the best of two worlds, retaining the surface respectability of "independence" and cautiously sharing all the fervor of communist activity?

Throughout this period little pressure was being exerted on me to sign up. Since it appeared likely that I would be made editor of *Spectator*, the communists may have decided it was better strategy to let me coast rather than jeopardize my chances. Then, just a few days before the *Spectator* election, I was formally approached. I had attended a meeting of the Social Problems Club at which preparations for the impending anti-war strike were discussed. When the meeting ended, Mark Graubard, a diminutive, intense man who was an instructor in zoology, left with me. We chatted aimlessly for a few minutes and then he got to the point. Wasn't it time, he asked, for me to become a communist in fact as well as in spirit?

He had me there. I had been asking myself the same question and I hadn't found a satisfactory answer. I did, however, have one last query. It is a mark of the naïveté of the communist novice that I asked it, and accepted his response. I said that I expected to be named editor of *Spectator* in a few days and that I wanted to write as I pleased and to be able to say that any opinions expressed on the editorial page were my own. How could I reconcile the concept of an independent editorial page with formal membership in the disciplined YCL?

Dr. Graubard, like many other participants in the Columbia revolution, has long ago repudiated communism. But on that April day he was a zealous recruiting agent and the innocence of my question did not fluster him. He unsmilingly replied that the answer was very simple; I would henceforth be a member of the Columbia unit of the Young Communist League. All issues confronting the Columbia unit would be freely and fully discussed. Since I would be an active participant in the discussions, I would clearly (the sequitur escaped me at the time, as it does now) be in agreement with the final decisions. Moreover, he added persuasively, it would be a far more satisfactory arrangement than continued non-membership; if I were not present, decisions might be made with which I disagreed and I might then be in the unhappy position of having to comment adversely on the work of men with whom I was in fundamental agreement.

Despite this egregious sophistry I signed my card, thereby pledging allegiance to the cause of the working class of the world and, incidentally, to the defense of the Soviet Union which was, in the communist view, the same thing. There was no longer time to argue or to betray symptoms of "irresponsible individualism."

It was easier to get in than to get out.

Not until summer did I confess to my brother: "One other thing I want to clear up because I think we have had too many misunderstandings about it. It is something I should have told you some time ago, but I have been shamefully hesitant about it. For several months, since just before the *Spectator* elections, I have been a member of the Young Communist League. I should not have kept this from you. . . . I should hate to think this would make any difference in your feeling toward me. . . . I hope you understand this. In the course of the coming year as editor of *Spectator* I'll probably be called 'idiot,' 'adolescent,' 'sensationalist,' and I think you should at least know what's been going on in my head. However unpleasant the consequences, I am a communist; any alternative course would be more unpleasant."

I feverishly recapitulated all my conclusions and that halted our correspondence. Until then he had always displayed affectionate patience, perhaps indicated by the way he saved my most exasperating letters. During my ensuing communist interval the line of communication was broken. I had stopped listening and he was understandably depressed by the sound of my voice. When I heard he was being pressed by his Law School associates to do something about me, I simply viewed that as a sign of Columbia's decline; brotherhood, it seemed to me, could not take precedence over communism.

With my brief colloquy with Graubard, the ceremonies were over, save for the informal congratulations tendered me by other members of the sect when they heard the news. They welcomed me with expressions indicating they were glad to greet me but could not help wondering why I had taken so long.

One other aspect of this proceeding should be noted here because, sixteen years afterward, it has seemingly fascinated both a Senator and a gossip columnist. That was my use of an assumed name on my membership card. When I testified in a libel suit brought against the *Post* and me by Jack Lait and Lee Mortimer in 1952, I was asked whether I had ever been known by any name other than my own in my communist days. The question sounded as if it were designed to elicit the disclosure that I was really William Z. Foster, or his first cousin. I responded quite truthfully that when I joined the YCL I signed my card as "Arthur Lawson" in line with the prevailing revolutionary theory that all of us should have incognitos in reserve for some future day of danger when YCL lists would be scrutinized. But from that day on I was never known by that alias or any other. I was "Comrade Wechsler" in the Columbia unit and in all other communist affiliations. It was as Comrade Wechsler that for several months later on I occupied the exalted and public position of membership on the National Committee of the Young Communist League. The only reason I recall the pseudonym is that in 1937 I collaborated on a play (blessedly unproduced) in which I used my YCL name for one of the characters. That was the only function my unimaginative alias ever served.

I became editor of *Spectator* on the day before the first nation-wide student strike against war. My first editorial was a page-one manifesto summoning students and faculty alike to join in this momentous demonstration.

To the hardened communist chieftains such a strike, I suppose, was primarily a dress rehearsal for what they anticipated as days of domestic upheaval to come. Since they viewed the outbreak of "imperialist war" as one of the great inevitabilities of history, they could hardly have deluded themselves into imagining that our campus capers would deter the "war makers." But to many of us —communists and non-communists alike—who participated in it, the strike was seen as a way of somehow persuading the hidden villains that they could no longer count on American youth to fight their predatory wars.

If we took ourselves with painful seriousness, we received encouragement from distinguished sources. Once again Roy Howard's *World-Telegram*, now so persistently uncharitable to sinners of the thirties, must be quoted as having delivered the benediction on our desperate deeds:

> For generations students like these in many countries have marched off to the bugle call to give their young lives for profiteers, imperialism and aggression. Now they are learning that wars are not all fought for glory and honor.
>
> President Roosevelt has declared that 90 per cent of the people are opposed to war. That helps. But it is the opposition of the cannon-fodder that counts most.

We could not help being impressed and gratified by this analysis of our works.

The editorship of *Spectator* spanned part of two academic years, running from April to April. In the first interval I was involved in only two moderately controversial episodes. The first occurred when the retiring managing board of *Jester*, the college humor magazine, declined to publish a cartoon by the incoming editor,

Ad Reinhardt, in which he burlesqued Dr. Butler's opposition to the child-labor amendment by picturing the university president in the act of wielding a stick against helpless children. When Herman Wouk, *Jester's* outgoing editor, and more recently the author of *The Caine Mutiny*, arbitrarily (in our opinion) decreed that this was not a work of art, we promptly borrowed the cut and unfurled it on *Spectator's* front page. Twenty-four hours later my associates and I were summoned to a conference at which Dean Hawkes patiently suggested that we had gone a bit too far. Like a father whose errant sons have repeatedly confounded him by the mounting seriousness of their follies, he seemed no longer capable of being surprised by anything and determined to keep his temper under any provocation. He neither threatened nor cajoled; the mellowness of his manner was definitely confusing, if not disturbing.

The other incident was an abortive attempt by some campus patriots to "kidnap" me. This scheme was forestalled by Chandler Grannis, a law-abiding citizen who lived next door to me in John Jay Hall and overheard the masked plotters as they were making their way toward my quarters. Upon discovery they fled in disorder and that was about the end of that, except for an anonymous threatening letter adorned by a swastika which I received shortly afterward, and several excited stories in the downtown newspapers which terrified my mother.

That summer brought my first intimate relationship with the "vanguard of the working class," otherwise known as those toilers who had the foresight to join the Communist Party. With communist operations at Columbia largely suspended until the fall semester, those of us who remained in the city were assigned to an all-university communist unit, including, because of the limited manpower available, both Communist Party members and YCLers. Among the party members were two workers in the Teachers College cafeteria who constituted, up to that moment, the only truly working-class representatives in the Columbia brigade. The other eminent member of the group was V. J. Jerome, who was becoming known even then as the "cultural commissar" of communism and whose assignment to our unit was regarded as a sign that we were being taken very seriously in the higher echelon. It is possible that his presence signified nothing except that all communists were supposed to belong to some group somewhere, and as a floating cultural specialist, he may have had no other place to exercise his dialectics in the summertime.

Jerome, one of the defendants in the recent Smith Act prosecutions of communist leaders, was a sad-eyed, ascetic figure who created an atmosphere of deadly discipline. He was clearly a man with whom one did not deal lightly, as we had learned a few months before. Earlier that year "Tuffy" Cutler had written a book review for *Spectator* largely laudatory of Lewis Corey's newly published *Decline of American Capitalism*. To novices and innocents, Corey's work was a scholarly, well-documented application of the Marxian critique. There was only one trouble with Corey's book, from a communist viewpoint; Corey was an ex-communist who had been expelled some years earlier after a bitter clash with the dominant party clique. Consequently he was an evil man, and all his works sinister. Cutler was sharply rebuked by Jerome for his errors of analysis.

So we all measured our words in Jerome's presence, and the result was my introduction to the deepest intensities of communist boredom. It was an experience often to be repeated. To be disappointed and disillusioned on some grand scale can be an unforgettable human adventure; but to be forced to fight off drowsiness in the inner circle of the noblest cause on earth was a dismal augury of things to come. My sharpest recollection of those clandestine gatherings, held in the sweltering tenement living room of one of the Teachers College "prols," is that they were almost irresistibly soporific.

My other tangible remembrance is of the self-consciousness and uneasiness we experienced in our relations with our two working-class comrades. They were the only real workers who had been recruited among the rather large staff of Columbia employees and there were some mildly acrimonious exchanges over their failure to unionize all Columbia University. They countered that they could hardly display more valorous zeal on the job without being fired. Columbia's industrial management had reportedly organized an efficient spy system to discourage any experiments in unionism on the campus, and it would have been foolhardy for our two lonely brethren to defy it. They felt that it was the responsibility of students and faculty members to lead the way. This idea made some sense but it had its limitations. Students could circulate union organizational leaflets indefinitely but somehow at some point somebody would have to stand up and form a union. By all the rules laid down in the classics of proletarian literature that duty devolved on men like our two comrades who had had the prescience to sign up with communism early. But they hadn't read the prole-tarian novels. At the summer's end we still had two working-class members—no more, no less.

We had, however, Comrade Jerome. Though I would vow under oath that I cannot remember a single phrase he recited, I can testify that he was an authentic caricature of a communist scholar. Somehow the music of his tedious voice remains in my ears even though the lyrics are utterly lost. When the Government many years later placed him in the dock in the Smith Act case, it was peculiarly hard for me to believe that his advocacy of anything could constitute a clear and present danger to the republic. What-ever his original talent as a poet, he was a singularly uninflam-matory revolutionist. He later achieved renown as communism's missionary to Hollywood. To have heard him whispering listless Marxist nothings to some wide-eyed film heroine would, I am sure, have been nothing short of colossal.

Had I been more perceptive, I might also, however, have de-tected the tragic quality in the man, and learned something then of the destruction of human material in the communist movement. For Jerome unquestionably possessed genuine intellectual ca-pacities and once he may have been a promising poet in whom a flame burned brightly. Now he had become a pedantic purveyor of stilted communist slogans, a hunter of heresy and a lonely, bitter man.

In August the American Youth Congress was founded in New York City and I was a participant in what was subsequently described as one of the major communist coups of the decade, if not of the century.

The Congress wasn't originally inspired by the communists. It was the brain child of a large, energetic and highly un-Marxian young woman named Viola Ilma who thought it would be nice if young people, whether Boy Scouts or YMCAers or National Student Leaguers, got together to combat "cynicism" and raise everybody's spirits. Youth must be heard, she declared, without any preconceived or exact notion of what youth ought to say. The vagueness of her view as to the Congress's ultimate mission led to some doleful leftist warnings that she was plotting a dark fascist enterprise; but she had no plot. She was a friendly and ambitious young lady with a yearning to do something constructive. Her Congress was a pushover for the communists, who knew what they wanted to do and were organized to do it.

From the communist view, Miss Ilma's timing could hardly have been improved. The communist line was already in process of change, a change to be formalized and proclaimed the following year in Dimitrov's call for united fronts everywhere to halt the onrush of fascism. In the United States and elsewhere there was already increased emphasis on finding "broader bases" of operation and on abandonment of "sectarian" ways. The communists were sure the moment was at hand for bigger ventures than ever before, and that they would no longer be talking to themselves.

The basis for selection of delegates to the assemblage wasn't too precise and, in advance of the three-day session, the communists had assured ample representation for themselves. All varieties of youth groups were invited to elect delegates; young men and women who displayed most eagerness about attending found it easy to get themselves elected and many of them conveniently

turned out to be young communists who had received advance
notice about the importance of the conclave.

After some sharp parliamentary skirmishes and a few uproars
the communists fastened their grip on the new organization. In
their own fashion they had earned it. After the evening sessions
each day most of the delegates went out to roam around the city
and enjoy themselves. Those of us who were communists slipped
off to a "fraction" meeting at which plans for the next day's developments were carefully rehearsed. All the top brass of the Young
Communist League was on hand for these left-wing skull-sessions.

By the time the Congress was formally opened Miss Ilma was no
longer its leader. She and a number of her bewildered conservative
adherents had fled the scene; the socialists, who knew what was
happening but were powerless to prevent it, were reduced to a
secondary role. The communists, while granting various consolation
prizes to assorted representatives of pacifist, religious and other
groups, carefully allotted the key positions to themselves. From the
time of that convention, the machinery of the Youth Congress
was securely in communist hands, but that fact was disguised more
skilfully than in many other front organizations.

A YMCA Midwesterner was elected chairman for the first year.
He was generally pictured as a spokesman of "grass-roots" youth,
as a "moderate" and as a fitting spiritual leader for so true a cross
section of the younger generation. It was not generally announced,
however, that he had been present at the communist fraction
meeting the night before at which it was decided that he would
be spontaneously chosen chairman the next day.

Although the seizure of Miss Ilma's Youth Congress seems a
cold and bloodless revolution in retrospect, most of us viewed it
then as an inspiring achievement in the world-wide fight against
creeping fascism. We did not think of ourselves as communist
"infiltrators" stealthily invading someone else's property; we were
persuaded that Miss Ilma was a potential tool of American reaction and the very vagueness of her thoughts was regarded as sufficient proof that she was dangerous. Our coup, we were certain,
had halted fascism on its own five-yard line. We could not believe

the obvious—that she and her group might be just mixed-up Americans earnestly, if ineptly, trying to grapple with complicated troubles; there always had to be a plot.

So the communists captured what was left of Miss Ilma's long-planned movement and from that point on they ran the show. Great issues were either resolved along communist lines or deftly sidestepped; at times the most vexing question confronting the Congress was to determine the age at which a man ceased to be a youth, and therefore no longer eligible for leadership. When the dignitaries began to lose their hair, this was no minor tragedy to the movement.

From 1934 until that day in August, 1939, when the Kremlin signed its pact with nazism, the Youth Congress was a relatively successful communist project. Then the masquerade suddenly ended as, one after the other, Youth Congress leaders who had been impersonating liberals abruptly revealed that they were committed to follow the communist line no matter where it led. It was not until then that many who had worked with the Congress finally walked away from it.

This sounds as if the deception had been magnificently clever. In some isolated cases it was; some of the most cherubic, wide-eyed and simple faces turned out to have been communists all along. But the camouflage would never have worked so well if the times had not been favorable for the flowering of such a movement. There was often no conspicuous rift between what the communists proposed and what many other Americans independently believed.

It was not what the Youth Congress did, but the deceit on which it was based that seems in retrospect most significant. The fraud began that summer of 1934 when members of the communist fraction posed as simple peasants from the hinterland to obtain top posts in the structure of the organization. Those of us in the YCL were taught never to pause to contemplate the meanness of the artifice. Political chicanery is hardly novel, but the communists made the living of a political double life a commonplace. Lenin had said the end justified the means and, on that premise, the communists scorned any conception of personal honor in political relationships.

Mrs. Roosevelt gave warm and generous help to the Youth Congress in the years preceding the debacle of 1939. The communists who held strategic posts in it responded to her benevolence by lying to her about themselves and seeming to enjoy the hoax. As a result she has often been held up to ridicule as a hopeless innocent who was fooled by politically precocious children. But that is another half-truth about the era. For the sympathy she had manifested for the proclaimed good intentions of the Congress won her the reverence of many youths who did not know what it was about. When the crisis came in 1939, many listened to her and not to the communists. If the youthful commissars had "used" her, they were punished when it mattered most to the country. Hers was the last word.

Nancy and I were married on October 5th of my senior year, two months before her eighteenth birthday and a few weeks before my nineteenth. Because neither of us had attained the age required for a license, we were subjected to the indignity of having our parents accompany us to City Hall to signify their approval.

Many earnest dialogues preceded our decision. We had already begun to think of my devoting the rest of my days to The Movement; although we were foggy about the details, we assumed I would be assigned to some revolutionary post after graduation the following June. The life of a "functionary" was unpredictable and certainly unremunerative. Where would I be twelve months from now? But time, as usual, won the argument. Since all our prospects were uncertain and likely to be brief, it made no sense to wonder whether any personal arrangement was practicable. If communism was to be outlawed (a subject of almost continuous speculation), we might as well plan to go underground together.

Our courtship had been intense and involved with myriad outside alarms and excursions. Our dates were always adjusted to meetings and conferences. Yet, with all our sense of urgency and with all our presentiments of impending disaster, we were enjoying life.

A decade earlier the beautiful and the damned were trying to live as frantically as possible because they did not want to confront what they blandly called the futility of life. We were convinced that, though we were living on the edge of catastrophe, we had been uniquely blessed with a knowledge of what was happening to us. It was a shock to our parents that we married when we were so young, but we were sure time had lost all its conventional meanings. How could one postpone anything when there might be so few tomorrows? This is not to suggest that we pitied ourselves. We lived on a keyed-up plane of continuing adventure and we rather pitied those who could not share the cosmic fun. Only the meetings—the endless, repetitive meetings—intermittently reminded us that we too had our moments of boredom.

Our honeymoon was a one-day trip to New Haven for the Columbia-Yale game. Possibly the seeds of my disintegration as a Bolshevik were already there; despite *Spectator's* continued disapproval of big-time football, I couldn't stay away from the game. Dave Cook and Carol Fraenkel, Nancy's older sister, went along with us. It rained most of the afternoon but we festively immunized ourselves with alcohol. Columbia won 12-6. Then we went back to New York to the one-room basement apartment on West Tenth Street which our families were subsidizing for us.

The remaining months of my term as *Spectator* editor were intermittently stormy and, in retrospect, appallingly grim. Most of the time I reiterated the view that war and fascism were upon us, and that Dr. Butler was fiddling while civilization burned. My fear that I might find myself at variance with communist policy on any weighty matter proved largely groundless. This lack of conflict I must partly ascribe to my own uncritical acceptance of the bulls handed down by the *Daily Worker* rather than to any leniency in the communist hierarchy. If I had chosen to cast any stones at the Soviet dictatorship, I no doubt would have heard from headquarters. Actually much of what I wrote was not identifiably communist doctrine. It reflected the prevailing left-wing intellectual fashion of the day. Most of the editorials were as acceptable to the socialists and their sympathizers as to the communist set. At no time did I try to advance the "theory of social-fascism"— the communist decree that socialists and trade-union leaders were just as wicked as the fascists because they "objectively" aided them. Even in my more submissive communist days I could not embrace the doctrine that Norman Thomas was a vassal of reaction. And anyway, as the year wore on, the United Front was temporarily improving communist manners.

We battled unmerrily on, alternately tilting with the munitions makers and the college officials. When student fees were raised, we believed we had at last found an issue which touched the deepest economic nerve and which, according to our dogma, should have stirred the largest indignation. But far more students attended anti-war rallies than ever gathered to decry this attack on their parents' pocketbooks. Then the *Nation* revealed in a series of articles that the Casa Italiana, the Italian cultural center on the campus, was a hotbed of fascists. We jumped at that, thereby landing once again in the awkward position of demanding academic freedom for communists and the simultaneous suppression of fascists.

The intensity of our activity was in almost inverse ratio to the amount of thought that accompanied it. We must have been particularly obnoxious to those serious undergraduates who had failed to see the Marxist dawn and who were living out their undergraduate days without benefit of the faith we had found. On one occasion Philolexian, the campus literary society, held a poetry reading by candlelight. In a *Spectator* editorial I proceeded, with the fury of a precocious philistine, to chide these youths for their blind escapism, their failure to perceive that the artist's future was on the picket line and their attempt to get away from it all by turning out the lights. One of the young men assailed in this manifesto tartly retorted that it was an old custom of Western man to witness plays in a darkened theatre and that just conceivably men might find poetry stimulating under the same conditions. We scorned his answer and dismissed the participants as frail souls incapable of facing the rugged realities. And we went downtown to applaud *Stevedore*, a blood-and-thunder proletarian drama founded on a "solid" Marxist analysis of good and evil. We read the proletarian novels of Grace Lumpkin, Fielding Burke and Jack Conroy and of countless others who had sprung to their typewriters to herald the final conflict.

We also officially deplored Columbia's acceptance of the first Rose Bowl bid in its history, but some of us sat a little furtively in the lobby of Hartley Hall on the day of the game, listening to the radio broadcast and enjoying every minute of Lou Little's proudest triumph.

At a couple of intervals Dean Hawkes tried to calm our editorial passion. So did Abe Sirkin, my editorial associate, who occasionally winced in public at some of my louder words. Abe was a notable example of a student who took a very good look at communism and refused to be stampeded. A campus Socrates, he had the exasperating habit of continuing to ask questions, no matter who said what.

Throughout my tenure as *Spectator* editor there were periodic rumblings of dissatisfaction among some student leaders. Ever since Reed Harris's year, an increasingly vocal body of undergraduates had been asserting that *Spectator* did not "represent" student opinion, which was true, and that some formula for obtaining a less cantankerous product was needed, which was difficult. At one point Student Board, dominated by critics of *Spectator*, decided to conduct a student poll to establish beyond dispute that nearly everyone felt it was time for a change. But it turned out to be a stalemate. A substantial majority of students neglected to vote, indicating simply that some of them couldn't make up their minds and that a great many of them didn't really care one way or another. We publicly hailed this plainly inconclusive result as victory. Actually the poll taught me the elementary lesson that the bystanders far outnumber the participants in almost any conflict.

The recurrence of this phenomenon has been a constant shock to this day. The degree to which some of us become more deeply involved than others may be as much one of temperament as of

belief. Many people instinctively recoil from controversy and turmoil; some of us seem incapable of remaining in our seats.

Just a few weeks before my term was to end, the *Spectator*
argument was suddenly renewed. A faculty-student committee
which had been appointed to consider the status of student publications issued a report recommending a series of changes in the
constitution and by-laws under which *Spectator* operated. The
most important proposal was that the editorial policy of *Spectator*
be determined jointly by the four members of the managing
board, rather than by the editor himself. The theory was that in
the ordinary course of events it was an arithmetical unlikelihood
that four radicals would win the highest posts.

So it happened that in April, 1935, there were two student
strikes, rather than the annual one to which the campus had become habituated. In addition to the now annual peace strike,
there was a strike voted by the full staff of *Spectator* in protest
against Student Board's decision to impose the constitutional
changes whether we liked them or not. We published a special
edition of *Spectator* with all its columns blank except for a page-
one editorial declaring that we had taken this step to dramatize
the threat to *Spectator's* independent existence. Whereupon Student Board promptly suspended publication of the paper.

We proceeded to raise funds all over the campus to publish it
as a private venture. We came out on schedule the next day, with
the word "Columbia" omitted from the masthead, and we sold
more than a thousand copies of the hastily prepared edition.

Over the week-end there were truce negotiations. The administration was fearful that another big mess was on its hands. We
were getting more support than had been anticipated, not, I suspect, as a tribute to our opinions but as a protest against any
form of interference with our right to express them. The proposal
in dispute hardly constituted direct censorship; it merely provided
that four men, rather than one, fix policy; but we argued that
arbitrary imposition of any changes in *Spectator* without prior
approval in a student referendum could set a precedent for more
drastic censorship. Finally Student Board's spokesmen agreed to

permit a referendum while we promised to abide by the new rules in the meantime. The accord was accepted. In a somewhat anticlimactic aftermath to this furor, the referendum resulted some weeks later, after my term had expired, in approval of the Student Board proposals by a margin of about 6 to 5.

That year the peace strike was nearly twice as large at Columbia as it been a year before. I led 3500 students in a solemn recitation of the Oxford pledge and numerous faculty dignitaries participated. Dr. Reinhold Niebuhr warned that war was steadily nearing, but added: "We do not inevitably have to participate in that war. If war should come now Columbia would have the worst kind of fascism. We must build a civilization in which war is impossible."

Dr. John Herman Randall said: "The immediate cause of war is that people like yourselves can be fooled into thinking that war is worthwhile." We vowed never to be fooled.

In April, 1931, the great Reed Harris strike had evoked little tangible faculty support. Now, four years later, the great peace strike was almost a community festival, blessed by many of the university's outstanding faculty figures. Our elders, we told ourselves jauntily, were learning the facts of life.

The next day I wrote my farewell editorial as editor of *Spectator*. If I had discreetly omitted serializing the Communist Manifesto in previous editions, I now told nearly all.

"Capitalism was a phase of history," I intoned.

> It lived a full life and it will be die hard. But surveying its frail structure today, its prolonged illness which has brought such suffering and misery for the world, we can only bid it Godspeed. For the great body of people—students, workers, farmers and the sinking middle class—capitalism offers only a postgraduate course in unemployment, war and reaction. . . .

Now there were less than two months of college left and, for what seemed like the first time in years, I slowed up long enough to look around. Even for a campus communist, those final weeks could be a curiously sentimental time. Suddenly I began to go to classes with desperate and eager regularity, as though I had be-latedly remembered that was why I was at college in the first place. I felt warmth and affection toward professors whose classes I had been perpetually cutting and I had an uncontrollable impulse to tell Dean Hawkes that I was really glad to have known him. In a vague way I began to conclude that I had had a magnificent time, possibly the time of my life, amid all the noise and violence and bitterness. Perhaps there was in all this a dim awareness of a kind of make-believe that shrouds even the most epic campus struggle. One did go back to a bull session at John Jay Hall, rather than to a fascist dungeon, when the evening's tumult was over; the hangovers were sometimes more memorable than the head-cracking.

I had little—perhaps too little—fear for my economic future. I had never really had to face the problem of going it alone, and I suppose I was at least subconsciously sure that someone would take care of my immediate wants as long as our staggering society endured. I do not know how generally true this was; certainly there were some undergraduates who were deeply troubled by the prospect of postgraduate unemployment. In the economic realm I think that at that time I feared success more than failure—success that would be empty and corrupt, and illusory anyway because the world as we knew it had so little time to live. More-over, how could any man seek "success" in the old terms while wars raged and humans starved?

The uncertainty and nostalgia of those final weeks may have been partially created by the realization that I was now face to face with the real thing. The luxuries of undergraduate rebellion were over and now came the great tests. I was married; I was also wedded to a movement which, I had to acknowledge, I knew only by name and reputation. I had seen little of it outside Co-lumbia. Now, whatever I did, I would be moving into a rougher and bigger league where the V. J. Jeromes played.

The reverie was interrupted by a final fling. Shortly before Commencement, eleven members of the Anti-War Committee at the College of Physicians and Surgeons—Columbia's medical school—were suddenly expelled.

As a result of these expulsions I did not join my class at Commencement Day exercises. I was picketing the campus. This was, perhaps, the appropriate climax to the four years I had spent on Morningside Heights.

4

Once the locale shifted from the congenial Columbia landscape to closer quarters downtown I sensed fairly quickly that I was not at home in The Movement. I remained a communist for a little more than two years after graduation from college. For a few months of that time I was a member of the Executive Committee of the Young Communist League. Yet even as I was presumably rising in the communist setup I had the intermittent sensation that I didn't belong there. I could not know until much later how many others who were going through the same public motions were equally uncomfortable. It was not that we had discovered evil in naked form. Indeed, we saw much individual goodness and selflessness. It was primarily that the atmosphere was suffocating; we had come to communism in a spirit of rebellion and we found ourselves imprisoned in the most ruthless orthodoxy any political faith ever imposed. We seemed to be living in a strange, faraway country ruled with iron rigidity by men quite unlike any we had ever known. Secretly many of us began to yearn for more familiar territory almost as soon as we entered this weird underworld of fanaticism and heresy hunting. Yet few left overnight and some tarried for a long time and a few are still locked in. The longer one stayed, the more difficult it became to leave; there was a sort of law of diminishing departure, depending upon the length of the period of servitude.

For some weeks before graduation it had been agreed that I would go to work full-time in the national office of the National Student League after Commencement. In late spring I was summoned downtown to discuss my future. That was, I think, the first time I ever visited the "Ninth Floor," then regarded as the inner sanctum of United States communism. Actually it was the top floor of a loft building on East Thirteenth Street where communist headquarters was then located, but it was surrounded with an aspect of awe and mystery. There the dignitaries of the party and the Young Communist League had their offices. Access to them was not supposed to be easy, and it was a true sign of ascension when one was called to the Ninth Floor level.

I was interviewed by Max Weiss, a light-haired, pedantic YCL chieftain. He had been expelled from City College after one of the innumerable political wars there a few years earlier and had plunged at once into full-time communist activity.

"Isn't it time you decided to become a professional revolutionary?" he asked. I remember his use of the phrase; it had a portentous sound. I told him that I was ready to decide. He suggested that for the next couple of years I should remain in "student work." As things turned out, I never graduated; that was my first and last mission. Since I still considered myself a journalist, he suggested that I prepare to assume the editorship of the National Student League magazine.

It didn't work out exactly that way because, at just about Commencement time, I was asked to write a book on the student movement, then the subject of almost continual public debate. It was agreed on the Ninth Floor that this would be a useful propaganda venture and I was freed for the summer for that enterprise. I wrote it in our basement flat on Tenth Street; during the steaming summer nights I sat at the typewriter in my shorts and made the acquaintance of numerous Village inebriates who came to our window to investigate the clatter.

The book was published that fall under the title *Revolt on the Campus,* and it got me into my first ideological scrape with the communist scholars. I cavalierly forgot to submit a copy of the original manuscript to the Ninth Floor for inspection, where all communist works were supposed to be scrutinized for "deviations" before they were unveiled in public. This Marxian lapse was called to my attention by Adam Lapin, a genial, pink-cheeked YCL leader who had been editing the NSL magazine and later became a bigwig on the *Daily Worker*. By that time the book was already in proof and was being rushed to press. I hastily assembled the galleys for Lapin. He confronted me with the bad news the next day. There was, it seemed, one inexcusable error, along with certain other minor flaws. I had devoted two pages to some indignant comment on the campaign that had been waged by the Hearst press against Professor Sidney Hook of New York University. Dr. Hook was then (as now) held in low esteem by both Hearst and the communists. He was an anti-Stalinist radical, which made him, in the judgment of the Hearst analysts, "more radical than the communists," and, in the view of the Stalinists, a "Trotskyite agent of fascism." Now here was a pretty ideological problem. The communists (and a lot of other people) said the Hearst press was pro-fascist; but since Hook was officially proscribed as a Trotskyite agent of fascism, how would we explain the Hearst attack on him? Surely these passages would just create confusion, Lapin exclaimed, and I would be well advised to omit any reference to the Hook episode. He did not say this too severely; he was almost apologetic about it. Then, as on so many ensuing occasions, I had the feeling that he suffered as he translated the official absurdity of the party line. Fortunately, I had the only unanswerable answer; the publishers had told me it was too late for any further amendments and certainly the elimination of two pages was out of the question. So the references to Dr. Hook were published as written. My error, however, was not lightly discounted. It took several days for the Ninth Floor to decide whether the book could be promoted through official communist channels in the light of this grievous mistake. When a dispensation was finally granted, it was accompanied by clear admonitions not to go around publishing any more such works without advance consultation on the highest level.

That autumn, working for the National Student League, I had my first personal adventure in what was known as a capitalist court. It did not quite conform to our gloomy expectations. Hollywood had just released a film called *Red Salute*, a B-movie described in the advance notices as a slashing, satiric attack on undergraduate radicalism. When the picture arrived in New York for presentation at the Rivoli, it was decided that the only appropriate greeting for this affront to student manhood and womanhood was a picket line. I was one of those in charge of the demonstration. The police lacked sympathy for the picketing and finally decided to disperse the line. At that point I was hoisted to the shoulders of some of my embattled comrades and began to deliver a somewhat intemperate harangue on the destruction of human liberty at the corner of Broadway and Forty-ninth Street. By then a fairly large crowd had assembled and the police decided the moment had come to shift the scene to Night Court. As the orator of the evening I was arrested first and about twenty others were tapped with me.

We sang out our revolutionary defiance in the patrol wagon. By the time the case was called an International Labor Defense attorney was on hand. It was nearly 3 A.M.; the magistrate, after a long evening reviewing the nightly parade of pimps and prostitutes, seemed benevolently disposed toward our gallery of youthful faces. He indicated early in the proceedings that he did not believe any grave crime had been committed and that he was inclined to send us home to bed. Our attorney was less mellow. He clearly felt that no chance should be lost to use the courtroom as a sounding board for the ideas of revolutionary youth. Ever since Dimitrov had recited his speeches at the Reichstag trial, it was agreed that he had set the pattern for behavior in any courtroom struggle, large or small. So while the judge tried to curtail the script with broad hints of a merciful verdict, the ILD's barrister thundered on, describing the iniquitous character of the film and the infamous oppression practiced by the police. He insisted on calling me to the stand and leading me through a series of questions; my answers were supposed to explain for the whole world's enlightenment why I felt an overwhelming moral compulsion to protest against *Red Salute*. But my responses were lamentably guarded and uninspired because, like most of the demonstrators, I hadn't seen the movie. As the attorney persisted, the magistrate seemed finally to be growing impatient. I had the feeling that the loquacious passion of our lawyer's defense might finally win us jail sentences. When at last he paused briefly to reload, the magistrate abruptly halted him and released us.

That Christmas Nancy and I, along with a contingent of New York delegates, traveled to Columbus in chartered busses during a bitter all-night snowstorm. There the National Student League and the socialist Student League for Industrial Democracy were to merge into the American Student Union, the first unification of American communists, socialists and liberals in the manner prescribed by the theorists of the Popular Front. The ASU became the major student affiliate of the American Youth Congress.

The young men and women who journeyed to Columbus from almost every area of the country that Christmas week were the troubled children of an anxious age. About half of them were communists or socialists; some were guilt-ridden sons of wealth, some were playboys craving new diversion and some undoubtedly had had unhappy childhoods. But, viewed as a group, they would probably have borne close resemblance to any undergraduate class photograph of the time. I know some died soon afterward in Spain and others found serenity in religion. Some became labor organizers and some have grown up to be pillars of their local chambers of commerce. A few have remained trapped on the dreary communist island and a few others probably belong to the McCarthy fan clubs. But many—perhaps most—of them have grown up to be thoughtful, independent citizens who renounced their sectarian dogmas without becoming reconciled to injustice and oppression.

The convention was high-spirited and harmonious. There were some objections voiced to the inclusion of the Oxford pledge in the ASU program and a few liberal students felt the language of the draft platform was too severe. But on the whole the event was heralded as a great landmark in left-wing political life. For that fleeting moment we really seemed to be making radical history. In one respect, of course, the communists conducted business as usual. "Fraction" meetings were held each night after the sessions.

At the convention's end five national officers were elected. Joe Lash, one of the early student socialists and previously Executive Secretary of the SLID, was named to that post in the ASU. The socialists realized this was the decisive office, since it involved steady and direct communication with all the chapters; the communists yielded the position because they were still wooing the socialists. Molly Yard, a Swarthmore graduate and a determinedly nonconformist socialist, assumed the agonizing role of Treasurer; Celeste Strack, who had been a revolutionary heroine at the University of California at Los Angeles, was to be in charge of organizing the high-school chapters; I was designated Director of Publications, which chiefly meant editing *The Student Advocate*.

In the mood of surface congeniality which characterized the communist attempt to convince the socialists that they could live amicably with us, we also agreed to the election of George Edwards, a socialist Phi Beta Kappa from Southern Methodist, as National Chairman. George, who later went to work in an auto plant, became a UAW organizer and won election as President of Detroit's Common Council, cast a distrustful eye at the whole "amalgamation" experiment. He was regarded by the communists as a troublesome character almost from the start.

The communists had stationed me in the ASU on the assumption that I would zealously carry out the communist line there. But I soon found myself far more interested in promoting the Popular Front idea than in performing factional communist assignments. I was sure Joe Lash and I could prove something to the world by working together harmoniously. He felt the same way about it.

I had the general feeling that communists and socialists, pacifists and Quakers, single-taxers and dedicated civil libertarians were on the side of the angels in the conflict against the mighty battalions of reaction, and that it was pointless for us to quarrel among ourselves so much of the time. When the Popular Front program was proclaimed in Moscow, I felt better about being a communist. I deeply believed that the Popular Front was not a momentary tactic but a great turning point in political history.

Actually the whole concept of trying to reconcile so many theoretical irreconcilables was too simple-minded. A strategic decision fashioned by a few men in Moscow was supposed to make the workers, liberals and radicals of the world one big happy family and wipe out the heritage of factional disunion, philosophical disagreement and psychological incompatibility. In reality this effort merely tended to suppress serious discussion of great issues. In the year and a half I edited *The Student Advocate* we rarely touched upon long-range political dilemmas. Our pages were dedicated to "immediate issues" because that was the only realm in which we could maintain the precarious structure of unity.

Even then new cleavages were developing. Until 1936, many students had been most deeply roused by the slogans of opposition to war. To most of the participants in the peace strikes of that period, a stand against war meant just that and no more.

But now, for those who were communists, a drastic change in orders was being formulated. Recovering slowly and groggily from the disaster Hitler had inflicted on the German Communist Party, the Kremlin was beginning to hum a new tune called "collective security." Maxim Litvinov was looking at Geneva as hopefully as was Nicholas Murray Butler. Russia, which heretofore proclaimed its solidarity with the "anti-imperialist" workers of all lands, was now signing mutual defense pacts with the government of capitalist France.

Steadily the communist accent became more anti-fascist than anti-war, and especially so after July, 1936, when General Franco launched his rebellion against the Spanish Republic.

Nancy and I had gone to Nantucket for two weeks; I was finishing my section of a book on which Lash and I collaborated, called *War Our Heritage*. It had been conceived as a kind of handbook for the youth anti-war movement and our joint authorship was supposed to signify the truce between young socialists and communists in the fight against militarism. But I was apparently fated for ideological misfortune in the communist literary set. By the time the book was ready to appear under the imprint of International Publishers, there was grave question in communist circles as to whether it should be released. It suffered from an unmistakable cultural lag; it was an anti-war tract and the new setup called for an anti-fascist battle cry. It was nevertheless published after Lash refused to countenance proposed revisions in the tone and conclusions of the work.

The outbreak of the fascist revolt in Spain stunned the Left. For nearly three years we had been waiting for the news that the German working class had at last risen in the long forecast rebellion against nazism. Now fascism had again seized the offensive. When we first scanned the dispatches few of us fully fathomed what was happening. Reading the news in Nantucket those first few days Nancy and I could barely guess that this was the beginning of the larger war we had been anticipating.

That autumn the American Left became steadily more preoccupied with the Spanish conflict. The long, lonely trek of the International Brigade had begun. That was also, however, the period of Franklin D. Roosevelt's campaign for re-election which ushered in months of confusion for the communist faithful. I began to murmur indiscreet dissents and to receive quizzical, reproachful glances.

We had previously been told to consider Franklin D. Roosevelt a willing creature of capitalism, to damn his NRA as an incipient form of fascism, to burlesque his advances and retreats as symptomatic of the bankruptcy of reformist thought. To those who contended that he was slowly getting somewhere and that the American economy was showing signs of new life, we responded by citing the still unpleasant unemployment figures. Up till then we had just about written off the New Deal as the final, feeble attempt of capitalism to resolve the inner "contradictions" which were to bring its doom.

This was the orthodox communist doctrine of the moment. As every communist some day or other learns, however, the slogans of February can become the deviations of October. By fall a new communist portrait of Franklin D. Roosevelt was unveiled. Moscow's foreign-policy line had changed, and that changed everything. Since FDR seemed favorably disposed toward amicable relations with the Soviets and the Kremlin was now looking for allies in the strangest citadels of capitalism, the American communists had to revise their estimate of that man in the White House. He admittedly fell far short of communist standards; he was still moving too hesitantly in many domestic areas and the communists had not yet fully abandoned all interest in home-front policy. Nevertheless, on the great issues of world affairs, there was much to be said for him, and more every day. Thus was evolved one of the most hilarious campaign slogans of any year: "Defeat Landon at All Costs, Vote for Browder!" It was almost too much for some of us. How, we whispered privately, could one argue in one breath that the supreme duty of progressive mankind was the defeat of the amiable Kansas Republican and simultaneously urge our followers to cast their votes for Browder? Suppose Browder got 100,000 votes, strategically located in close states, and thereby swung the electoral vote to Landon? Weren't we saying in effect: Defeat Landon at all costs but don't help his opponent?

George Orwell has defined in brilliant detail the anatomy of communist double-think; certainly this was our dramatic introduction to it.

At about that time all good communists were being reminded anew of the haunting menace of "Trotskyism." Trotskyism was a miniscule, ineffectual army insofar as it constituted an organized movement; only a handful of Americans knew anything about the teachings of the exiled Soviet hero. What the communists defined as Trotskyism was any serious questioning of the validity of the communist position at a given moment. The mere expression of doubt was the seed of "Trotskyite treason." Nothing is more comparable to the intellectual overtones of present-day McCarthyism than that communist crusade against Trotskyites, real, imagined and alleged. The purge was waged inside and outside the communist movement. It was a total obsession. It destroyed reason and restraint. It often proved as fatal for the hunters as for the hunted; in the grand search for unorthodoxy, men lost all interest in everything else. The innocent, of course, were recklessly labeled along with the guilty. The word "comrade" became a bad joke as one communist eyed another with suspicion. The real objective of the crusade was to crush any vestige of independent thought inside the communist apparatus. Any question raised could be quickly branded as proof that the questioner was a carrier of the dread germ known as Trotskyism. Why else was he asking questions?

The "anti-Trotskyite" vendetta was used to impose the wildest changes in party doctrine on a bewildered membership. Thus the Trotskyist label was affixed to all radicals whose opinions were to the left of the communists, circa 1936-39; actually many of the targets were merely guilty of clinging to positions the communists had just abandoned. Anyone who continued to use the language of revolution in the era of the Popular Front invited the epithet "Trotskyite." To deny that FDR was "a progressive force" was now as serious an error as to have implied a couple of years earlier that he might be a man of reasonably good intentions.

The communist attitude toward Mr. Roosevelt had no connection with the success or failure of any efforts to infiltrate the Government. It was responsive only to the whims of Soviet foreign policy. Once Moscow decided that collective security was the order of the day, communists everywhere were commanded to alter their opinions of the "bourgeois-democratic" governments and to detect new virtue in old devils. Small children may now be under the impression that the communists of the thirties were telling Mr. Roosevelt what to do. The fact is they were largely engaged in a new game of follow the leader and, until further notice, the leader was to be FDR. This is not to say that they weren't trying to obtain positions of power. Obviously they were and in some scattered areas of Washington they succeeded. But collective security was not a communist idea. Dr. Butler was preaching it and Mr. Roosevelt was moving in that direction long before the Kremlin assumed its new world view. The New Deal, far from being the dark design of Moscow, was obviously the program which extinguished any real possibility of communist revolt before the communists temporarily dropped the slogans of revolution.

To many present-day adolescents the only significant event of 1936-37 is that a man named Alger Hiss was transmitting State Department papers to a communist courier named Whittaker Chambers. But to most communists of those years the disheartening fact was the failure of our campaign to convince the State Department and the White House to lift the embargo on Loyalist Spain. The retrospective version of communist strength in the mid-thirties has been as much distorted by ex-communists with romantic recollections as by reactionaries grinding political axes. They have attributed to the gray mediocrities who dominated the communist movement a majestic Machiavellianism bearing little resemblance to any real characters of the time.

I met Earl Browder for the first time in that fall of 1936. The Student Union, after a blissful beginning, was running into trouble; the communists were increasingly annoyed by the stubborn pacifism they met in their attempt to "reorient" the movement toward collective security. The socialists and some other groups were accusing the communists of plotting to undermine the anti-war program and even some of us could not keep pace with the changing line. It was decided that we'd better have a talk with Browder, the Communist Party's General Secretary, to "get ourselves straightened out."

So several of us went up to his refuge on the Ninth Floor one evening and spent long hours listening to him resolve our dilemmas. This former Kansas bookkeeper was a mild-mannered, affable man who seemed almost surprised by his own eminence but who did not let humility modify his opinions. He used that strange, stilted speech common to most communist leaders which usually made their remarks sound as if they had just been roughly translated from the original Russian. He rambled on at length and out of his discourse emerged one of those involuted communist rationalizations. It was true, he said, that we had entered a new period in which collective security was the keystone of communist policy. On the other hand (the discussion always shifted from hand to hand in any true communist analysis), this did not mean abandoning certain of the anti-war positions on which the student movement had been built. It was, he insisted, the communist position that collective security would prevent war; therefore, while agitating for it, we must continue to agitate against the war preparations of the United States Government since only the "war makers" favored such preparations because they didn't want to join hands with the Soviet Union in preserving peace. And so on, far into the night.

I left the gathering unconvinced that everything was clear. If we were committed to the proposition that the free nations ought to band together with Russia to deter fascist aggression, much of the deterrent effect would depend on how strong they were. Neither Hitler nor Mussolini was likely to be impressed by a program of resistance based on unpreparedness. Any effective stand against aggression surely involved the risk of war; but we were now embracing a stand which called for the assumption of all the risks without any of the preparations. At the same time Browder admonished us to intensify our vigilance against "Trotskyism." Most of our troubles, he observed, really stemmed from the spread of that dangerous infection.

When we left the session several of my associates expressed their ecstasy over the flashes of illumination to which we had been exposed. I said nothing. All that seemed apparent was that the communist movement had devised a wide range of sublimation for the experience hitherto known to mankind as thinking.

The communists were trying harder than anyone else at that point to get on speaking terms with the rest of the country. Whatever they did, however, was invariably marked by a furious and comic extremism. Now they announced that "communism is twentieth-century Americanism" and that they were the true sons and daughters of the American Revolution. One of the most serious offenses a communist could commit was to cast any aspersions on the validity of the American tradition we had so long debunked.

Meanwhile there was strife within the Student Union. Just one year after it had been formed, its second convention became a bitter battleground on the issue of peace. The communist bloc vainly shouted that most of the old anti-war slogans were outworn, and all that mattered now was halting fascist aggression. But the socialists and pacifists clung tenaciously to their initial positions. The conflict was resolved in a generally unsatisfactory fashion; it was agreed to take no position at all on the problem of collective security.

One may too easily caricature the debate that was dividing the Student Union. To many of the participants these were grave issues involving difficult choices. While the communists had nothing but contempt for those who were slow to relinquish their previously held anti-war positions, some of those who clung to the banners of the past were hurt and heartbroken by our desertion. One day during that stormy transition I debated Gus Tyler at Hunter College. Tyler, now political director of the International Ladies Garment Workers Union, reaffirmed the socialist position of opposition to any entangling American alliances with other capitalist governments. I defended the communist view that a new day was at hand, and that the Oxford pledge had lost its meaning in this "new situation." When the debate ended a tearful Hunter College girl came up to me and, quivering with anger and disappointment, said: "How could you say those things? When you administered the Oxford pledge to me, you said we must never back down."

Seldom has a man felt more justly rebuked by a wronged woman for forgetting his most sacred vows.

As a full-time employee of the Student Union I received $17.50 a week in those weeks when the ASU's treasury could meet the payroll. Soon after the organization was launched we became aware that raising funds for its modest budget would be our hardest and most continuous task. Although I am sure the communist financial structure was intricate, we never got the impression that there was a great deal of money around. On a few occasions, when we were literally bankrupt and facing eviction from our headquarters or suspension of *The Student Advocate*, we appealed either to Mary Fox of the socialist League for Industrial Democracy or to Gil Green, the Chairman of the Young Communist League. I would guess that in the long run Mary secured us more help than Green did. There were a couple of times when the communists did miraculously produce something like a $500 "loan" to pay the printer's bill, but it always required a long fight.

The problem was complicated by the fact that Joe Lash and I were surely the least talented financial operatives in radical history. Neither of us had any trouble making a collection speech at a public gathering, but to confront a single wealthy contributor (from whom all large blessings really flowed) was an almost unbearable assignment. One afternoon Molly Yard told us a potential sponsor was coming to the office to inspect our headquarters and, if impressed, to give us a genuinely large donation. As the hour set for his arrival neared, Joe and I became more and more flustered and unhappy. The prospect of rising to that social challenge proved overwhelming and we fled the office before he got there.

Thus the life of what was called a "functionary" was often lived on a desultory plane. A characteristic day at the ASU headquarters began with a staff meeting attended by Joe, Molly, Celeste Strack and me. We discussed plans for new chapters, ideological matters and financial trouble. After that the day might be quite vacant and aimless. Although *The Advocate* was supposed to be a monthly, we could rarely afford to come out that often, and it was hard to sustain a schedule when deadlines were so vague. Sometimes I spoke at an ASU chapter meeting in the afternoon or evening; sometimes we sat around for hours with visiting Student Union members who had come to town; a lot of the time Joe and I held long discussions about the condition of mankind in general. Between conventions the pace was not exactly furious. Once in a while I went out of town to speak at regional conferences or local rallies. But most of the time I appeared regularly at our office at 112 East Nineteenth Street, wrote letters requesting articles for *The Advocate* from various celebrities (lamely explaining that we did not pay for contributions), read newspapers, books and magazines, and tried to remind myself that the outward listlessness of the day did not reflect its inner meaning.

As a communist functionary in the Student Union I was periodically invited to attend a "bureau meeting," a weekly conclave of Young Communist League leaders. These sessions were held by about a dozen YCL dignitaries each Saturday morning. They gave me my closest glimpse of the inner wheels of United States communism. What I saw and heard would make an unexciting script for a Senate inquiry. Perhaps I should amend that testimony slightly, for I can hardly claim to remember much of the dry and dreary verbiage of the youthful commissars. I have referred earlier to the monotony which saturated many communist cell meetings. These Saturday-morning conclaves touched the bottom of boredom.

The participants included Gil Green, the small, boyish-faced YCL Chairman who was by far the most attractive character in the room and who seemed to have a degree of authentic humanity denied to many of his comrades. There was Carl Ross, who succeeded Green when the latter was deemed aged enough for a post in the Communist Party. Ross's major qualification appeared to be his Nordic physique, an admittedly important asset at a time when communists were tracing their genealogy back to the American rather than the Russian Revolution. Unfortunately, Ross was a mumbler. It was almost impossible to follow his words; when one did catch up with him, he was invariably reciting the most banal slogan of the day like a small boy sleepily reciting his prayers. There was Henry Winston, a large, genial fellow whose sincerity seemed only equaled by his lack of comprehension of some of the more obscure theoretical clamor. There were Jack Kling and John Little, two clearly tough Bolshevik hombres whose scowls, roars and heavy-handed ironies always made one feel they had just seen a movie about the early leaders of Russian communism. There was Max Weiss, who still looked a little like a shy college professor but who could raise his voice authoritatively when he detected a deviation in the air. And there was Celeste Strack, who vocally dreamed of growing up to be La Pasionaria and deemed it incumbent upon herself to prove that a middle-class college graduate could be as zealous in unearthing "Trotskyism" as the most vigilant proletarian.

And there was "Max." One always uttered his name with quotation marks. I never knew him by any other name; I learned quickly that one did not ask about it, or about him. He was just there. When we faced any ideological quandary, he laid down the law. It was indicated—but never explicitly stated—that "Max" was the representative of the Young Communist International and, from the behavior of the others, one might have deduced that Stalin himself was in our presence. No one ever quarreled with "Max."

He was a squat, heavy-jowled man somewhere in his late thirties. Most of the time his face was extremely morose, as if in contemplation of all the sorrow he'd seen. Once in a while he would appear at a small social gathering and have a few drinks. After that he would inevitably reminisce about the role he had played in the great Soviet purges of incorrigible kulaks. He went back to that story so often that I wondered whether he suffered some lurking remorse about the whole business. But the moral of his story as he told it was that Bolsheviks could not afford to be sentimental about individual human life because the revolution often called for ruthless deeds to achieve greater goals.

I assumed that "Max" was a Russian but we did not think of him as a "Russian agent" or of ourselves as his innocent instruments. Rather we looked at him with a certain awe and respect. He was a real, full-dimension, self-made world revolutionary whose opinions were obviously superior to those of novices like ourselves. The suspicion that he was a Russian merely gave weight to his judgment. After all, the Russians had made a revolution, hadn't they? As the Popular Front concept became firmly established,

"Max" did exhibit occasional perplexities. The newfangled talk about Jefferson and Washington must have sounded strange to his ears. He gradually became adjusted to it and before long he was clamoring for bigger and better Fourth of July ceremonies.

On big occasions "Max" also attended student fraction meetings. At such events as ASU conventions he would hide himself in a rooming house some blocks from the meeting hall. He would meet with us in late evening to review what had been done, uncover the day's errors and plan the next day's maneuvers. I often wondered where he spent his afternoons. He never seemed to have much fun and there must have been times when the tedious, repetitious details of life in the American youth movement seemed far removed from the epic events of his earlier revolutionary existence abroad.

The YCL bureau meetings were long-winded, wearying affairs. Most of the time we seemed to be rehashing the gains and losses of the most recent American Youth Congress or Negro Youth Congress or Student Union convention or student peace demonstration. The caucuses usually began with a long, dull report; then there was what passed for discussion, never to be confused with debate, and then some consideration of what other congress should be held where and when, and what "cadres" should be assigned to it.

This was the dreary face of the movement I knew. We were told nothing of espionage and spy networks and undergrounds. There seems to be clear evidence that the communist apparatus carefully divided its operations so that those who were functioning in the realm of agitation and propaganda were given no access to the murkier layers of intrigue. We never knew about Whittaker Chambers or anyone else holding similar assignments. While there was an atmosphere of furtiveness around communist headquarters, it always had an element of play-acting. The only real concealment I knew of was that of the identities of some of the Youth Congress leaders who were still presenting themselves to the world as serious-minded, groping idealists. We met with them in a special unit devised for their benefit. Often non-communists were invited to

attend those gatherings where, again, we talked about some forthcoming congress or aid to Spain and then, if time permitted, we
sharpened our theoretical wits by turgidly discussing Marxism as
a science for a half-hour.

It is now being said that the meetings of the YCL bureau were
episodes in the conspiracy to seize America. To complete the
record, they must also be set down as stale, flat and exasperatingly
prolonged conclaves in which my major problem was to occupy
my mind while seeming to pay attention. I may as well acknowledge that I met that problem, then and in other circumstances,
by learning to play baseball in my head. The game is perfectly
simple; it requires only a knowledge of the names of players on
two teams. Once you have constructed the batting order, anything
you wish can happen. It is, of course, more interesting if the game
is close and you can order as dramatic a finish as you desire. The
real challenge is to remember, without use of pencil and paper,
the record of each player throughout the game so that you can
visualize the box score when it's over.

Occasionally there were special events to enliven the proceedings. I recall, for example, the trial of one bureau member whose
name had been recommended for expulsion. He was a Negro accused of the high crime of "black chauvinism" which probably
meant, at that juncture, that he had refused to accommodate
himself to the moderate line of the Popular Front. Until that
period the communists had been promoting the doctrine of "self-
determination for the black belt"—the rather spectacular notion
that Negroes should have the right to set up their own republic in
any area where they constituted a numerical majority. Like many
other planks in the early communist program, this was a literal
attempt to transplant the Soviet pattern of ostensibly autonomous
republics to American soil. The idea gained little favor with either
Negroes or whites, and with the advent of the Popular Front it
was quietly pigeonholed. But on this, as on other issues, some who
had been drawn to the communists by specific "advanced" positions were reluctant to join the retreat. This was apparently such
a case.

The trial was strictly a formality, as everyone knew it would be. Once an expulsion was initiated, the outcome was as certain as in any Russian prosecution. This time the defendant did not bother to appear; he knew his number was up. Nevertheless the routines of a judicial proceeding were enacted. One of the bureau members served as prosecutor, solemnly reciting a long list of accusations. There, as in every communist crucifixion of a heretic, it was not considered adequate to show that the man had erred; it was essential to prove that he had been a sinister character all along, that his motives had been venal and his intentions politically dishonorable from earliest infancy. Ugly references to his personal life were inserted as indicative of his general decay. Not many months earlier he had been heralded as a promising fellow representing the flower of revolutionary Negro manhood. Now he was a traitor, opportunist, careerist, an irresponsible individualist and Trotskyite wrecker.

The actors seemed to regard this drama as their own equivalent of the big productions in Moscow. No one raised his voice in behalf of the comrade who had fallen from grace. It seemed a long time since the days when communism symbolized man's protest against inhumanity and injustice.

# 5

When did the decisive doubts begin? Possibly they were always there, even in the high times at Columbia when I was discounting all uncertainties as dread symptoms of middle-class frailty. But perhaps the answer is simpler: every communist is a potential ex-communist. When I was a communist we often attributed defections to the impact of "bourgeois propaganda and prejudice" on simple minds. But that was just another way of saying that in a climate of freedom the communists were extremely vulnerable.

The communists were constantly engaged in a fierce effort to immunize their followers from alien ideas. A devout communist was not supposed to read "anti-Soviet" books and was obligated to discourage others from reading them. As in most censorship crusades, the effect may have been to stimulate curiosity about the forbidden works. By 1937 Nancy and I were defiantly reading Eugene Lyons' *Assignment in Utopia* and it did, I am certain, hasten our exit.

The communist taboos applied not only to reading; they were designed to restrict association with "the enemy" and especially with that hated band loosely described as "Trotskyite." One did not, according to the communist rules, consort socially with such specimens and one did not debate with them in either a public or a private place. This interdict grew steadily more severe as the succession of Moscow trials was presented to the world.

The atmosphere that resulted was stifling. It became more oppressive each week as new sets of Soviet heroes proclaimed their lifelong villainy. But there was also a war in Spain and, for many months, the emotions it created counteracted the doubts created by the news from Moscow.

To the Left, the early stages of the Spanish conflict were a time of hope and excitement, of passions revived and faith rejuvenated. Earlier in the decade there had been the swift, crushing triumph of Hitler, and all the ensuing recrimination as to the blame for that disaster; and then there had been Dollfuss's victorious onslaught against democratic socialism in Vienna. Now the issue was drawn again and this time it would be different. As far as we could see at a distance, socialists, communists, anarchists and just ordinary freedom-loving men were united in the great stand of the century. "Make Madrid the Tomb of Fascism" was the cry heard around our world. "No Pasaran" was to be the triumphant theme song of a generation. In Spain, at least, the air was clear and the battle lines plainly marked, so we believed, and there could be no doubt where every man of good will—that eternally homeless figure—must finally take his stand. Our involvement was personal, too, for some of our friends had headed for the front to join the International Brigade. Those who remained behind could not let them down.

Early in 1937 I learned that Dave Cook, who had returned to England after graduation from Columbia, was in Spain. I received my first letter from him late in March: "I came here because life in England was too useless a one to be living at such a time as this. If I'm to be among those who don't get back, I'll have concentrated so much into the last short space that it will be as good as having lasted for a normal span. I have no military experience of course and this would have kept me home if I had found a place in the movement back there. . . ."

Then, three weeks later, came a scrawled post card: "Still alive and kicking faintly in hospital in Madrid where I've been two weeks. Not seen much of the war as I was hit after first day at front. Getting about on crutches now. Expect to be O.K. soon. All the best."

In the face of such communiqués one tried harder than ever to stifle doubt and to serve selflessly in the movement which produced such men. As if he had read my mind, Cook wrote me late in April, after emerging from the hospital: "The feeling of being neither flesh nor fish, which so many of us in the middle class know only too well, is, it is true, resolved over here. There are occasional discouragements, disappointments, shattering of false ideals—but those one retains are all the stronger and tougher. When one sees this war in its historical perspective, one is filled with a feeling of tremendous pride, and a joy in the privilege of taking part in it. . . . It is a sort of war and peace which passeth all understanding. There is a danger of becoming priggish, like a saint who knows that his own salvation is assured."

So there it was again: the stealthy apprehension that one's dissatisfactions in the communist movement could be traced to the stain of middle-class birth which only the fullest sacrifice could eradicate.

Others I knew—non-communists as well as communists—joined Cook in Spain. Thoughtful, generous Joe Lash, who liked to talk to students of the philosopher's good life that transcended the vulgarities of politics, made the pilgrimage. Perhaps he hoped to find in Spain a truer coalition of enlightened spirits than the faction-ridden ASU. Then one day Gil Green told us he was journeying to Spain on a "political mission." What impressed me at the moment was not the vaguely explained nature of the assignment but the fact that he was leaving just before his wife was to have a child. When he told us the news, someone suggested that he might have requested a postponement of his departure date. He laughed.

"I'm a soldier. I go where I'm told and when I'm told."

Reports of deaths and casualties began coming in and somehow victory remained elusive. In the capitals of America, France and England non-intervention was still official policy and for many weeks nothing seemed remotely as important as the propaganda campaign to change that policy.

But the beginnings of discord behind the Spanish lines could soon be detected. There, as seemingly everywhere, the problem, we were told, was Trotskyism. Gradually the crisp air of noble, clearly defined combat was being polluted by the ancient fratricidal struggles. The Spanish communists had begun to denounce their political opponents in the Loyalist camp as "agents of fascism" and the cry was swiftly taken up here. There were real disagreements about the conduct of the war, but the communists everywhere transformed honest differences of opinion into massacres.

At about that time André Malraux, then a communist literary idol, came to the United States on a lecture tour in behalf of the Loyalist cause. At one of his first meetings here communists were carefully planted in the audience to ask him leading questions about the allegedly dark deeds of the POUM, the anti-Stalinist bloc loosely identified by the communist analysts as the embodiment of "Trotskyite-anarchist" evil. Wasn't it true, Malraux was asked, that the POUM was sabotaging the Loyalist Government? His reply was coldly devastating:

"I will not say anything critical of any human being who fought and died in the defense of Madrid."

And he would say no more.

His response dismayed most of the communists in the audience. I felt uncomfortably removed from those of my comrades who cast dubious glances at him and seemed to be beginning to wonder whether he too was falling victim to the black plague of heresy.

Soon afterward, Andrés Nin, the POUM chieftain, was suddenly kidnapped. Socialists and "Trotskyites" set up a great clamor of protest, charging that Soviet agents had engineered the crime, and communists were placed on the defensive anew. It was said by the orthodox communist spokesmen that Nin was probably safe and secure and that tales of his fate were imaginary, but they also said that he was probably a fascist agent who deserved the improbable punishment he was getting.

And it was said most emphatically that anyone who betrayed real concern over Nin's condition was a furtive Trotskyist sympathizer posing as a believer in justice.

I was saying less and less, thinking of Cook and Lash and others and trying to be a good home-front soldier in an army where I found myself increasingly out of step. Yet something about my demeanor must have given me away. I was under suspicion and so I was ordered to face the great test. I was chosen to deliver the speech on "The Danger of Trotskyism" at the student session of the impending Young Communist League convention. It was "Max" who told me I had been honored with this assignment. When he gave me the news I had the certain feeling that he was watching my face for some betrayal of weakness or dismay. I simply assented. I had, for the moment at least, decided that I could face so small an ordeal while others were enduring far greater punishment at the Spanish front.

I had to write my speech in advance; no oration could be delivered at such a conclave without having been inspected by the higher-ups. And as I wrote it I found I was engaged in an almost whimsical attempt to say what I thought and yet couch it in phrases that would be acceptable to the communist brass. My thesis was that, despite everything said about us, we communists possessed the Marxian key to history. Our prophecies of crisis had come true; our warnings had been justified; we had no reason to fear debate with anyone because history had amply demonstrated that we were right. We were, I intoned, under fire from the reactionaries and the pseudo-revolutionists alike, but we could meet their arguments with a sure sense of the validity of our own stand.

I thought such an address would invite early doom. I was saying in effect that no communist need fear exposure to the ideas of the heretics because truth was on our side; we were history's favorite sons. But the irony missed fire; probably it was not quite as well aimed as I had assumed it to be. When I finished the speech the students applauded lustily and "Max" warmly congratulated me, adding that it was imperative that these unhistoric remarks be published in pamphlet form at once. Even the most vigilant hunters of heresy told me I had really scored. My embarrassment was accentuated when I was promptly elected to the Executive Committee of the YCL amid the acclaim evoked by my analysis of the ideological perils confronting us.

My troubles with Trotskyism, however, were not over; they were just reaching a crisis in a somewhat different area.

The first big Moscow trial had been staged in August of the previous year. At that ghastly circus Kamenev, Zinoviev and other Soviet immortals had abjectly told the credulous communist multitudes that they had been wickedly plotting the overthrow of the Soviet state for a long time. Thus began the debate that was to rock the communist world. But the timing of the first trial was fortunate for the commissars; it came soon after the outbreak of the Spanish war and, for some months at least, many of us brushed off discussion of the Moscow mystery, choosing instead to think about the less demoralizing struggle in Spain. This is not to say that there was no uneasiness. While it had been possible to dismiss earlier reports of famine and failure in Russia as mischievous inventions of the kept press, the self-denunciations delivered by ancient heroes could hardly be written off the same way. And the shocks had just begun.

In January, 1937, came the second mass trial. Karl Radek and other venerated Soviet figures similarly vied with each other in confessing the most implausible crimes. Within communist circles men and women talked in hushed tones about the news or, more frequently, sought other topics of conversation. The *New Masses* and the *Daily Worker* published interminable explanations. Only the simple-minded, we were assured, could be startled and shaken to discover that the heroes whose glories we had sung were all turning out to be pro-fascist schemers and Trotskyite wreckers. Only middle-class minds, it was alleged, could be disturbed by the spectacle; every revolution had its discordant aftermath. As long as capitalist encirclement confronted the USSR, there would be disappointments and betrayals. Then came the editing of history on a more lurid scale then ever before. Day after day the revolutionary roles of the fallen leaders were revealed to have been less distinguished than previously reported. It began to sound as if Stalin had done it single-handed and that others hitherto listed as architects of the Soviet state had been incidental characters, and probably obstructionists.

The gnawing questions persisted and some of us were unable to seal our minds. One of my close friends at that time was Joe Starobin. As a student at CCNY Joe had been one of the founders of the National Student League. He had gotten into some ideological skirmishes with communist officialdom in those early days, however, and had quietly retired from the fray. He was now a privately employed chemist, suffering from restlessness and nostalgia. He wanted to write and he wanted to get back into The Movement and he was terribly earnest about both ambitions. Yet he was clearly not quite trusted in the higher echelons, and for the best reasons; he had qualities of whimsy, imagination and independence of intellect uncommon to "integrated Bolsheviks." He liked to talk and argue, to revaluate hypotheses long considered sacrosanct and ask questions that were supposed to have been firmly settled long ago. Joe was as close to being a maverick communist as one could imagine. To the mirthless men in high places this was an obvious contradiction in terms. Joe clearly felt that his life was being wasted; he was forever talking of finding an escape from chemistry and a return to activity, preferably in communist journalism.

Possibly the proof of our friendship is that we talked freely to each other, which was not usual among communists. Joe and his attractive dark-haired wife Norma, who had been a school-mate of Nancy's at New College, had almost nightly sessions with Nancy and me, talking about the trials. We confided our darkest apprehensions to each other. But we were still unprepared to give up, perhaps partly because the Spanish war was still being fought and partly just because one did not light-heartedly abandon communism. We groped for clues; we sought better explanations than the communists were offering; we clutched for rational straws and hidden meanings in all the shadowy corners of the fantastic Moscow puppet-show. Finally the printed record of the Kamenev-Zinoviev trial was published here. We pored over it, trying to convince ourselves and one another that there was logic and authenticity in the stories the defendants had told, and that this was simply one of those cruel post-revolutionary sequels which cast no fundamental reflection on the Soviet idea.

Out of those discussions came our decision to write a pamphlet sifting the testimony and attempting to prove that there were no important inconsistencies in the evidence unfolded at the trials. It is difficult for me to say now whether Joe and I were persuaded that such a case could be made, or whether we felt that in actually writing the document we would finally—for better or for worse— uncover some glimpse of the truth for ourselves.

We talked to Gil Green and a few others about the project and we were tentatively authorized to undertake it. That the suggestion was greeted with less than enthusiasm was understandable. We were proposing to deal with the most delicate issue confronting the movement. Moreover, our preoccupation with it may have been recognized as a sign of our own unspoken dissatisfaction with the inept fuller-explanation department conducted by the *Daily Worker*.

Our inquiry had a brief, unhappy life and died a sudden death. As soon as we started work it became apparent that we were engaged in a perilous task. The terrible truth was that there were gaping inconsistencies and contradictions in the tales told in Moscow. We were chiefly endeavoring to refute those critics who had uncovered damning flaws of detail, involving dates, places and other issues of fact. The deeper we got into the maze, however, the greater our own confusion became. So, after considerable writing and much anguish, we decided we had better seek lofty guidance on the Ninth Floor. We submitted the fragment we had written along with a request for an interview at which we could explore certain perplexing questions of fact which we lacked the wisdom to resolve ourselves.

"Max" rendered the verdict. It was an unappreciative one. He was angry and contemptuous; we had, he said heatedly, fallen into a "Trotskyite trap" by attempting to deal with factual discrepancies in the trial. I recall his words almost exactly, perhaps because I felt at the time that those words finally proved I had enlisted in the wrong crusade.

"What we need is not an analysis of facts," he shouted. "What we need is a political analysis which will characterize Trotskyism as the other face of fascism. We have to show that this treason was the inevitable result of the political nature of Trotskyism. That is all we need, not dates, places, facts."

That is what the man said.

That evening Joe and I decided to scrap the project. But the incident remained with me; I kept hearing "Max's" words. They seemed finally to have bared the communist mind. One either had to accept everything on faith or fall into a Trotskyite trap. Reason, logic and evidence had no place in this system of thought.

There was, of course, a deeper doubt stirred by all this. For if one stopped arguing about factual details and began thinking about the larger implications of the trials, the consequences could be even more subversive. Suppose one assumed that the charge of frame-up was unjustified, that the defendants were guilty as charged and their confessions valid. Was it really preferable to believe that the fathers of the revolution had been arch-villains from the start? Didn't that merely prove there had been a great hoax played on humanity? It was almost worse to believe that so gigantic a fraud had been perpetrated than to believe the confessions were a fantasy.

The blunt words that "Max" had recited were like the self-revelations of a beautiful but vulgar woman who has heretofore remained mute; once she has spoken, she never looks quite the same again and one wonders how it was ever possible to have considered her an enchantress. "Max" was the most dramatic symbol of world communism I had known. Now in effect he was accusing us of attempting to apply reason to a problem in which faith alone mattered. It is not that this was the first time I had heard a call for total intellectual surrender; I had simply never heard it stated that baldly.

That was nearly the end of my fidelity to communism. If there had been nothing else going on in the world, I would probably have walked out at that moment. But too much was still happening. Although I realized I was on the verge of insurrection, I was still reluctant to say so out loud. There were still, for example, letters coming from Cook; how could I explain to a man who was fighting in Spain that I had decided there was something essentially corrupt in The Movement?

Moreover, there was still one thing to be done, and until it was done I could not be sure that, politically, I was ready to end it all. For several months Nancy and I had been advertised as the leaders of the Student Union's annual summer tour. In return for the responsibility we assumed, our expenses were to be paid by the Open Road, a travel agency which sponsored the trip with the ASU. A portion of the fare paid by each traveler was allocated to subsidize our voyage. The itinerary called for six hectic weeks of European travel, including ten days in the Soviet Union. I had never been abroad before; Nancy had been to Europe as a child accompanied by her parents and governess, but Russia had not been on her route. Now at last we were to see the shrine of communism. Possibly—I think we clung to this as a faint, forlorn hope—we would see something that would bolster our vanishing confidence. So we remained grimly quiet about the disintegration of our beliefs. There had been travelers who had been to Russia and come back with renewed hope for humanity. Even in ten days we might find the fountain of revolutionary youth.

In June, the month before our departure, Nancy was serving as a counselor at a progressive-school camp. A letter I wrote to her then gives some picture of the mood in which we were embarking on this private mission to Moscow. The news of the Tukhachevsky trial and execution had just descended on us; I thought wryly that it was lucky Starobin and I had abandoned the pamphlet because we would scarcely have been able to keep up with the process of extermination at its accelerated pace. These were some of the random heresies I communicated to Nancy:

"I suppose you have read of the latest wave of executions in the USSR. Dick stopped by the house last night full of questions and presumably expecting me to answer them. It becomes increasingly embarrassing to have to reply by invoking 'faith' and 'trust' and other irrational symbols we would normally reject. One can acknowledge, I think, the military factors which produce the Russian tension. But it's certainly painful to read of the five-year-old Russian kids who write manifestoes saying: 'All hail the patriotic executions of the wretches, diversionists, scoundrels, and sons of bitches.' Such children should be drowned, not boasted about. The only defensible argument in this whole mess is that this is a hell of a time in history for us to speculate about the refinements of human decency. There are too many immediate things to be done. I know the fact that people like Cook and Lash are in Spain makes me humble about random criticism and dissatisfaction. But nevertheless I think it is crucial to recognize that the trials raise profound problems affecting the future and all the things we claim to be fighting for. When idiots rub their hands in bloody glee at each new execution as if our side had just scored another touchdown, it makes me physically sick; one can't help wondering what would happen to any society if such people take it over—and whether they are really representative of what is called the 'integrated Bolshevik.' Of course we've both said all these things before; the question still is what we do about them. I suppose somebody will interpret that last sentence as evidence of my subconscious drift toward counterrevolutionary terrorism. Anyway, that's enough poison for today. . . ."

Only one mildly entertaining obstruction threatened to disrupt our voyage. I obtained visas to France, England, Austria, Poland, Finland, Norway and Sweden without difficulty; but a few days before our sailing I learned that some question had been raised about my Soviet visa. I had described myself as a "journalist" on my passport and was informed that the Soviet consul wanted to see samples of my writing before reaching his decision. Although I was then publicly known to be a member of the National Committee of the Young Communist League, that did not suffice; or, perhaps—in the light of the general tensions then gripping the world communist movement—that just increased his nervousness. I dutifully submitted copies of *Revolt on the Campus* and *War*

*Our Heritage* and that was the last time those volumes received any solemn notice until I was called before a Senate committee sixteen years later. On the eve of the sailing, I got the visa.

There were fifteen college students and one middle-aged man who sought the company of youth in the group that Nancy and I had been designated to chaperone. The students were undergraduates from Yale, Smith and other fashionable colleges; seven were males and eight were females. Not one was a communist; many of them were congenial, fun-hunting and somewhat spoiled children of wealthy parents who had sent them along for this ride because the advertisements indicated that education would be mingled with sightseeing and the other commonplaces of European travel. When we met the parents at a pre-embarkation party sponsored by Open Road, several of them expressed concern at the visible youthfulness of Nancy and me, and were even more distraught when I confessed that this was my first trip. They were a little reassured to learn that Nancy had been there before and we did not labor the point that she had been twelve when she made the grand tour.

For some of the participants, the trip marked their first exposure to any kind of left-wing politics. Nancy and I often found ourselves in the ambivalent position of lamely striving to dissipate their anti-communist stereotypes at the moment we were preparing to renounce the faith. This was a trifle confusing for us as well as for the pupils.

En route to Russia—the circuit was Paris, Vienna, Prague, Warsaw, Kiev, Moscow, Leningrad and then to England via Scandinavia —there were crises wholly unrelated to the deepening ordeal of left-wing life. As soon as we reached Paris, the group sharply divided on sexual lines; the co-eds launched their pursuit of European man while the males hunted French womanhood. One of the young ladies established contact with an Argentine polo player and seemed determined to pursue both him and his horse to the end of the earth.

But we also encountered a more serious situation. At each step along the way there were local guides chosen by Open Road to lead the expedition. In Paris we had two; one was a devout communist, the other an equally ardent pacifist. One of our co-ed voyagers promptly fell in love with the communist trail-blazer and he turned up some days later in Vienna to keep pace with her. The romance flared intermittently all summer; we began expecting him to greet us at each station, and he frequently did. This was, I believe, the most flagrant example of communist infiltration throughout the trip.

While in Paris Nancy and I attended a local Young Communist League convention as well as a communist-directed international student congress. Although I did not purport to be a French scholar and could barely follow a French play, I could understand the orations at this assemblage without much difficulty; one simply added an "e" at the end of "Trotskyism" to identify the true danger confronting humanity. The student congress had one unforgettable scene; its sessions were dominated by a huge portrait of John Cornford, the brilliant young British communist who had been killed in Spain. One looked at the picture and felt a twinge of sadness at the awareness of one's own widening separation from The Movement. This was the cruel reawakening of sentiment. How did one equate the valor and nobility of this portrait with the dismal dictum handed down by "Max" in a drab room on East Thirteenth Street? Which was the communist reality—the young man of flaming spirit and great promise who had lost his life in Spain or the dour commissar warning against the use of one's own mind?

Fortunately, our student flock kept creating diversions. As an episode in their education we took them to a communist mass meeting on the outskirts of Paris. They were unmoved by the rhetoric but they seemingly absorbed the singing. When we all returned to our quarters at the Cité Universitaire after a few stimulants along the way, some of them felt they could best exhibit their passion for Paris by singing the Internationale, or what they remembered of it, on the steps of the dormitory. What they had not been told was that the French universities were strongholds of fascist emotion. They were momentarily threatened by the French equivalent of Columbia's egg-throwing brigades. I advised them to drop the song, at least until they were prepared to face the consequences of the music.

To European students we met, the Americans in our charge were a baffling array. They were likable, friendly and exuberant; but it required supreme effort for most of them to feign any real interest in politics. Since I was a leader of the American student movement, our hosts tended to assume that the entourage consisted of dedicated militants, and it was hard to explain that most of them were there simply because their parents could afford to finance the journey.

Sixteen years later it was equally hard to explain all this to Senator McCarthy who seemed convinced that the group I had led was composed of hardened communist operatives conducting a large-scale espionage junket through Europe.

In the moments when I could abdicate the functions of tour leader, I found Paris sad and disquieting. We were there on Bastille Day, and in the evening we watched the long display of French military preparedness, climaxed by the marching columns of men whose fathers had died in a world war only two decades earlier. Our pacifist guide, Grischa, seemed almost ready to burst into tears as we watched the show. He did not pretend to be a politician; he said only that he knew war would bring incalculable suffering to great numbers of people who just wanted to be allowed to live out their lives in peace. He told us he did not care under what banner war was fought because in the end the victims were helpless anonymities who were forced to fight against people they did not hate. Grischa had not learned to speak that ruthless language of history which enables communists to picture themselves as the protectors of humanity in general while inflicting their destruction on single human beings who happen to get in their way.

The next day Grischa took us to Chartres and there, amid the exquisite tranquillity, he talked again of the approaching catastrophe. At home we had glibly said that collective security involved the risk of war, but that those who feared to take the risk were doomed. It was easy to say so. But to Grischa war meant simply that life was no longer worth living, even if one somehow managed to survive.

Grischa's attitude seemed far more impressive than that of the communists who coolly accepted violence as the accepted method of social advance, regarding each battle as just one more skirmish in an endless chain of strife that was finally supposed to usher in peace on earth.

During that July in Paris I was further removed from the communists than ever before. They seemed to be saying everybody would be happy and all torments of existence removed once the communist dawn was reached, which is an absurd oversimplification of the nature of human sorrow. They also seemed to be saying that only soft souls could be disturbed by the prospect of another big bloodletting. Their analysis of human unrest seemed as faulty as their prescription for eventual joy; it was always tomorrow and tomorrow.

In Prague we took the students to see Paul Hagen. I had met him through Mary Fox of the League for Industrial Democracy some months earlier in New York. A communist as a youth in Germany during the twenties, he had rebelled against the communist bureaucracy long before Hitler's triumph. Now he was a dedicated anti-Nazi, working actively with the anti-Hitler underground, risking his life on intermittent missions to Germany to maintain contact with his comrades. He was about forty and he seemed to have lived a dozen lifetimes. Despite all the defeat and disaster that had overcome the German Left, he was patiently starting over again. The group with which he was identified was quite accurately described as "New Beginnings"; it represented an effort to achieve a rebirth of independent German socialism freed of the bitter factional feuds and the narrow dogmas which had fatally divided the German Left. Those who were trying to raise American funds to finance Hagen's work were socialists and independent liberals. The communists had no kind words for him and, shortly before we saw him in Prague, he had been in Spain hunting for a member of his group who was reportedly being persecuted by the Soviet secret police.

Hagen was dramatic proof that the virtues we attributed to the communists—tenacity, courage, selflessness, resolution—were not the exclusive property of Stalinism; that a man might remain faithful to equalitarian ideals long after he had mutinied against the communist machine. Indeed, such a man might be a more inspiring example than the obsequious revolutionaries who never dared to raise their voices in criticism of the American communist hierarchy and the holier-than-holies in Moscow. Obvious as it may seem now, this came under the heading of revelation then. Within the communist movement it was generally assumed that the true men of the future must perforce be communists; all other forms of radicalism represented weakness or depravity.

A strikingly handsome man whose face seeemed to reveal all the hope and heartbreak of European anti-fascism, Hagen enthralled the co-eds in our entourage; they seemed to take renewed interest in the politics of the Left when he was talking. The warmth and imagination so conspicuously missing among most veteran communist chieftains were possessed in abundance by this heretic. Although he was an inescapably romantic figure, he was devoid of revolutionary exhibitionism. He had a nimble, lively mind, and he did not hand down opinions in the flat, final tones that characterized the commissars. Certainly his life had been as full of adventure, peril and crisis as "Max's." What he had learned was that there were few simple answers and slogans, and that man may fight best if he is fully aware of the complexity of the struggle.

I write of Hagen at some length partly because, sixteen years later, I was to be closely questioned about my association with him. Had he not been a communist as a youth? Yes. And, having come to live in America after World War II broke out, was he not barred from the OSS and then, at the end of the war, excluded from any participation in United States Military Government in Germany? Yes, he was; the treatment accorded him was an outrage apparently engineered by a fanatic German emigré who had never forgiven him his youthful communist enterprises, and who had succeeded in convincing our often credulous Intelligence experts that Hagen was untrustworthy.

But the bleak facts were there. Once upon a time Hagen had been a communist; the past he never tried to conceal had caught up with him in our own Intelligence files. How did one explain in 1953 that my meeting with him in the summer of 1937 had exactly the opposite significance of that now attributed to it; that he was one of those who most influenced my renunciation of communism, not merely because of what he said but because of what he symbolized—the existence of real alternatives for disenchanted communists?

There could be a "new beginning."

We reached Kiev in early August. The days we spent in the USSR did not shake the world. We saw as much and as little as average tourists were permitted to see in that twilight of the Russian travel era. What we saw in that brief interim scarcely constituted material for an extensive exposure of despotism; neither did we see anything calculated to revive our fading faith. We made the usual visit to a collective farm, which evoked the comment from one of our student group that he didn't see anything he hadn't seen in South Jersey. We visited hospitals and factories and schools; we attended open-air concerts. All that we were shown was evidence of some tangible material accomplishment, much, I suppose, as visitors to Nazi Germany were invited to marvel at the broad highways Adolf Hitler had built.

But I had begun to see that the issue was freedom, and nothing we saw or heard encouraged the hope that there were any fresh winds bringing any freer air to Russia's multitudes. We had heard it said ten thousand times that liberty was an "abstract concept." But when one encountered the countless ikons of Stalin in every public place and the withdrawn, uneasy faces of guides when one asked them questions, and when one went through the Museum of the Revolution where history had been carefully revised to conform to the Stalin legend, there was no abstraction involved. This was the concrete triumph of the monolithic mind; this was the rigid pattern of the communist movement expanded into a whole society. In New York, after listening to "Max," one could go out in the street and seem to get away from it all. How did one escape here? How was one to know whether one's neighbor was a friend or an informer and whether one's children were eavesdropping so that they might file a report on one's whispered deviations?

On the train from Kiev to Moscow our guide was a nice but nervous Russian professor of literature. He spoke English fluently and, after we had shared a bottle of vodka, he spoke almost freely. We were talking about the party line in fiction; how could men write creatively if they lived in hourly fear that their works might be damned for failure to conform to the unpredictable decrees of the cultural commissars? At first he defended the system with a kind of feverish gibberish, but after the vodka had been consumed, he began making admissions. There were difficulties, yes. There were times when he was troubled about what they were doing; perhaps the functioning of the mind should not be dealt with in the same terms as factory output. . . . I wondered how many others suffered from these anxieties in the privacy of their rooms, and how often the loose tongues produced by vodka led to the arrest of "fascist-Trotskyite wreckers." The next morning our guide had a hangover and a haunted look, as though pondering his indiscretions and wondering whether I would turn him in. I tried to reassure him by saying the evening had been so gay that I could barely remember what we had discussed.

In Moscow we were led about by an attractive blonde schoolteacher. She was friendly, gracious and communicative—until we tried to get her to talk about the trials. I asked her as casually as I could what the public reaction had been. Her face froze. She suddenly acquired a blank look, as though she had lost her ability to hear. I started to repeat the question and she walked slowly off, giving no sign that she knew I had said anything.

I had mentioned the unmentionable. I tried the same question on others; the response was identical. One didn't discuss the Moscow trials in Moscow unless one had an exit visa.

We were still resisting the ultimate conclusion. One morning one of the Yale students in our troupe told us he and a companion had walked the streets of Moscow late the previous night and, on a side street, had seen a man dragged screaming and protesting out of his house and hurled into a police wagon. What they had seen—we learned later—was just one of innumerable such scenes being enacted that summer. Although we didn't know it at the time, the quiet purge of helpless thousands of "deviationists" was reaching a fierce peak that August. Great demonstration trials had been staged for the luminaries; the lesser victims were hauled away without such public spectacles. But when the Yale boy, who had no political interests and simply seemed to enjoy taunting us, told his story we expressed total disbelief. Nancy and I warned him his imagination had run wild as a result of the anti-Soviet fiction to which he had been subjected so long, and that is what we tried to persuade ourselves.

Our efforts to uphold the virtues of the Soviet Union in the face of undergraduate derision were beset by comic interludes. Upon arrival in Kiev three of the co-eds were assigned to a lavish suite at the hotel. It had a royal flavor; they were really delighted and were beginning to look with new understanding on the Soviet experiment. But shortly after dawn the next morning they were awakened by loud pounding at their doors. Excited voices told them to pack and get out of the suite at once because there was a leak in a pipe and the flood was expected at any moment. They got dressed, packed and fled; as they were leaving, a Russian general was ushered into the suite amid great pomp and circumstance.

Despite my membership on the YCL National Committee, I was not given access to any inner-council meetings in Moscow. Indeed, our only contact with any communist officials was an evening spent with several Young Communist League leaders. It was a stiff, austere gathering, and when one of the students tried to start a discussion of the Moscow trials, there was a hasty retreat into other topics.

So there we were in the workers' fatherland, living in a hotel room that overlooked Red Square, and in this majestic setting we felt a nervous desire to reach Finland. There were no really untoward incidents. The sightseeing proceeded on schedule; but the sense of imprisonment was inescapable. We were in the communist citadel, and in place of exhilaration we had only the depressing sense that we ought to watch our words, and that our room was probably wired.

Sixteen years later a Senator was to say that he suspected I had had a private audience with Joseph Stalin and that Stalin had ordered me to return to America, pose as an anti-communist and prepare for the great day of warfare against Joe McCarthy. And I was to swear solemnly that it didn't happen.

In a sense, of course, I did see Stalin—everywhere. He gazed at me from every billboard. I saw far too much of him. I had come to Russia as a communist but, once there, I had not the slightest sense of belonging to this gray, monolithic civilization. I remember thinking how close I was to full entrapment, and how I would have felt if I had been sent to Moscow for training, as some Young Communist League leaders were. What if I were there without the certain knowledge that I could and would leave within a few days?

Somewhere in Red Square lay the body of John Reed, the Harvard man who had cast his lot with what he thought were the legions of emancipation. What would he have thought of the iron oppression his dream had become? In a little more than a week one could scarcely find out everything. One could only say with certainty that the air was stifling on the coolest, clearest day. It was being said over and over again that the Russians did not care as long as they were eating. They were, one might have said more precisely, subsisting on a diet of bread and dread.

Four months after leaving Moscow Nancy and I were both out of the Young Communist League.

This is a political biography, not a detailed personal memoir, but again I am reminded that there are moments when the dichotomy becomes artificial. Nancy and I were married at a time when we were both reasonably devoted communists; we have often thought with some horror of what might have happened if either of us had held steadfast to the faith while the other groped for escape. Neither of us intellectually dominates the other. We can both be quite firm and stubborn about our opinions; Nancy is as contemptuous of my study of batting averages as I am of her view that automobile-driving is a sport rather than an emergency form of transportation to be utilized only when there is no saner means of getting somewhere. Yet the graphs of our political emotions throughout that period were almost completely parallel. That may merely suggest that our cycle of belief and doubt and final estrangement from communism was not unique; many others were going through the same process with the same feeling of loneliness.

Perhaps it was easier for us to leave together than it was for anyone to leave alone. The bigger exodus did not occur until two summers later when the Soviets signed their treaty with the Nazis; those of us who left the "locomotive of history" at the earlier station called the Moscow trials have sometimes tended to view ourselves as especially perspicacious, just as many who had left before us wonder why it took us so long to get off or why we got aboard in the first place. After all, there had been ex-communists before we became communists, but we refused to heed them; we had to find out for ourselves.

There are those who say that it is wrong to display any more patience for communists than for Nazis. The communist movement is no less dedicated to the destruction of human liberty; its crimes have been no less monstrous, its bestialities no less hideous. And that is true. There is only this difference, and it is the difference, as Dr. Niebuhr has suggested, which makes the world communist threat in some ways more formidable than the Nazi assault ever was. It is that the communists have appealed to men's loftiest instincts, while the fascists frankly addressed themselves to men's cruelest impulses. The communists raised the banners of liberty, fraternity and equality, and then pitilessly perverted these symbols; the fascists said openly that they stood for conquest and subjugation and, eventually, for the triumph of "superior" races. The communists preached an internationalism as old as the simple credo of the brotherhood of man; the fascists invoked no such pretense.

It may be said that only retarded pupils or hopeless cases can still be lured into the communist fold by the illusions that ensnared earlier generations. But that is to assume that experience is simply and directly communicated from one decade to another, that teachers are free and imaginative, and that there are inspiring alternatives for those who refuse to accept as incurable the recurrent crises of our time.

I write with some feeling about tolerance and sympathy for the youthfully benighted communist, because if there had been no such sentiments in the America of 1937, Nancy and I might have concluded there was no escape, and so might many others. It has often been said, and with some justice, that the communists in the Student Union cynically exploited people like Norman Thomas, Roger Baldwin and Mary Fox and others who tried to help that abortive Popular Front adventure. But, as with Mrs. Roosevelt and the Youth Congress, the communists finally lost more than they gained. It was the existence of such people—and of Paul Hagen abroad and others like him—that helped to convince many of us that the communists had no monopoly on sincerity and selflessness, and that it was possible to fight for decency in the world without yielding to the communist machine.

We sailed back to America from Southampton in late August, 1937, after a swing through Scandinavia and a fortnight in London, including a blessed week to ourselves after saying farewell to the students we had led. It was assumed that they could make the crossing without our guidance and they all brought themselves back alive.

Our voyage brought reminders that nothing was yet entirely simple. Aboard the aged *Berengaria* were wounded Loyalist veterans, and the lonely pathos of their return made one halt in mid-

ocean and debate again one's right to abandon communism at so
desperate a moment in history. The spiritual discomfort of the
journey was augmented by the presence of a sociologist whom I
had known in the left-wing set on Morningside Heights. He and
his wife had just led a group through the Soviet Union and they
seemed entirely delighted with what they had been allowed to
see. A short, solemn man with the countenance of an earnest
poodle and a wild bundle of insistently preserved long hair, he was
the supremely orthodox Stalinist; he considered it his duty, for
example, to conduct symposia on shipboard at which he could
recite his Russian travelogue and bring at least some glimpse of
light to those who had spent their summers in territory west of
Utopia. At one point he demanded that I deliver a brief talk to
supplement his remarks; I reluctantly consented and my words, I
fear, were drably noncommittal. Nancy and I knew he was troubled
by our lack of spontaneous support for his recital. We had the
sensation that he was applying his ideological stethoscope to our
chests and listening for Trotskyist murmurs. After a while, whenever we saw him approach, we would gaily whisper "Chickie" to
each other, in the fashion of school children warning that teacher
is about to descend on the scene of illicit activity.

Actually we tried not to talk too much, even to each other.
We both felt this passage really marked the end of our communist voyage; but we were uncertain as to where we would
go from there, and we tried to give the trip something of the
carefree quality of a huge farewell party. Nancy was planning
to enter Columbia Law School in September, so she at least had
a physical destination; my school days had been over for two years,
and I was officially scheduled to return to my post at the Student
Union. But I knew I would not go back there; I was about to be
twenty-two anyway, and I had seen enough campuses and enough
student groups. I could not keep on trying to rally thoughtful,
warm-spirited and sometimes excessively guilt-ridden undergraduates into a movement that served as a recruiting ground for the
communists.

When we got back I told Gil Green I wanted to leave the Student Union and find a place in journalism. That was all I told him and he did not seem disturbed by the announcement. He was friendly, and he tried to be helpful; he said he thought he could arrange for me to work for Tass, the Soviet news agency. I politely demurred; he did not try to order me about. I said I thought I would just try free-lancing for a while.

He said that would be all right, but that I ought to get settled pretty soon. I told him I hoped to get a regular job on some newspaper or magazine and then devote myself to active work in the Newspaper Guild, which was then beginning to make real strides. That was all right, too, he said. I thought he was humoring me but that was fine with me; if I was merely being considered a temperamental individualist, that was nothing compared to what I would be called if and when I finally got out. Meanwhile the Spanish war was still dragging on, with disheartening news from the front. I kept faintly telling myself that perhaps a change of locale would make it possible for me to remain a communist; as long as I wasn't a "leader," I would be responsible for no one but myself and I would not carry the burden of deceit which haunted me every time I made a speech. In those weeks I talked to few people. When I hinted to Joe Starobin that I might decide to leave The Movement, he looked at me with the hurt astonishment of a father whose son has just confessed he is about to run off with the maid; he had always known it was possible, but it just couldn't be true.

Not long after our return from Europe I got a letter from somebody at the magazine *Soviet Russia Today* asking me whether I was planning to write my "impressions" of the USSR; I ignored the communication and received no further inquiries. Strangely enough, the YCL did not exhort me to deliver any lectures about the wonders I had presumably seen. Although later on Gil Green was to express astonishment when I formally resigned, there may have been some wariness about pressing the point even at that early date. Some time during the Soviet junket I had sent one of the student YCLers a post card bearing a picture of Stalin on one side and a brief written message on the other in which I said this man's face was everywhere and I was still trying to find out his identity. I learned later that this poor joke was passed around by the recipient and elicited unfavorable comment about the state of my political health. The person to whom I had addressed the card was an especially orthodox co-ed comrade who, not many months earlier, had told me how moved she was when she saw a photograph of Stalin handing a flower to a child; this was, she said, proof of his essential tenderness, and I could not bring myself to tell her that I had seen Tammany politicians hand out equally touching gifts without even getting their pictures in the papers.

It was a long, harrowing autumn. Each time I now read an ex-communist's account of his break, whether it occurred in 1926 or 1953, I am fascinated by the universality of the experience. Just as communist rhetoric sounds almost the same in any tongue, so the phenomenon of communist disenchantment seems to be duplicated in all its excruciating details, whether it occurs in New York or Paris or Peking.

Soon after I returned I wrote two articles that were accepted— with extensive revision—by the New York *Times* magazine section. So that the record may be clear, let me say that neither essay could be construed, then or now, as communist propaganda. They chiefly described the mood of fatalism with which young men in Europe were awaiting the arrival of a second world war; they contained neither exhortation nor program; they represented the most candid writing I had done since my pre-communist days. They were so lacking in communist spirit that Gil Green sought me out shortly after they appeared to tell me they had been de- plored on the Ninth Floor as expressions of a pessimism utterly at variance with the communist outlook. I accepted the reproach without protest, knowing that—from his viewpoint—it was well deserved. I was still unable to phrase the final words that would end the suspense.

It was Lester Markel, the Sunday Editor of the *Times* and one of the most gifted men in our profession, who accepted the articles, and I am eternally indebted to him. If his day of judgment should come at some future senatorial inquisition, I suppose the appearance of my by-line in his section at that time will be held against him. How could I explain to the ex-Democrat from Wisconsin that Markel's acceptance of those earnest, if unmemorable, reports gave me some confidence that I could write for the "capitalist press" without having my copy dictated in Wall Street?

That fall Markel sporadically gave me other assignments. At his request I did a portrait of B. Charney Vladeck, the veteran socialist who was then presiding over New York's City Council. To the communists, Vladeck had been a despised "social democrat" for a long time. I interviewed him at length and found him a wise, compassionate man, as thousands had learned long before me; that is what I wrote, and again there was criticism on the Ninth Floor.

Despite Markel's generosity there were long gaps that fall when, for the only time in my life, I experienced the panic of the unemployed man who begins to doubt that he is employable. What I wanted most was a regular job, with a place to spend eight or ten hours a day. Sitting at home in our apartment on Charles Street gave me too much time to debate what then seemed to be the insoluble issues of personal choice. I knew that I didn't belong in the communist bureaucracy; but I did not know whether I was fully ready for the separation, with all the upheaval that would surely entail. In those weeks I facetiously described myself as an anti-Stalin Stalinist, which was a way of saying I believed the communist position on immediate world affairs was probably sound but I could not endure the oppressive complacence of the communist mind. I could not consider the Moscow trials a minor episode in the splendid march of progress. I detested the repetitive sound of communist "formulations." I was for collective security but I resented the unwillingness of the communists to recognize the risks involved; I was for Loyalist Spain but I refused to equate anarchists and Trotskyists with the fascist enemy. I thought the Soviet regime had probably improved the living standards of the populace but I could no longer pretend that it had any of the characteristics of a free society. All of which simply means that I at last dimly understood that the "either-or" formula of political analysis was infantile. The lines were never drawn as plainly as the communists said they were, the villains we booed off the stage often seemed to recite rather devastating exit lines, and the heroes had inexplicable lapses.

Amid all this meditation the drab fact was that I was unemployed and seemed likely to remain that way for quite a while. There was a rather absurd incongruity in my problem because I knew it was already being whispered that I had "sold out." There were rumors that my absence from communist functions and my presence in the pages of the *Times* magazine were strangely and significantly coincidental, and that a pot of gold was being delivered with the milk at my doorstep each morning. I did not try to explain myself; I was still too unsure of what the explanation really was.

I applied for jobs at *Time* and *Newsweek*, making it perfectly plain that I was prepared to start as office boy or doorman. I had become obsessed with the notion that everything would come clear once I found regular employment. It seemed essential that I go to work for a living in some obscure place and then reconstruct my political future, if any. At both magazines I was given extremely cordial receptions and then, a few days later, came crisp notes rejecting me. I suppose these followed brief inquiries which established without the aid of detectives that, on the record, I was a communist hothead.

There was one moment in that interval when my resolve to escape momentarily wavered. One day, while walking around Greenwich Village headed for nowhere, I met Joe Freeman, then the editor of the *New Masses*; I knew him slightly and liked him a great deal. A Columbia graduate of an earlier radical generation, he was a gay, lively man who did not wear a communist leer or speak the language of pious certitude; I had even heard rumors that he was intermittently accused of nonconformity. He asked me what I was doing and I explained rather vaguely that I was looking for a job in journalism. He stared at me a trifle uncertainly, and then suggested that I go to work for the *New Masses*. I conjectured that he had guessed I was in a troubled state and was trying to be helpful. What I did not guess was that at exactly that time he had asked to be released from his post at the *New Masses* (for reasons quite similar to my own retirement from the Student Union) and had been told he would be permitted to step out if he found some promising revolutionary youths to provide new manpower for the magazine. So Joe, having served long and faithfully, was on the way out and hoped I would help speed him. Not till many years afterwards—when both of us had long severed our connections—did I find out what that conversation was really about.

I trudged back to Charles Street seriously considering his proposal. Possibly the *New Masses* would be different; perhaps I could start anew there, and take a fresh look at The Movement. Then I read that week's edition and abandoned the idea; what the *New Masses* offered was simply a somewhat more erudite presentation of the crudest communist positions. Granville Hicks (who left the train in 1939) might present a defense of the Moscow trials more adroitly than the *Daily Worker's* Mike Gold, but the intellectual content was exactly the same. There simply was no room for debate of any sort; the function of a *New Masses* writer was to find good words for bad arguments.

I did not acknowledge even to Nancy my deepening concern about whether I had joined the ranks of the unemployables. I wrote several magazine pieces that were rejected and I paced the floor of our apartment. With the passage of each week I had the growing certainty that I was headed for WPA. I have never forgotten those weeks and nothing now enrages me more than the smug announcements of well-fed citizens that a lot of human beings really prefer unemployment—with relief payments—to genuine labor. We faced no peril of starvation—our families were quite prepared to feed us—but the frustration and vacancy of those weeks are unforgettable. The dreary joke was that the only way I could have quickly gained employment was to re-enlist as a communist active, whether at the ASU or the *New Masses;* that was the one thing I could not bring myself to do. I wanted out, but I still wanted to slide out without creating a tempest; that, I thought, I owed to Cook and others like him.

Technically I was still a communist. I was still a member of the YCL National Committee. There had been no attempt to force me to assume some new assignment; there had been no official recognition of my curious conduct beyond the occasional puzzled or injured glances of those with whom I had worked.

By November Nancy had resolved her own position. She simply stopped attending communist meetings at the Law School; she was buried in books at Kent Hall. When some of the comrades finally challenged her to account for her delinquency, she blurted out the explanation; she told them she couldn't stand the doctrinaire atmosphere, and she had decided to try thinking for herself. Soon afterward we learned that the Law School communists were whispering that she had deserted The Movement because she was a contemptible careerist determined to devote all her time to winning election to the *Law Review*.

This kind of talk was really the hell of it. We knew it would grow louder. We knew people we had considered our friends would echo it. We knew that as soon as I walked into exile with Nancy the ugly gossip would mount and the accusations become more reckless. There was no frenzy any meaner than that which the communists unleashed on the "renegade"; it was a cardinal principle of the sect that no one ever left except for the most loathsome motives of personal advantage. The communists could never agree to disagree with a former comrade; whether in Moscow or Union Square, the ex-communist must be labeled a venal, deformed monster who had been bought off by imperialist agents or whoever happened to be the devils of the day.

Now there is a ludicrous quality in these assaults, but they did not seem funny then. For we had been brought up to share the suspicion that anyone who left communism did so for "opportunist" reasons. We had undoubtedly said unkind things about others who had preceded us to the exit. And even when we felt ready to depart we were still shadowed by self-accusation. The communists had brilliantly succeeded in making us distrust ourselves. We were middle class; we were intellectuals; we had no "proletarian roots." We had always been warned that such "elements" were most prone to flee in hours of crisis. How could we be sure that what we were doing was the reassertion of our own reason rather than the proof that we had failed to overcome our "bourgeois background"? We were suspicious of everything—and, perhaps most of all, we suspected ourselves.

To those who have never been close to communism, these introspective musings may seem far-fetched. By the fall of 1937, it will be said, the depression was over and the original motivations for enlistment in the Stalinist ranks were lost. But were they? In fact 1937 was the year of the "recession" which was gloomily analyzed by some Marxist and non-Marxist economists as the harbinger of another disastrous decline. There were still several million unemployed. In the spring of that year one of the most savage class-war episodes in our history had occurred in Chicago where the striking Republic Steel workers were shot down by the police. Although Mr. Roosevelt had delivered his momentous call for "quarantining" fascist aggression, the democracies were letting the Spanish Republic bleed to death. The Russians were still pictured as the only true friends of the embattled Loyalists; not till later did we learn the price of the alliance. There was little serenity on the horizon. Did it matter decisively that the communists themselves were guilty of sadistic excesses, and even that their revolution was devouring its children? In the long view, which is the rationalization of all oppression, weren't they still on the side of the angels?

The questions seemed hard. Yet once doubt has really set in, it is incurable; this the communists have always known, and that is why they wage such relentless war against the slightest manifestation of heresy. For it was possible to believe everything about the harshness of the times and still choose to walk alone rather than march blindly in formations led by the communist drill sergeants. One did not have to become a storm trooper on leaving the communist army; Paul Hagen and many others proved that.

In December what I had hoped for finally happened. I had

written to Freda Kirchwey, the *Nation*'s editor and publisher, applying for a job on the *Nation*. She asked me to come in and after we had talked a while she suggested that I start writing articles for them and indicated there might be a position open soon. It would be, she emphasized, a lowly post, requiring, among other things, that I clip each day's papers for the editors and run the magazine's "morgue." We talked quite frankly about my politics and I told her I was planning to resign from the YCL. Then I discussed the same problem in greater detail with Bob Bendiner, the *Nation*'s managing editor, who had served for about six months in 1936 as a staff member of the *New Masses* and hurriedly departed. A staunch and witty anti-Stalinist, he felt strongly that I should not come onto the *Nation* unless I had completely severed my communist ties; it was an independent magazine and anyone on its editorial staff ought to feel free to voice his own opinions rather than recite the morning line of each day's *Daily Worker*. I warmly agreed; the notion of working in a place where people said what they thought, rather than what someone told them to think or what they assumed they were expected to think, seemed as close an approach to emancipation as I could achieve in this life.

I was also informed that the job which was about to become available would pay $30 a week. I heard the modest sum with great relief. It was true that this would be more than the $17.50 I had received in the Student Union, and would no doubt be paid more regularly; yet I thought I could hardly be accused of selling myself to the highest capitalist bidder if I received so low a wage from the palpably non-capitalist liberal weekly.

I went home and wrote my letter of resignation from the YCL. It was not a scintillating document but it was final. In it I said I had not felt at home in the communist movement for a long time and that I was embarrassed to pretend to be one of the boys; I did not feel like one. While I agreed with communist positions on world issues such as Spain and collective security, I could not work effectively in an atmosphere which seemed completely intolerant. Moreover, since I was now going to work on the *Nation*,

I wanted to be in a position to think for myself, even if that meant disagreeing with the communists or anybody else. The letter was defensive and almost apologetic in tone; but this was it.

I mailed it to Gil Green and he called me the next day and asked me to have dinner with him. His voice was quiet and not unfriendly; perhaps partly for that reason, I did not look forward to the interview. I knew Gil had invested a good deal of time and energy and hope in me, and in a restrained, awkward way, we had become friends. Although still in his early thirties, he had been a communist for many years. He had worked hard at it; he had done a lot to educate himself; and he had never been quite capable of exhibiting the self-righteous fury displayed by so many of his comrades when confronting the problem of disaffection.

We met at a cafeteria on Fourteenth Street and we had a long, unhappy dinner. He surprised me a little at the start by saying he had been stunned by my letter. He had not even guessed, he said, that I was dissatisfied; he had assumed that my wanderings in the previous months merely reflected my desire to get established in my craft, which, he thought, was a perfectly understandable ambition. Quite earnestly, he said he simply could not fathom what my letter was about; with the kind of wide-eyed youthfulness which was natural to him, he pointed out that he had always listened patiently to my words. He could not imagine what I meant when I referred to the denial of freedom in the communist movement. And then, oblivious to the paradox, he repeated what he had said before he left for Spain: that a good communist was a soldier and did not question directives; and that "individualism" could be a disastrous disease.

It was a hopeless meeting and a painful one. I liked him, and what I had to say had to be an indictment of him—he was, after all, the top man in the YCL—as well as of others whom he considered his comrades. I told him of the meeting with "Max" about the trials and I tried to indicate something about the general condition of bondage in which we all found ourselves. He smiled faintly and condescendingly a few times, as if he were hearing a child's small talk, and he gave no ground. I do not know to this day whether he had the slightest comprehension of what I was talking about, or whether he had long ago managed to shut out all such uncertainty.

We walked to the corner and he extended his hand.

"I just want you to remember one thing," he said in an even, final voice. "When anyone leaves The Movement, he goes the whole way. Watch out."

What he was saying in one sense was that some ex-communists had ended up as bitter, bedraggled reactionaries, having deserted not only communism but the valid ideals which had first attracted them to it. But I had fought that out with myself. There was no such determinism in history; it was the smugness of communist Babbittry to assume that there was. He was saying something else, however, that was true. One may leave the communist movement feeling that it is possible to maintain a relaxed sympathy toward it; but once the break is made, antagonism develops swiftly. That is not merely because the communists begin a personal onslaught, questioning the heretic's motives, intentions and ancestry. It is because the heretic himself is finally free to examine honestly and with some detachment the nature of the order from which he has fled. This doesn't happen overnight; for weeks and months he may still be reluctant to look back critically, and to risk the epithet of "red-baiter." Then gradually, as if returning to the real world after incarceration in an asylum, it becomes possible for him to contemplate the inmates and their curious customs almost as though he had never been there himself. Some ex-communists never quite achieve that state; they function like communists in reverse, and they establish what Richard Rovere has called "the Bolshevism of the Right," mimicking the intolerant frenzy of the thing they profess to have renounced. But the great majority slowly acquire something that may be reasonably described as sanity.

Two days after I resigned from the YCL, a friend of mine who had been working for the ASU dropped in to see us. He said he had heard of my decision and we discussed it rather quietly. Then he told me he had seen "Max" that day and that "Max" had angrily told him to visit me, demand that I withdraw my resignation and, if I failed to do so, literally spit in my face. The visitor laughed when he told the story and, not too long afterward, joined us in exile.

As a college freshman the first major Marxist tome I had ever read was Nikolai Bukharin's *Historical Materialism*. For some reason that now escapes me, I started there, rather than with Marx or Lenin. A couple of months after I left the YCL, Bukharin joined the growing company of fallen archangels, abjectly proclaiming in a Moscow courtroom that he too had really been an enemy of the people all the time. The coincidence seemed like a footnote to my communist travels. It was pleasant to realize that it was not incumbent on me to burn his book.

# II

# The Age of Responsibility

# 6

To leave the communist movement at the age of twenty-two is quite different from escaping twenty or thirty years later in life. Of course, even the youngest ex-communist may find it hard to shake off the experience for a long time; as in any emotional binge the aftermath can be prolonged. But for the young man who has recoiled from communism there is the sense that his real life still lies before him and that what has happened was an exhausting adventure rather than the whole story of his existence. What seems most important is to start afresh, and not to be paralyzed by memory.

One of the virtues of American society in the thirties was that it appeared possible to do so. We did not have the apprehension then that everything would be shadowed by the past and that we would have to spend the rest of our days defending or explaining or reciting plaintive recantations. The immediate problem seemed to be to make peace with ourselves rather than with society, and to become reconciled to a new and quieter mode of living.

In the first months, rejection by our former comrades, who happened to be most of the people we knew, was a more painful problem than acceptance by the free society to which we were returning. With rare exceptions, the end of communist affiliation meant the end of friendship with communists. Many of them believed the official assumption that base motivations of personal self-interest had precipitated the break; others simply decided it was indiscreet to prolong the association since eyebrows were always being raised by the more doctrinaire fellows when our names came up. Conversely we tended to assume that those who continued to see us were in a state of diminishing devotion to The Movement.

I did not issue any public manifesto on the day I left the YCL, and sixteen years later I found a Senator regarding my silence as a suspicious circumstance. Yet in fact few people recite eloquent repudiations in a public square at the moment of departure from communism. In the first phase the common impulse is simply to get away from it all, and to try to figure things out. One has a rather glorious sense of applying one's own intelligence to one's own problems for what seems like the first time in years; but that exultation is modified by a kind of grueling ethical self-examination which continues for some months. We live now in a time when the cardinal requirement is to justify even a remote link with the communists; at that time anyone who had been touched by communism felt primarily obliged to justify leaving it.

A circumstance of history aggravated the difficulty for those of us who left at that point. Until the Nazi-Soviet Pact the ex-communist was still regarded in many areas as a puzzling figure. Among fellow-travelers the real communist still commanded a healthy respect as one who had the courage of the fellow-travelers' convictions. "Red-baiting" was considered a grievous sin in a large portion of the liberal intellectual populace; a "renegade," by his very act of apostasy, had rendered himself guilty of the offense. It was fashionable in some circles then to say that the trouble with ex-communists was that they were obsessive, and possibly some case histories warranted the charge, but often this simply meant that the ex-communist had the habit of reminding the innocent that some of the things said about the communist apparatus by the darkest "reactionaries" were lamentably accurate.

More serious considerations inhibited the former communist in those days before the summer of the Nazi-Soviet alliance. They were the same factors that had kept some of us in after we had lost the faith. In Spain the war was nearing its melancholy end; in Europe Hitler was marching his legions into Austria and thundering his threats against Czechoslovakia. In the face of these terrors the case for collective security and the Popular Front still seemed to have entirely reasonable foundations, even if one no longer believed that the communist movement was a tolerable place to inhabit and even if one were unable to share the communist ecstasy about the living conditions of Soviet man. From afar it still looked as though the Soviets were genuinely trying to avert World War II while Western statesmen (with the exception of Mr. Roosevelt) floundered, and some hoped that nazism would fight on the Eastern Front and leave the West in peace. Both the *Nation* and the *New Republic*, while voicing some uneasiness about the Moscow trials, still looked to Moscow for international comfort. So too did many thoughtful conservatives who believed that only the unity of the non-fascist powers could save the world from total war. It will be said comfortably now that nearly everyone underestimated the cynicism and ruthlessness of the Soviet rulers, but it is easier to say that now than in 1938 when, on the surface, only Moscow and Washington seemed to be displaying any resistance to the course of appeasement that led to Munich in September.

Thus the communists held together some semblance of the Popular Front they had created at home and abroad, and those of us who could no longer remain communists had the loneliest time of our lives. For we had really resigned on philosophical rather than tactical grounds; we had walked out because we could no longer dismiss words like freedom and justice and mercy as "bourgeois" ambiguities; because the oppressive quality of Stalinist thought control, always crudely disguised as a new triumph of dialectics, had become unendurable. But expediency still gave a certain prestige to the communist program. The other radical sects were forlornly saying that the world war on the horizon would be just another imperialist conflict and that the workers of the world should prepare to resist their own governments when the explosion came. The doctrine seemed peculiarly far-fetched, however, in the absence of any sign that the German workers would or could do anything about the Hitler regime.

In this interim Nancy and I remained politically homeless. We were enrolled members of the American Labor Party, which was then the common, often strife-torn political machine of anti-Stalinists and Stalinists. But we were entirely inactive in that or any other group. We had not abandoned our interest in politics, as some do when they finally turn away from communism with a bellyful of disillusion; neither were we searching for any emotional equivalent of Stalinist dogma, as others do when they are appalled by the sudden loss of certitude and purpose. We found a real joy in reacquiring intellectual independence. It was tangible pleasure to remind ourselves that no thought was a heresy any longer; our minds were our own.

In the *Nation* office I found many ideological arguments and personal tensions. Max Lerner, who was to resign as editor a few months later to join the Williams faculty, was just finishing *It Is Later Than You Think*, a fiery last call for Popular Front anti-fascism; critical as it was of communist rigidity and harsh in its analysis of the simplistic Marxist fallacies, it was nevertheless the testament of those liberals who until August, 1939, believed that the strategy of the Popular Front could check the fascist advance. Bob Bendiner and Peggy Marshall had little sympathy for this view, while Freda Kirchwey, who still looked like an animated and lovely college senior, seemed to be wavering between the two camps and trying to keep everyone contented. There was also Maxwell Stewart, a tall, phlegmatic man with an academic demeanor and a propensity for signing communist petitions and refining merit from crude communist positions; and there was Louis Fischer, the *Nation*'s roving foreign correspondent, who had not yet reached the point of no return for fellow-travelers and who, booming in and out of the office between trips to Spain and other places, seemed like a strange hybrid of Richard Harding Davis and John Reed. The arguments were sometimes violent and even bitter; much political and personal history had preceded my arrival. But while Freda often seemed upset by the controversy, I must confess that for many months I just enjoyed listening; whatever the rights and wrongs, there was the atmosphere of minds working. To a twenty-two-year-old who had just left the monolithic communist world there was a certain music in the discordant sound of the weekly editorial conferences.

As I had been warned, my chief duties at the start were to clip the day's papers, file them in the magazine's improvised morgue and produce them in some order on Fridays and Mondays when the editorials were written. I also did special research for Lerner and got to know him well in the brief months before he left. Since then we have worked together on *PM* and the *Post*. Though we have occasionally disagreed, his is one of the liveliest and most stimulating minds I've ever encountered, whether he is discussing politics or sex or some connection between them. There is never a dull moment when he is around.

Clipping newspapers is a tedious occupation but I got a certain private satisfaction from the humbleness of the chore in those initial months. I had wanted to start anew, in a role far removed from the loftier summits of the youth movement, and with some sacrificial gesture that might denote the authenticity of my convictions. For in the aftermath of leaving the YCL one felt a compulsion to prove a purity of motive at least equivalent to what one still regarded as the ultimate grace of the communists. To me this drab daily labor in the *Nation's* morgue seemed like a pretty clear demonstration that I had not yielded to the fleshpots or chosen some sinecure above the battle.

From the outset I was invited to attend editorial conferences and even encouraged to speak. Gradually, while continuing to serve as keeper of the archives, I began to write signed articles.

With the passage of months the sense of uneasiness I had felt when I quit the YCL steadily receded. The *Nation's* editors were quite dedicated and serious people, most of whom could undoubtedly have amassed more worldly goods in some other venture. They took their own varieties of liberalism seriously—but not always mirthlessly—and they felt just as strongly as the communists did about the woes of the underprivileged. What troubled me about a couple of them was that at times they were so defensive about not being communists. In those days, the communist unknown seemed to have a mysterious attraction for those who had never entered it. This was particularly true of I. F. Stone who, to this day, persists in regarding the communists as just a colorful if eccentric group of political daredevils cast in more heroic mold than any other sect, and therefore to be forgiven their admittedly strange conduct. In the years I knew him I always had the feeling Stone could remain a fairly regular apologist for the communists, with intermittent sorties to the left and right, only by staying out of the organized movement; like other instinctive mavericks, he would not have lasted very long inside.

In the early months of 1939 there was a lull on the Left. The Spanish war was over, and the recriminations about its outcome were overshadowed by the prospect of the new and bigger storm. Everywhere the fascists and their fellow-travelers seemed to be riding high. In the United States Charles E. Coughlin was intoning his hymns of hate to growing multitudes and the echoes of his message were being heard on the sidewalks of New York. In that spring and summer I spent many evenings covering meetings of the Christian Front and related groups as the basis for a *Nation* article called "The Coughlin Terror." Frankly emboldened by the Nazi successes, the Coughlinites for a brief period really appeared to be making headway in several neighborhoods; the street brawls, sluggings and anti-Semitic forays that we once stamped as strictly European were finally being enacted in our own country.

There were striking similarities and contrasts between these meetings and the communist conclaves I had attended. There were the gray, disappointed faces, the monotonous chants, the feverish sense of self-righteousness, the almost sexual release produced by some familiar slogan or the mention of some well-known scapegoat. But there was this difference: at the end the communists promised peace and justice and a better day for everyone; the Christian Fronters offered the image of a vast pogrom. The young men who attended communist rallies were roused by the age-old equalitarian ideals; to the youths at the Coughlinite gatherings, the prospect of some violence before the evening was over seemed the main attraction. But they had this in common: the communists, like the fascists, attributed each man's woes to the existence of devils, and assured him his troubles would be over if he followed the leader.

The Christian Front hysteria reached its peak in midsummer. There was genuine fear that a fascist movement had finally taken root in New York, and that its counterpart was developing in other areas under the stimulus of Coughlin's weekly sermons. Liberals were generally exercised about what was happening; it seemed clearer than ever that the Nazi plague was finally spreading to our invulnerable continent, and that our stake in halting Hitlerism abroad was greater than ever. What limits would there be to the arrogance of these street gangs if nazism conquered Europe? In the tension of those hours there was undoubtedly exaggerated apprehension over the progress that the Christian Fronters were making. But nazism was crashing ahead on a world scale.

Then, on August 22nd, came the horrible letdown for the local fascists and communists and for the fellow-travelers of both. Berlin and Moscow signed their treaty of friendship and non-aggression, thus announcing to the world that their great ideological war had been a sham battle. The Nazi warriors against "Bolshevism" and the Soviet "fighters against fascism" clasped hands like old acquaintances.

One of the most obnoxious qualities of the Marxist mind was the conviction that there is order and predictability in history. To some degree the ailment afflicted all Marxist sects. It was an underlying assumption of the Stalinists and of others who claimed to be the true disciples of Marx that they had found the key to all social evolution in the struggle of classes, and that there was an inevitability about how most men would behave, depending only upon their relationship to the ownership of the means of production. Thus the propertied classes would invariably react with violent fury against any attempt to reduce their holdings, and, no matter what the ostensible values of the age in which they lived, would resort to the most naked barbarism to preserve their privileges; and the dispossessed, having nothing to lose but their chains, would almost certainly recognize their plight and eventually rise up to overthrow their oppressors. There were other corollaries of this thesis: that the "contradictions of capitalism" were ultimately insoluble and that, regardless of palliatives, the end result—internal explosion—was inevitable. An individual might try to hasten the process or he might seek sanctuary far removed from the turmoil; what one man did was not particularly crucial because the process itself was foreordained. The element of surprise was thus reduced to a minimum. To say that "anything can happen" was the mark of an untutored bourgeois mind; the possibilities were drastically limited by economic "forces" which governed events.

To such classic doctrine, Stalin's communists brought one new element of decisive proportions. That was the existence of the Soviet Union, generally described as the workers' fatherland, and the first earthly embodiment of the Marxist dream. Here the ownership of the means of production had supposedly been placed in the hands of "the people"; for a certain intervening period the will of the people had to be formally expressed by the machinery of a state which would, in the course of time and in the process projected by the Marxist saints, finally "wither away." Even in this transition period, however, it was safe to assume that there was at least one country on earth which was always on the side of justice and peace and the suffering multitudes of the world. It had to be that way, according to Stalinist scripture, because the transfer of control of the means of production had been accomplished, and that was the key to everything. This "socialist state" could not have any delusion of imperialist grandeur because its imperialists were wiped out. It could not be aggressive because, as every Marxist child knew, aggression was the result of the pressures created by the "contradictions of capitalism." It could never align itself with such enemies of the workers as Adolf Hitler because it was a workers' state, and the workers everywhere had common interests.

The new state had automatically produced a new kind of statesman, so we were told, whose only concern was the welfare of the
proletariat; though the Moscow trials indicated there had been
a few monsters left over from the old days, no imperfection could
be attributed to Stalin himself, who was the very personification
of the new "socialist man."

Stated simply, the Soviet Union could do no wrong because
the source of all evil—private ownership of the means of production—had been eliminated.

Armed with these premises, the true communist *knew* that Moscow could never sign a pact with Germany. This was not a matter
of conjecture; it was a law of international politics as elementary
and unchangeable as the simplest law of science. In November,
1938, Earl Browder had declaimed: "The reactionaries openly
speculate that the Soviet Union may try to beat Chamberlain at
his own game by joining hands with Hitler. But even those who
hate the land of socialism cannot believe it, when they see that
the Soviet Union alone rounds up the traitorous agents of Hitler
within its own land and puts them beyond the possibility of doing
any more of their wrecking, spying and diversions for fascism."

And less than three months before the fatal day, the *Daily
Worker* had said:

> The whispered lies to the effect that the Soviet Union will
> enter into a treaty of understanding with Nazi Germany are
> nothing but poison spread by the enemies of peace and de-
> mocracy, the appeasement-mongers, the Munich-men of fas-
> cism.*

But on August 23rd the impossible was officially announced
from Berlin and Moscow, and the believers were called upon to
believe what had hitherto been classified as the unbelievable.

For some hours the communist chieftains here and in other
countries writhed helplessly. Moscow had not taken them into its
confidence; it had let them go on until the last moment angrily

* Quoted in Eugene Lyons, *The Red Decade*. Bobbs-Merrill: 1941.

crying that any talk of a Nazi-Soviet agreement was a falsehood conceived by diabolical fascist agents. At Christian Front meetings speakers had insisted with equal vehemence that the rumors were the invention of crafty communist operatives. On August 14th, some four hundred intellectuals had joined in an open letter assailing the canard that there were any basic points of similarity between the Nazi and communist regimes; such talk, they declared, was instigated by "fascists and their allies" to undermine the "united anti-aggression front."

The letter was a reply to a manifesto issued by the Committee for Cultural Freedom affirming the opposition of free men to all those tyrannies—Germany, Italy, Russia, Franco Spain and Japan alike—where "creative independence is suppressed and punished as a form of treason." This document, signed by John Dewey, Sidney Hook, George S. Counts and about 150 others, including some recent refugees from the fellow-traveler front, contained the central heresy; it charged that the Soviet dictatorship, like the Nazi despotism, had hounded and imprisoned and tortured men whose only offense was their refusal to accept the omnipotence of these super-states in the realm of the mind. While the fellow-traveling four hundred agreed that such terrible things did occur in Germany, Italy, Spain and Japan, they emphasized the importance of "answering those who attempted to destroy the unity of the progressive forces by spreading the false idea that the Soviet Union and the totalitarian states are fundamentally alike." Professors, journalists, playwrights and actors affixed their names to the statement. Some were devout communists, but a substantial number were those who had enlisted as allies in the Popular Front and had come to accept the fundamental communist thesis that Moscow was the last best hope of anti-fascist man.

When the news of the Nazi-Soviet Pact came on August 23rd, the communist leaders at first refused to answer their telephones. Then Israel Amter, one of the elder communist statesmen, hopefully announced that he was certain the text of the agreement would contain an "escape clause," permitting the Soviets to fight in Poland's defense if Hitler's armies marched. Twenty-four hours later the text arrived and the clause was missing. And when the Germans struck against Poland, the Russians marched too—against Poland.

It seemed unlikely that the communist movements of the West could survive the blow. But while defections occurred, total collapse was somehow averted. In the case of the leaders, many probably felt they had nowhere else to go; that is the trap and the tragedy which ultimately confronts the communist bureaucrat. What was more remarkable was the tenacity of a significant section of the rank-and-file members.

Immediately after the invasion of Poland, the communists called a mass meeting in Madison Square Garden. I was preparing an article for the *Nation* on the impact of the Nazi-Soviet alliance on American left-wing groups and Nancy and I went to the meeting. It was a fantastic assemblage. For one thing, although there had been predictions that the Garden would be half-empty, a throng of about twenty thousand jammed the place. Obviously they did not yet know exactly what to think and the party leaders were unable to relieve that condition because they hadn't been told themselves. The uncertainty created some ridiculous interludes; for example, on the few occasions when Hitler's name was mentioned, it was plain that the audience did not know whether to boo or whether, in the light of recent developments, such an expression of hostility might henceforth be defined as "imperialist warmongering." Any mention of Mr. Roosevelt's name evoked the same irresolution; his reincarnation as international villain was not yet complete. Finally, however, the crowd got a real chance to jeer; the speakers began denouncing "Trotskyism" and everybody knew that, no matter what else might change, it was safe to boo.

The meeting was a caricature of Stalinism. Here were twenty thousand people, many of them adults, assembled in a time of total crisis. The Second World War had begun; it had been touched off by the Nazi-Soviet agreement. The communist leaders had virtually nothing to say that was relevant to the great issue. Yet while the cheering section no longer knew exactly what team it was rooting for, it was one of the most enthusiastic rallies I had ever seen. There was not a heckler in the house.

Perhaps to compensate for the lack of ideological clarity, the audience was permitted to sing some old revolutionary songs that had fallen into disuse during the discreet years of the Popular Front. This seemed to give many of the participants a nostalgic thrill. One of the reasons the communists may have been able to avert wholesale rebellion in the ranks was that a considerable number of communists had never fully accommodated themselves to the polite amenities of the Popular Front era; now they scented a return of truly "revolutionary" rhythms and their feet seemed to be tapping the floor in anticipation of more and better old tunes.

Nancy and I left the Garden flabbergasted and depressed. We had not been out of the YCL long enough to be entirely impersonal about the spectacle. We knew that people whom we had once considered our friends were undoubtedly in that hypnotized, hysteric crowd, and the awareness that we had ever been a part of it was almost terrifying. Communism had professed to be the supremely rational science which coldly dissected the ills of society, rejecting mysticism and supernaturalism, but the Garden rally was a kind of intellectual voodoo dance.

In the process of leaving communism, most people pass through an indecisive time in which they choose to call themselves "noncommunists" rather than "anti-communists." So deep is the hated stereotype of "red-baiter" that one's first resolve as an ex-communist is to avoid that stigma. In the months since we had resigned from the YCL we had taken no major part in any public political arguments; if we had quietly helped to undermine the faith of some of those whom we had known well, that was probably more by osmosis and example than by agitation. Most of what I had written for the Nation before the pact had no direct bearing on the communist issue. Our defection was well known and the usual stories had been told, but we had not been the center of any loud controversy. But shortly after the meeting I wrote an article for the Nation called "Stalin and Union Square" which rather pitilessly described the post-pact communist performance, reported some conspicuous resignations and summarized the confusion and dismay that afflicted the fellow-traveler set. The article also reported that a number of former Stalinists and independent radicals were talking of forming their own "New Beginnings" group, comparable to Hagen's German organization.

The *New Masses* replied angrily:

> Clearly Mr. Wechsler is a bright young man who has grown a trifle giddy and Gitlowish from the fact that he was once briefly on the inside. . . .

This was the vital epithet; Ben Gitlow was a former communist leader who had, all good communists were taught, become a "red-baiter."

The *New Masses* rejoinder continued:

> The Wechsler article marks a new low in liberal journalism. . . . Powerful currents are running in America and the world. A new offensive against civil liberties is under way. It finds expression not only through specifically reactionary channels but through individuals or groups who out of weakness, confusion or opportunism provide weapons for reaction.

My reference to the "New Beginnings" project proved especially inflammatory:

> Mr. Wechsler doesn't know it, of course, but his reference to the "New Beginnings" group was none too happy. That group arose within German Social-Democracy, professing to be dissatisfied with the policies of its official right-wing leadership. But its very first manifesto was strongly anti-communist and anti-Soviet. Today it is a reactionary little sect, working closely with the Brandler group, the German counterpart of American Lovestoneites, doing its bit to keep the German people divided.

Fourteen years later a Senator from Wisconsin was to declare that my interest in Paul Hagen's "New Beginnings" venture was a link in an unbroken chain of "communist" association.

148

Among a few former communists the Nazi-Soviet agreement appeared to stir a measure of perverse relief. They had been sincerely troubled by what they viewed as the excessive trust the West was placing in Moscow's proclaimed "anti-fascism"; they probably felt that Stalinist influence on liberal thought could not be finally broken as long as the Russian illusion persisted in any form. I suppose that all of us who had left the communists before the pact experienced some emotion of vindication; the myth of Soviet incorruptibility which we had earlier rejected was at last exploded, and the argument—we thought—was over. But any such gratification also seemed indecent; for the pact had destroyed the last chance of preventing world war. In the face of that fact no other consideration had much importance. The onslaught against Poland debunked all the communist rationalizations for the pact. All the agonized attempts to prove that the alliance was a superior piece of high anti-fascist strategy were cruelly blasted by the clear evidence that it was Stalin who had given Hitler the signal for his aggression, and that the frail structure of collective security had now finally crumbled. It was said in belated explanation that Stalin had done this to protect his own national interest, and done nothing worse than Chamberlain and Daladier had done a year earlier at Munich; but the earlier Western capitulation had been met with outraged cries of protest from the Kremlin and all its followers. Wherein was Stalin's offense a lesser one?

The communists were finally forced to a wall, and they had to employ candor in their defense; at last some of them conceded that the only thing that was crucial was the security of the Soviet Union, and Stalin knew best. Everything else was inconsequential; if a war had to be fought everywhere else, the "citadel of socialism" could meanwhile live in peace and get stronger and stronger so that, eventually, it would be able to help what was left of humanity live happily ever after. One man's fairy tale was another's nightmare.

With the passage of each month after our departure from the YCL, Nancy and I found ourselves increasingly boycotted by those who had been our comrades, and we had no real desire to invite the awkwardness of seeing them. One of the few with whom we had retained any social contact was Joe Starobin, and I think that was largely because we momentarily expected him to join the ex-communist legion. But he didn't. A few months after I resigned from the YCL, he became a member of the staff of the *New Masses* and, shortly thereafter, its foreign editor. He survived all the ensuing crises; as late as 1953 he was filing dispatches to the *Daily Worker* from Indo-China after a series of private audiences with the communist leaders there.

Soon after the Nazi-Soviet Pact and the Soviet attack on Finland Joe made what seemed like a final attempt to recapture me for communism. We had not seen each other for quite a while; then he suddenly called me and suggested lunch. He was contemptuous of the *Nation's* criticism of Soviet policy. He contended quite agitatedly that we had all missed the point of history; a great new "revolutionary" era was at hand and the Red Army was the instrument of liberation. The wave of the future, he assured me, was red, not brown.

I wanted neither one. We parted a little stiffly and we no longer tried to sustain any kind of social relationship. Once we had enjoyed arguing with each other; I had found him a far more flexible adversary than most of his associates. But now I was being denounced in the communist press as a reactionary renegade and he was becoming a communist celebrity as a result of his loquacious rationalizations of the Nazi-Soviet alliance; there was no longer any mellow margin for informal debate.

In 1951, more than a decade after that meeting, he telephoned me again and asked to come in and see me. By that time I had been editor of the *Post* for about two years and my first thought was that he had finally reached the end of the communist road. I was quite wrong. He had a mission. He wanted to persuade me to write an editorial asking that the second group of Smith Act defendants be released on bail during their trial despite the fact that several of those convicted in the first case—including Gil Green—had jumped bail. Then he embarked on a rather discursive analysis of the American scene, the moral of which was that liberals would have to join hands with communists in a new united front to fight "American fascism." I told him I thought it was much too late to try to recreate the Popular Front; that as far as I was concerned, the real test of liberal nerve was our ability to wage a two-front battle against the reactionaries and the communists.

We talked of other things. He asked me what I thought of the way the world was going and I told him, perhaps a little provocatively, that I expected Tito's revolt against the Kremlin to spread to other areas of the communist empire. He assured me that I was exaggerating a minor episode; there was no basis of principle in Tito's rebellion; it had all occurred because Tito wanted to run the international communist show and Stalin did not believe in such domination. I looked at Joe and smiled and said that, if he really believed that, there was not much point in our trying to conduct a conversation; and if he was just saying it for the record, the exchange was equally pointless.

He left a few moments later. I do not suppose that I could explain to the junior Senator from Wisconsin that I felt sad, rather than angry, about the meeting, and reminded myself that there but for the grace of God . . . And perhaps, even after all these years, the surviving rulers of the Communist Party would be as suspicious as Joe McCarthy about a meeting between Joe Starobin and me.

From any viewpoint September, 1939, was a dismal time for rejoicing over the befuddlement of the local communists; their troubles were a fragment of the larger desolation facing mankind. I knew there were some quite earnest interventionists who felt at least a partial release when the attack on Poland precipitated World War II; at last, they said, the age of surrender was over. War with fascism was inevitable anyway, they reasoned, unless the democracies were to submit to total slavery; it was better that it came before any more bloodless Nazi conquests. At the time of Munich many men had quoted Eliot: "This is the way the world ends, Not with a bang but a whimper." Now some faint will to resist had finally been awakened; the whimpering was over and

Hitler knew at last that he could not seize the world without a struggle.

This was a perfectly plausible contention and, intellectually, many of us shared it. But it did not at once overcome the feeling of despair which accompanied my realization that the Second World War was on. We had said to ourselves often that the prevention of war was the only true test of our civilization, and we had said the military resistance to fascism in Spain was justified because it might help to avert the greater catastrophe of world war; even in the years when we talked light-headedly and carelessly of "class war," we rationalized such talk on the ground that it would lead quickly to the overthrow of the system which bred wars. Now another great struggle between nations had begun and, though this time the enemy unmistakably wore the ugly countenance of despotism, who could be sure that any greater good would come of this conflict than of the earlier crusade for democracy we had so scornfully debunked?

The war had to be fought and won, but no one had the right to greet it with simple songs or to pretend confidently that humanity's big day was on the horizon. The outbreak of war was the announcement that another generation had failed in the quest for serenity, and that once again the methods of the jungle would be used to defend the values we considered synonymous with civilization. It was my firm conviction that anyone who regarded this as a happy hour was a sad species of man. Like the communists, those who were enthralled by such a spectacle had acquired, in their zeal to save humanity, an extraordinary capacity for ignoring the suffering of lonely humans.

The newly fashioned pacifism of the communists was even shabbier. Until a few weeks earlier they had been saying that only the faint-hearted could falter in their resistance to fascism; they kept repeating the battle cry of the Spanish Republic, "It is better to die on your feet than live on your knees." But now their view of the proper posture for the valorous man was abruptly revised to meet the specifications of the new Soviet era.

Amid the raucous sounds and double-talk that marked the early months of the war, what seemed to me the most tenable attitude was voiced in a small volume by Irwin Edman called *Candle in the Dark*. It was written immediately after the outbreak of hostilities and subtitled *A Postscript to Despair*. For the second time in a generation, the "brutal futility of war" had begun:

> Whatever be the causes, whatever the necessity, the fact that there could be such causes and such necessity has already eaten like a canker into the bloom of every value we enjoy and every ideal we cherish. It has seemed to make a mockery of all our hopes, and nonsense of all our knowledge. It has turned the faith in education into an irony and has reduced to triviality the arts on which men have lavished their technical mastery and their lyric flame. It has made even private joys seem precarious and shame-faced. What do all these things avail, when they end in deliberate death and incalculable chaos? Men in the nineteenth century were sad that they could no longer believe in God. They are more deeply saddened now by the fact that they can no longer believe in man.

How then, he asked in Æ's phrase, could men turn now from "the politics of time" to "the politics of eternity" so that they might retain their sanity in a time of madness? Only by acquiring a sense of history—not the ruthless, mechanical concept of the commissars who pretended to know where man was headed, and thus to dismiss his current ordeal as a trivial episode in a long, predictable drama, but rather the awareness that even in the most blissful time there is the commonplace of frustration and the fear of tomorrow. It was to know what the communists and the demagogues of every stripe could never acknowledge: that "the death's head at the banquet is a grim but true image for the most radiantly happy life." It was also to know that men before us had believed that everything was lost, when in reality they had merely been at some turning point in history. "The darkness now seems absolute. Men before us have forgotten that it hides the morning star."

This was not the testament of an isolationist preparing to enter his storm shelter. Nor were these the last dour words of one who had lost faith in man. Indeed, even as he urged us to confront war without expectation or despair, he called for a renewed vision of men's capacity to dwell in a nobler universe:

> The battle against entrenched privilege, against authoritarianism, against snobbishness of race or caste, has been steadily going on. It is a battle quite as important in the long run as that in China or Europe. Only when that subtler battle is successful will the bloodier battles disappear.

This alone appeared worth believing in those first months after peace, or even the semblance of it we had known, was lost. I still believe it.

For a brief period following the Nazi-Soviet alliance there was an attempt to create some American replica of the "New Beginnings" group. Among the participants in the informal sessions that initiated—and terminated—this move were Max Lerner, Granville Hicks, who had just resigned from his *New Masses* post and plunged with great seriousness into the discussions, Louis Fischer, Matthew Josephson, I. F. Stone, Malcolm Cowley, Leo Huberman and I. Quite a few others dropped in to talk or listen. The first meetings were intense, if inconclusive. There seemed to be general agreement that the time had come for reconstruction of the American Left; the Communist Party, everyone appeared to feel, was finally exposed as a branch of the Soviet Foreign Office; the other radical sects in America were too involved with their own factional pasts to affect the future. But there was a good deal of ambiguity and disagreement about what was to be done next. Perhaps the underlying discord is reflected in the diverse paths that members of the group subsequently followed. Many of us became increasingly active anti-Stalinists, even in that period of comparative somnolence on the Left which followed the German invasion of Russia and the rejuvenated "patriotism" of the American communists; others reverted to a rather friendly, if not familial, relationship to the communists.

At the time the abortive United States version of "New Beginnings" perished, however, its death was not attributed to any serious ideological stress, but rather to the fact that too many members of the group were committed to write books in the ensuing year, and therefore too busy to get a new political show on the road. This whole experiment in disorganized politics lasted only a few months, never getting beyond the stage of mimeographed communiqués designed for circulation to a small élite of recently disaffected communists and perennially unaffiliated liberals and radicals.

It was through this circle that I first knew Huberman. He was a stocky, gregarious man with the wide-eyed, convincing manner of one who is always open to argument; he seemed kindly and sympathetic to the most untutored political soul and patient with the most benighted. He had taught at New College, where he had been an unusually well-liked teacher, and he was the author of some "popular" radical books, including an exposé of the labor-spy racket. It was through Huberman that I shifted from the *Nation* to that celebrated, chaotic experiment known as *PM*.

Just before that transfer I collaborated with Hal Lavine, now an associate editor of *Newsweek*, on a book published by the Institute for Propaganda Analysis. It was called *War Propaganda and the United States*, and I kept thinking as we wrote it that Professor Casey would have enjoyed this belated recognition. The book was chiefly an analysis of the battle of pressure being waged by domestic and foreign legions to enlist American sympathies in the European conflict. Its premise was that Americans ought to try coolly to examine their dilemma despite the heavy propaganda fire to which they were being subjected by both interventionists and isolationists.

As a nation we were instinctively pro-Ally and anti-war; was there any rational reconciliation of those emotions? Perhaps not, but we argued that this time the judgment should be made on our own, after an appraisal of the risks and the possibilities, rather than in response to the often disingenuous slogans that filled the air—whether the fake pacifism of the communists and their newly found Coughlinite allies or the insistent calls to duty of the Allied spokesmen. If we decided to go the whole way, let us know our war aims; if we proposed to continue giving all aid short of war, let us understand that this was a policy of calculated risk rather than a comfortable resolution of our conflicting desires.

The book dealt extensively with the crude effort of the Soviets to picture the Finnish campaign as a "war of liberation"; it also described the self-defeating attempt of pro-Ally journalists to suggest that the Finns were successfully smashing the invasion. All this was written during the months of the so-called "phony war" in the West when the Allied and Nazi armies were engaged in their winter of "*Sitzkrieg.*" In that atmosphere it still seemed possible for the United States to weigh its course calmly, and perhaps thereby exercise greater influence on the course of the war and the peace to come. But in May (shortly after publication), the Nazis stormed through the Lowlands and headed for Paris, and America was the last great arsenal of beleaguered democracy. Even though we were then not prepared to enter the war, the impact of events proved far more important than any propaganda of written word or public speech.

Despite the timing, the *War Propaganda* volume was fairly well received, at least in those areas where any doubts endured about America's role. The communists damned it, of course, because it burlesqued their pacifist pretensions and denied the holiness of the Soviet war on Finland; warmly pro-Allied commentators contended with some justice that it was an amoral book because it seemingly equated the propaganda of all sides and thus inferentially questioned the existence of a clear ideological conflict between nazism and freedom. To that extent, I think, it was a hangover of the era of debunking in which we had grown up. As we neared total commitment, all the cynicism produced by the wry and mournful aftermath of Wilsonian idealism gave us a moment's pause.

## 7

In a small, three-story structure in Brooklyn, Ralph Ingersoll was assembling the final members of the staff that would bring *PM* into the world. Among other innovations that were to distinguish his creature from anything newspaperdom had ever known, he planned to publish a daily page of labor news, supplemented by a picture page covering the same field. Apparently struck by Huberman's talents as popularizer and simplifier, Ingersoll hired him as labor editor, and Huberman in turn asked me to be his assistant.

It was a tempting project and I quickly agreed. I had enjoyed the *Nation* a lot; the two and a half years I had spent there include some of my happiest recollections. They had offered an ideal sanctuary after the private turmoil of departure from communism and given me exactly the assurance I needed that one did not have to choose in this life between serving in a communist regiment and enlisting in the predatory legions of finance capital, as the *Daily Worker* often put it. There I met some of the people whom I have come to like and respect most—Lerner, Bendiner, Fischer, Peggy Marshall, Keith Hutchison and others, and though I dissent from much of what she has written in recent years, I recall Freda Kirchwey as a compassionate, spirited and conscientious woman who seemed to suffer personal pain at each unfolding of this century's horrors.

But now I was twenty-four and, in a way, the *Nation* seemed almost too protected a place for someone my age. I was troubled, too, by that ancient disease of liberal journalism—the feeling that we were talking to ourselves, and to those who agreed with us, rather than to the great multitudes who daily received their guidance from Hearst, McCormick and the other conservative press lords. In his blueprints Ingersoll conceived *PM* as a great mass daily, fearlessly independent, applying all the established skills of such successful journalistic ventures as *Time* and *Life* to the task of creating a new, exciting kind of newspaper that would be as interesting as it was uninhibited.

I went over to Brooklyn for an interview with Ingersoll and became even more enamored of his idea and instantly devoted to the man. He was sitting in his shirt sleeves when I came in: a big, informal man in his early forties, with a quick, quizzical smile, a prematurely bald head and a self-confident, jaunty manner. Not until one looked closely were the dark circles under his eyes noticeable. He seemed full of ideas and energy in a disarmingly unpretentious way; he walked with the plodding, purposeful tread of a bear who knows where he is going, his head always tilted in front of him, as if unable to restrain its eagerness to get to its destination. He was, I later learned, also impatient, quixotic, stubborn and suspicious; he possessed an almost childlike egocentricity that permitted him to engage in some of the journalistic exhibitionism that later marred *PM*'s pages; his interest in ideas was that of a promoter rather than of a reflective man. But he had boundless spirit, as if he lived perpetually at the peak of a manic cycle and never allowed himself to lapse into moody reverie. He had tenacity and daring, and he never knew when he was licked. He was a great reporter, with a remarkable eye and ear for detail. He was, above all, an adventurer, breathing some of the bold pioneer fire that must have created the early American railroads. I was sure when he hired me that this was to be an epic chapter in American journalism which, in a melancholy way, it proved to be. I was also sure that this would remove me even further from that narrow, provincial world of feuding radical sects, of Stalinists, crypto-Stalinists and anti-Stalinists whose internal struggles seemed steadily more incongruous and diminishingly relevant to America. In that expectation I could not have been more wrong; from the start, *PM* was an ideological battlefield reminiscent of the Student Union, and often the adults seemed to be getting younger all the time.

The Big Idea had been conceived long before my arrival at the Brooklyn plant. Back in 1938 Ralph Ingersoll and some other ranking journalists had begun talking about "a new kind of newspaper"; gradually, however, Ingersoll assumed command of the project and by 1940 he was its prime mover. He was writing long prospectuses in an effort to arouse the financial enthusiasm of potential angels and in one of them he observed: "What we would have would be an organ of the United Front." The sentence was the clue to much of the later trouble. It also explains, perhaps, why any chronicle of *PM*'s life and death may contain more references to politics than to journalism. Politically, *PM* was born too late; by the time it was ready to make its widely heralded debut—the date was June 18, 1940—the Popular Front belonged to the past; the Russians had made their deal with the Nazis; Poland and Finland had been overrun; the American communists were chanting "The Yanks Aren't Coming," fomenting disorder in defense plants and denouncing as fascist beasts anyone who believed that America had a stake in the defeat of fascism. *PM*'s first headline carried the news that Paris had fallen to the Nazis.

But in the frantic days that preceded publication there were few overt signs of the battles that were to shake the building. Technical confusion dominated everything else; the trial-run editions were slipshod and incoherent. With the advance promotion campaign under way, we had little time to think about the content of the play we were producing; everyone was just trying to learn his lines, and figure out where he was to stand on opening night.

What Ingersoll had assembled was a weird array of incompatibles. There were expert editors and technicians, like Bill McCleery and Charles Tudor, both of whom had come over from *Life*; there were veteran refugees from the Scripps-Howard chain, like George Lyon and John P. Lewis; there were able Washington correspondents, like Ken Crawford and the late Nate Robertson; and then there was a large group of strictly non-professionals who had never been in a newspaper building before and who could not accustom themselves to the notion that deadlines were to be met rather than resisted. A number of those in the latter category, it developed fairly soon, had been hired chiefly on the basis of left-wing political eminence.

There was unquestionably immense talent mingled with the mediocrity in that strange city room. What precipitated the initial confusion was largely a technical problem; Ingersoll was determined to scrap all the old rules of journalism. He took the view, for example, that the conventional news lead—the device of cramming all the salient facts of "who, what, when, where and why" into the first paragraph—was fatal to creative newspaper writing. He had a good point there, but, like many others, the cure was administered with disastrous excess. For while everyone began to use the narrative form, with the climax of the news reserved for the last paragraph, as in an O. Henry story, the composing room held to its old rules; when a newspaper is being rushed to press and "trims" are required, the last paragraph is supposed to be cut first. Finally it began to occur to everyone that the news in each piece of news might be denied *PM*'s readers if we clung to the formula of the happy or unhappy ending.

In his critique of "journalese" language and method Ingersoll was nevertheless often on firm ground. He deplored the lack of detail in most newspaper writing; many reporters have a dull capacity for writing down all the names and addresses involved in some crime of passion and failing to look around at the scene of the crime. But Ingersoll, who had spent most of his journalistic life on weekly magazines—the *New Yorker* and then *Time*—continually underestimated the deadline pressure that haunts a daily; much of what he lamented in the other papers was simply a result of the fact that some stories were telephoned in by reporters to rewrite men twenty minutes before deadline, with no chance for either man to worry about the nicety of detail. When the problem was presented to Ingersoll, he first took the position that he didn't care when a story was published as long as it was better than the version offered by competitors; but *PM*, already suffering from a tendency to lag behind the news, could scarcely solve its difficulties by announcing that henceforth it would be even later but better.

Ingersoll was forever baffled and a trifle shocked by the improvisations which enabled the paper to come out every day. Late one night he was conferring with the department heads shortly after the midnight edition of the *Times* arrived. One editor proposed rewriting a *Times* story, a conventional, time-hallowed practice on all New York afternoon newspapers. "Is that ethical?" Ingersoll asked Hal Lavine, then the able, harassed national-affairs editor. Lavine explained that it was not only ethical but essential.

"Do other newspapers rewrite what we print?" Ingersoll asked.

"Not often enough," Lavine replied sadly.

What actually happened was that most of the fresh formulae Ingersoll had devised were steadily discarded in favor of standard operating procedure. Originally he had said there would be no editorial page; *PM* was seeking Truth alone, without fear or favor, and the Truth would emerge so clearly from its pages that no reader would need exhortation to decide what he thought about what he had read. But Truth was an early casualty. Soon after its initial appearance, *PM* was stridently voicing its opinions in the news columns and on the newly added editorial page alike. At the start there were no by-lines in the paper; before long everything was signed, including the editorials. Nothing went according to plan; soon, for a variety of technical reasons, *PM*, without changing its name, began coming out in the morning.

Much of the disorder that followed publication day was just the result of panic. When *PM* first limped off the presses, it had been blessed (or cursed) with such extravagant advance notices that people literally fought with each other in Times Square and other centers to buy the precious first editions. Such battle scenes were never repeated after opening day. The patrons suffered cruel disappointment; the product they received was inept, formless and uninspired. Novelty was an inadequate substitute for news and a warm heart could be quickly obscured by a heavy hand. If *PM* had been a legitimate play, it would have closed the second night. But the show went on. A new angel appeared, and *PM* remained on the boards as a philanthropic venture.

In the first stage Ingersoll had financed the paper by obtaining individual contributions, most of them in the $100,000 range, from a galaxy of interested sponsors, including Marshall Field, John Hay Whitney, Marion Rosenwald, Philip Wrigley and quite a few others. The first fund was quickly exhausted and for a moment it appeared that *PM* might perish in infancy. Ingersoll, however, was not a man who gave up easily. Perhaps defter in the use of the spoken than the written word, he persuaded Marshall Field to become sole backer. Field was a gracious, sensitive, modest man and the ensuing pain he suffered was not all financial. Undoubtedly *PM* offended his tolerant instincts and his sense of propriety, but he never gave public vent to his discomfort. He, too, believed there was an idea beneath the clamor, and his faith endured unimaginable reversals.

*PM* was the ultimate paradox of United States journalism. The familiar portrait of an American daily is that of a benighted reactionary gazette owned by a domineering conservative Republican and further constricted by opulent right-wing advertisers. *PM's* owner was a shy, unassuming liberal Democrat and, until the paper's last days, it accepted no advertising; yet it probably was the target of pressures as violent as any newspaper ever encountered. The most frenetic force was New York's surviving pro-communist legion which served as a growling watchdog around the premises and roared its rage whenever the paper seemed to be exhibiting signs of genuine independence. At such times the communist leaders would threaten boycotts, picket lines and other forms of reprisal. On one occasion the organ of the National Maritime Union, then controlled by communists, warned that it would designate *PM* a "scab paper" if a certain irreverence toward the communist line continued, and on another the *New Masses* published a premature obituary called "Death in the *PM*" to signify disapproval of some personnel changes Ingersoll had made which adversely affected a few Stalinist staff members. Regrettably, however, these clashes never resulted in a permanent estrangement and, when Ingersoll returned from war service for his final, desperate effort to realize the early dream, he was still thinking in terms of the long-dead Popular Front image. He had his great moments as well as his dreary ones, but politically he lived in the wrong decade.

PM had promised to be more dispassionate, possibly even more sedate than its rivals; it soon found itself compelled to shout to attract any attention at all. Ingersoll had decided that PM should be the voice of the total interventionists who favored immediate declaration of war on the Axis, but in domestic policy he was still unwilling to sever relations with the communists, whose major interest was the promotion of strikes in defense plants. Thus he found himself lustily championing such strikes on those days on which he wasn't urging immediate entry into the war. In effect he was striving to preserve a common front of deadly enemies: the liberal interventionists and the communist isolationists. On some days he employed what became known as the "all-out" formula, which meant that almost an entire edition would be devoted to a single theme, excluding all other matters of cosmic or human interest. After thus detailing some new phase of the fascist threat to America, PM would ask: "What Are We Going to Do About It?" The answer was a little puzzling, because the next day PM might be giving fulsome display to the views of the left-wing laborites engaged in staging plainly political demonstrations disguised as economic strikes in vital aircraft plants. Eminently sincere isolationists were often depicted as "traitors" and "appeasers" of the lowest calibre, but much of the time the communists were granted immunity from such abuse.

As his pro-Allied exclamations during the Nazi-Soviet Pact amply testified, Ingersoll was neither a communist nor an orthodox fellow-traveler. His closest approach to the communist circle was said to have occurred in the thirties when he was supposed to have attended one of the numerous Marxist study groups informally sponsored by the communists in Park Avenue salons. Some of his best friends, however, were communists and a few may even have admitted it. To Ingersoll this probably seemed unimportant at the time because all anti-fascists were supposed to be brothers. But it became very important when he allowed communists to do much of the hiring for *PM*. Soon after joining the staff I discovered that a man I had last seen as a high-ranking theoretician on the Ninth Floor had been brought in to head one of *PM*'s departments. There was no indication in his manner or his subsequent works that he had changed his views before joining us.

The labor section was inevitably one of the areas of fiercest controversy. Huberman was plainly not a communist and never had been, although he had been generally reckoned a fellow-traveler until the Nazi-Soviet Pact. In conversation he was flexible, detached and critical about the communist machine. Our clashes on *PM* involved both journalistic and political issues and he was understandably aggrieved about the way they turned out. Perhaps our fundamental difference—which was never clearly drawn—was that he retained a religious loyalty to Marxism at a time when I felt all the complexities and vagaries of history had undermined that creed. He persisted in regarding the communists as earnest exponents of one view of Marxism rather than as local representatives of an alien world power. Even that may be an oversimplification of a phenomenon that survives at home and abroad: the unaffiliated radical who still refuses to comprehend the record of Russian and communist performance and confuses the mythology of Bolshevism with its modern manifestations.

There were three other staff members under Huberman and all were generally identified with the left-wing faction; with the passage of months and the intensification of the communist drive against the arms program, I found myself more and more isolated from my colleagues, all of whom chose to interpret each communist-led strike as merely another episode in the workingman's quest for a better break. Admittedly the lines were not always clear; legitimate strikes, such as those at Ford and Bethlehem Steel, led by emphatically anti-communist unionists, were recklessly described by some commentators as chapters in the communist campaign of disruption. To draw the distinction seemed to me essential; *PM* rarely did. Left-wing labor leaders who were then engaged in a perfectly cynical attempt to create turmoil at any cost were treated in *PM*'s pages as if they were non-political martyrs of labor; it was considered improper to read into their hell-raising any motive except allegiance to the workingman's welfare.

Anti-communist liberal and labor chieftains began to open fire on *PM*, sometimes, it might be added, with a machine gun that was quite careless about the selection of victims. Huberman tried to counteract the criticism; more prominence was given to men on the non-communist side and I was permitted to write close-ups of such anti-communist union figures as Julius Hochman. But such formal balancing acts didn't resolve the difficulty; they simply accentuated the rather pathetic effort to publish a Popular Front paper long after the concept had become archaic. Huberman was harassed by the mechanical pressures of newspaper writing—a teacher and author by profession, he refused, for example, to meddle with that city-room gadget, the typewriter, and genially insisted on producing his copy in longhand, regardless of the imminence of a deadline. The political furor compounded his troubles, and he became defensive and impatient; the communists kept assuring him that he was producing the only worthwhile section of the paper, and I think he came to believe that.

It was not a joyous year, and I can almost hear the Senator asking me why I didn't give up when it became apparent that the communists had so firm a foothold. The answer, for one thing, is that matters on *PM* were always in a state of flux as well as uproar; the tide of battle between communists and anti-communists —with a lot of bewildered fellows watching on the side and wondering when we would start to put out a newspaper—raged back and forth, and there were moments, as I have indicated, when the communists seemed to be on the run. But there was a deeper reason. Believing, as many of us did, that the internal battle could eventually be won, we refused to abandon faith in the initial idea, distorted as it was in the product that reached the newsstands. And this goes back to an earlier matter. I have said that when I left the YCL it was with the conviction that there were more varied alternatives in life than serving either Earl Browder or William Randolph Hearst; a man did not have to give up fighting for what he considered justice and equality when he renounced communism; indeed, he might even say that he had just begun to fight. Yet for one whose craft was journalism the choices were meager. They still are. Even amid its bleakest misfortunes, many of us believed that *PM* might yet usher in a great new journalistic epoch. From the start it was circulated nationally and some of its most faithful adherents lived in cities where "the one-party press" was exactly that. One fine day, we dreamed, there would be special editions of *PM* published in such cities, with local news sufficient to meet the competition. Many newspapermen I knew who worked for Hearst, Scripps-Howard and other big complacent enterprises shared this dream. Even when *PM* seemed maddest, many of them cast envious eyes at those lucky enough to be participants in the noble experiment. They believed with us that somehow it had to turn out all right in the end.

It was said derisively at times that *PM* had revised the ancient definition of news to read: "Man Bites Underdog." That seemed to me a felicitous description rather than an insult; old man Scripps and some of the other heroes of our profession, whose memories seem to become more deeply enshrined in respectable places as their deeds are forgotten, would have reveled in the phrase. None of us who worked on *PM* need ever apologize, it seems to me, for the countless good fights that it fought in behalf of the weak and the unfortunate. *PM*'s instincts were lamentably sounder than its judgments, however, and the communists, who too often feel that a worthy underdog must have a proper ideological bark, contributed heavily to the lack of discernment which permeated *PM*'s pages.

By the autumn of of 1940—less than six months after the faltering premiere—*PM*'s internal disorders were becoming acute. On the labor staff, friction between Huberman and me had steadily increased. It revolved chiefly around that professional labor leader and amateur thespian, John Llewellyn Lewis. That was the year of Lewis's darkest discontent. His loathing for Roosevelt, mingled with his deepening isolationism, had separated him from most of his non-communist colleagues in the CIO. Sidney Hillman had gone to Washington to serve in the defense program; Phil Murray was quietly voicing his loyalty to the foreign policy of his "commander-in-chief" and the commander was Roosevelt, not Lewis. There was a rising rebellion in the CIO against Lewis's course. But to the CIO's communist bloc, Lewis was destiny's favorite son; he alone of labor's non-communist dignitaries was crying out in protest against the nefarious "imperialist war makers" and reciting, for reasons of longer standing than those of the communists, the allegedly nefarious deeds of Franklin D. Roosevelt.

Huberman was enthralled by John L. Lewis, personally and politically. He seemed sure the man could do no wrong and that he was, as Lewis himself often condescended to explain, the true and magnificent voice in labor's wilderness. Meanwhile Ken Crawford, the able Washington bureau chief, was filing exposures of Lewis's strange peregrinations and I was writing similar copy in New York.

The rift widened as the 1940 election approached. On the editorial page PM was supporting Roosevelt against Willkie, but Ingersoll's ardor wasn't matched by some of his subordinates, including Huberman, who shared the communist view that both nominees were servants of the war-bent forces of special privilege. Huberman's great hope was that Lewis would manifest a similar neutrality. Shortly before the election, however, Jim Carey, the CIO's youthful secretary and by then an outspoken anti-communist, told me he was sure that Lewis had decided to support Willkie. He indicated he had gotten that information from Lewis himself, who seemed like a pretty good source. When I broke the news to Huberman he said he just couldn't believe it. After Lewis took his stand for Willkie, I think Huberman honestly felt that it was I, rather than John L. Lewis, who had betrayed him.

Under mounting outside pressure, Ingersoll finally began to

make staff changes to reduce the left wing's power in the city room. Huberman was one of those dismissed and his became the most celebrated case. He was regarded by the Stalinist group in both *PM* and the city-wide Newspaper Guild as a sympathetic character who had tried to keep "red-baiting" out of *PM*.* Following Huberman's dismissal, Ingersoll called me in and told me that I was to head the department, an appointment intended, I gathered, to dramatize that anti-communists were at last taking over the paper. I immediately inherited an anomalous situation since the three other department members were still in the left-wing bloc, participants in the campaign for Huberman's reinstatement and convinced that my promotion marked the triumph of naked reaction.

Throughout the city the Huberman incident became a matter of bitter Guild controversy and I got no fun out of the proceedings. I felt personally sorry for Huberman and uncertain about the propriety of replacing him. Despite our differences, I had liked him and we had gotten along until the final weeks. Yet in a way it had been a case of mistaken identity; having met him in the abortive "New Beginnings" project, I had assumed we had no basic disagreements in outlook. Presumably he felt that way, too. But we had reacted quite differently to the events of the year; he drew steadily closer to the communist position, which he considered a true Marxist analysis, and—particularly after the fall of France—I was increasingly engaged in opposing the communist campaign of sabotage and pseudo-pacifism. He had found new justifications for the Nazi-Soviet alliance; I hadn't.

Within the Guild I had become active in the city-wide battle to wrest control of the organization from the communists. I was one of the supporters of the "Youngstown petition," which called on the Guild to declare its opposition to communism as well as fascism. The communists were fighting desperately to prevent the passage of such a declaration.

* Summoned before the McCarthy inquiry in May, 1953, Huberman swore that he had never been a Communist Party member. He described himself as "a Marxist."

The management's case against Huberman rested on technical grounds, and while it seemed certainly arguable that nature had not ordained him to be a daily newspaperman and that his very real talents were in other fields, his defenders maintained with considerable force that he was being victimized for his political attitudes. The dispute dragged on for many unpleasant weeks during which the communists made it clear to all who would listen that the forces of right-wing oppression, especially me, had decreed Huberman's ouster. The row was finally resolved by one of those wordy compromises which give lawyers a sense of accomplishment and bear no tangible relationship to the real issues. In the context of such an accord the dismissal was rescinded and Huberman resigned.

After exiling Huberman, Ingersoll seemed to suffer from an acute feeling of guilt about the whole matter, accentuated no doubt by the reproaches he suffered at the hands of his left-wing intimates. Indeed, as if to prove that communism could not have been even remotely involved in the dismissal, he spent a lot of time making sure that the labor section avoided any conspicuous alignment with the so-called "red-baiters." During my ensuing months as labor editor he stood over my shoulder with a copy pencil and was visibly disdainful of any material that deprecated the statesmanship of the communist labor chieftains.

By 1941 PM had officially declared war, many months in advance of Pearl Harbor, but it was still maintaining its uneasy romance with the left-wing laborites.

In deciding to issue his call for United States entry into the conflict, Ingersoll was not content to write editorial manifestoes in support of his stand. The decision called for total mobilization everywhere, beginning on PM. Thus it was that Ingersoll, in the manner of a prime minister addressing parliament, broke the news to the staff that PM was going to war.

The institution of the journalistic mass meeting was already well established on PM. As if to affirm his faith in the democratic process, Ingersoll had early hit upon the plan of holding periodic staff pep rallies attended by everyone from top editors to copy boys. At these conclaves the content of past and future editions was discussed, and informal expressions of sentiment taken. However, this town-hall technique had limits sharply defined by Ingersoll, whose vote tended to be decisive.

On one such occasion scores of us were dutifully assembled and he began the meeting with the dramatic announcement that *PM* was at war with the Axis, and was henceforth dedicated to persuading the Government to join that war. He added, however, that no employee would be required to compromise with his conscience; henceforth the staff would be divided into two groups—the "actives" and the "non-combatants." The actives would cover all stories in any way related to the war and would recognize that their supreme mission at the typewriter was to awaken the country to the desirability of an immediate declaration of war. The non-combatants would be assigned to fluffy stuff that had no bearing on the war-at-any-price program. After Ingersoll had outlined this scheme, Lou Wedemar, who had toiled for Scripps-Howard for many years and was still a little puzzled by some of the nuances of the new journalism, asked gaily, "Will the non-combatants have to wear white feathers?" I have no recollection that his question was answered.

Having decreed that *PM* would henceforth crusade for military intervention on a grand scale and welcome the epithet of warmonger, Ingersoll simultaneously devoted himself to placating the communist bloc in home-front labor matters. He chose the New York bus strike of 1941 as the occasion for reaffirming his belief in the proposition that communist labor leaders must be treated with reverence and communist labor causes examined "on their merits," as if only the most hopeless reactionary could imply that foreign policy dominated the trade-union policies of the communists.

Ingersoll's approach to the bus conflict was preceded by a great show of mock objectivity. In a twelve-hundred-word memorandum distributed to the staff (all his memos were carefully mimeographed for general circulation in the city room) he explained that the approaching bus controversy held the key to the success or

failure of the newspaper. It was his announced belief that once
*PM* found the true facts in the dispute, its conclusion would become binding on the metropolis; if the facts appeared to favor the
union, so be it, and if they seemed to favor Fiorello La Guardia,
the Mayor who was quarreling with the union, so be it, too. Once
*PM* had spoken, he said, there could be no further argument.
All this was elaborate nonsense and I suspect that Ingersoll
knew it. A bus strike was in the making and Ingersoll saw it as his
chance to recapture the affection of the pro-communist faction
despite his advocacy of total war.

As labor editor I was initially slated to be in charge of the Great
Bus Investigation, but I disqualified myself pretty early. One of
my first steps was an interview with the attorney for the Transport
Workers Union. I tried to get some evidence from him that the
bus employees had a compelling economic case, based on com-
parisons with working conditions in other cities and even with
equivalent employment. In a moment of remarkable candor the
attorney said that it would be hard to assemble such data. The
case, he admitted, was a close one. And then he added: "I think
a strike would be a good thing anyway because we're in a period
of imperialist war and the workers have to be toughened up for the
big fights ahead." He said this jauntily, as if even a poor fool
ex-communist ought to understand him.

The next day Ingersoll met with the labor staff and I reported
my skepticism about the union's position. Ingersoll said I had
totally missed the point, and that it would probably be better if
someone else conducted this phase of the labor section's activity.
He thereupon placed himself in charge of the project and named
an ardent Stalinist as his deputy. When the bus strike began, *PM*
went joyously into battle proclaiming that its objective analysis of
the dispute had demonstrated clearly that the union had truth and
justice on its side. I have often thought that Mike Quill, who was
then one of the stalwarts of the pro-communist CIO bloc (and is
now an anti-communist) must have been startled to discover all
the justifications that *PM* invented for his capricious strike.

The episode carried a great journalistic lesson. Throughout the strike *PM* acted as the unofficial house organ for the union; day after day it devoted pages of copy to the strikers' story, as translated by the union's glib communist spokesmen. But the members of the union gave Ingersoll a poor reward for his services. Quite a few copies of *PM* were sold at strike headquarters during the walkout but, when it ended, there seemed to be no evidence that any big body of new readers had been recruited. The anti-union *News* and *Mirror* were quickly forgiven their sins; they offered crime, corruption and comics in peace or war.

The bus enterprise was a failure because it was based on an essential dishonesty or naïveté—the notion that the communist-led Transport Workers Union was uninfluenced by the vaster politics of international communism and that its economic crusades could be divorced from its political designs. This is what Ingersoll wanted to believe and he may well have convinced himself it was true; he had tremendous respect for any conclusion that he reached, and an equally vast talent for forgetting the route by which he had traveled to his decision.

The death of a newspaper is always a sad event, not merely for the men who lose their jobs but for all who had ever invested their hopes in it. This is peculiarly true of newspapers which seemed destined, if only for a brief moment, to bring new light and independence to our profession. The passing of the New York *World* is still sentimentally recalled wherever old reporters reassemble; legends about the paper multiply each year, and to some survivors its final issue is still quite literally equated with the end of the world. *PM* has a similar aura and the circumstances of its death will be debated for a long time. All of us who worked there have strong views as to the day on which its doom was apparent. Yet despite all its technical deficiencies—and they were never overcome—*PM*'s fatal disease in my judgment was political. At the start and at the finish, it was the prisoner of Ingersoll's certainty that the Popular Front could somehow be brought back to life, and that everything would be simple when that happened. The corollary was that communists and fellow-travelers could be regarded as earnest playmates in the pursuit of truth. At one point he designated Dashiell Hammett to read all copy before it was published; the nervous thin man performed this chore dutifully but he could never bring himself to tolerate anything that the *Daily Worker* might have labeled "red-baiting." He was a mournful, taciturn man and hardly an autocrat around the city room, but his effort to impersonate objectivity was unconvincing.

When the Nazis invaded Russia in June, 1941, Ingersoll really got the old Popular Front gleam in his eye. This, he was sure, was the big moment he had been awaiting; now the bitter feuds that had haunted and harassed *PM* would surely be dissolved in a great resurgence of the old spirit of the thirties. It was astonishing that a man so worldly in so many spheres could remain a political adolescent so long. Certainly the Russian entrance into the war on the Allied side, even dictated as it was by the simple consideration of survival, altered American attitudes toward the Soviets. But that development scarcely resolved the deep, enduring conflicts between American communists and the liberals. *PM* was still suspect to anyone even moderately versed in the politics of liberalism. And the schoolboy wide-eyedness with which it rallied to the Soviet cause did little to allay the suspicion. Like Walter Winchell, who had been contributing columns to *PM* under the pseudonym "Paul Revere II," *PM* proceeded at once to label fascist anyone who expressed any reservation about the diplomatic sincerity of the Kremlin. The Nazi-Soviet Pact was filed and forgotten; he who remembered it was a sower of disunity and probably an agent of the enemy. Now, more than ever, Ingersoll stepped up his demands for an American declaration of war and violently pelted anyone who disagreed with him.

*PM* wasn't trying to be a newspaper. Human-interest stories were shelved; the only human whose interest was reflected in the paper was Ingersoll, and his total preoccupation was his call for war. Sometimes the result was salutary; during the Battle of Britain Ingersoll flew to London and produced some of the war's best dispatches. Although his judgments were feverish and faulty, his eyesight never failed him; when he wrote what he saw, he was superb.

Ingersoll may well have been right in his view that it was our duty to go all the way; but there was something frightening about the frenzy with which he belabored those who still hoped— especially after the Nazi attack on Russia—that the war could be won without American entry. As he saw it, there was nothing complicated about it. If liberalism in part means an awareness of the difficult choices that confront men at most big historical intersections, PM had little to do with liberalism. It exuded all the certitude that made communism so alien a creed; like the old judge, it was often wrong but never in doubt.

The degree to which the paper had become a daily pamphlet was illustrated in the days after Pearl Harbor. The Japanese had brutally resolved the American dilemma; we were in the war and only a few diehards refused to concede the point. In the days after that shattering event, Ingersoll walked about the city room in a kind of vacant trance. Finally he confessed at a staff meeting that he was no longer certain of the paper's excuse for existence. Its mission was accomplished: the nation was at war. What was there left for PM to do? He would have to "rethink" the whole project, he told us. Since the country was now united in the cause he had so long advocated, he had no other immediate message for his countrymen.

In the uncertainty about PM's future that beset Ingersoll after Pearl Harbor, it was agreed to abandon the labor section and to send me to Washington to cover wartime labor news in the capital. I welcomed the shift. Crawford and Robertson were there, and the bureau seemed like an island of sanity in the generally chaotic operation. Both were skilled newspapermen and both were fighting liberals who did not believe one had to pamper the communists in order to affirm one's liberalism; both had been prominent in the ultimately successful fight to end communist control of the Newspaper Guild. Nancy and I moved to Washington early in 1942 and Michael Wechsler was born there that year.

In those first months Crawford, Robertson and I were in a state of fairly continuous desperation about the paper's course. Ingersoll had decided that there was justification for PM's survival after all. The paper became the chief hunter for right-wing subversion; it proposed not merely to expose pro-fascism but to demand its suppression. This campaign reached its peak in a high-pitched drive to force Francis Biddle's Department of Justice to bar Coughlin's magazine, *Social Justice*, from the mails. At Ingersoll's call, *PM's* readers deluged Biddle with thousands of post cards clamoring for action and, at least partly in response to that pressure, the Postmaster General called a hearing on the case. Ingersoll did not let up. He announced that he was planning to organize a mass delegation to Washington to let it be known that no equivocation would be tolerated. By that time Crawford had suffered too much; he went to several top-ranking New Dealers and persuaded them to exert private pressure on Ingersoll to abandon his march on Washington. Reluctantly Ingersoll yielded; his relations with Crawford were never very genial after that.

The important point about this and comparable episodes was *PM's* surrender to the double standard that the communists have repeatedly tried to impose on American liberals. During the Nazi-Soviet Pact many of us had opposed demands for the suppression of the *New Masses* whose pro-Soviet apologetics were as subversive as Coughlinism. In that era, when the communists were dedicated to undermining the defense effort, *PM* generally took the view that no clear and present danger warranted a crackdown, and accorded the communist laborites a benign tolerance. It also bitterly decried the Government's prosecution of Harry Bridges. These were issues on which many anti-communist civil libertarians shared *PM's* opinions. By and large little was done to curtail communist activity in that period; the republic survived, and perhaps it was stronger because it refused to be stampeded into repression.

Yet pretty much the same factors were involved in the Coughlin case and here *PM* led the pack. Every argument of expediency advanced by the Right for total war on domestic communists was now invoked by *PM* as a sanction for the silencing of unpleasant pro-fascist voices.

*PM* suffered from the recurrent inability of some liberals to recognize that principles have no meaning unless they are applied without escape clauses. In *PM*'s case this was further complicated by Ingersoll's irrepressible affinity for communist illogic. Despite the communist abuse he had suffered because of his "premature" interventionism, he always seemed to have a soft spot in his head for the latest piece of communist double-think.

Ingersoll was inducted into the Army in July, 1942, and *PM* got a new, if impermanent, lease on life. It was a measure of the degree of political passion dividing the staff that his departure was weighed almost exclusively in terms of its impact on the rival factions. Those of us who were trying to shake off the Stalinist label attached to *PM* believed that a real new chance was at hand, especially when we heard that John P. Lewis would become acting editor. The left-wing bloc was openly displeased and dismayed. A long-time Scripps-Howard executive, Lewis had generally been a "number two" man. At *PM* he first served as assistant to managing editor George Lyon; when Lyon left, after vainly upholding the position that a newspaper should publish news, Lewis replaced him. Now, with Ingersoll leaving, the understudy was suddenly thrust onto the stage. It was a large assignment.

Lewis not only inherited Ingersoll's job; he was also bequeathed his staff and, despite periodic purges, the left-wing bloc had managed to retain a sizable proportion of posts. An unassuming, straightforward man with no great fund of ideological data, Lewis was quickly the target of communist sniping. He was neither a fellow-traveler nor an old-school intellectual; he was a hard-bitten veteran newspaperman with an inordinate capacity for work, steadiness under fire and infinite patience. Part of his difficulty was that he was torn between what he felt was his obligation to carry on the "Ingersoll tradition" and his awareness of some of the deceits that had been practiced. He tried to curb the pro-communists on the staff and under his regime men who were known to be anti-communist achieved a preponderance of control of the major departments. But he steadfastly tried to avoid a head-on collision; he was, after all, there on Ingersoll's sufferance.

Operating in a political world he never made, Lewis often resorted to half-hearted compromises in an effort to keep the ship afloat and the crew quiescent. But in the atmosphere prevailing then his problem was far more difficult than it might have been two years earlier. Some of the nation's most respectable figures took the view that any criticism of our Russian ally was a form of treason and that the American communists ought to be accorded new respect in view of their ostensible patriotism; the fact that this patriotism had been inspired by the Russian rather than the American war effort was considered secondary.

Those of us in the anti-communist camp conceded there was a double danger. The great national objective was the defeat of the Axis; yet at moments some voices in America still seemed more eager to wage a domestic war against Roosevelt and to turn their international guns against Moscow than to accomplish the defeat of fascism. In some quarters it is now considered a sign of prescience to have disparaged the validity of the alliance with the Soviets, but it looked then as if we might be fighting Germany, Italy and Japan for decades unless Roosevelt and Churchill could maintain that alliance until V-J Day.

On the other hand the preservation of military unity hardly required a moratorium on criticism and the abnegation of all realism in our appraisals of Russia and the communists at home. This was the running fight on PM and it was a fight in which Lewis often threw his weight decisively against the communist faction.

The Alter-Ehrlich affair sharply defined the conflict. When the news that the Soviets had executed these two heroic, world-renowned Polish Jewish socialists reached the United States, it seemed an elementary reflex of conscience to protest. The Russian "explanation" that these two lifelong foes of tyranny had "collaborated with the Nazis" was preposterous on its face; the fact that they were Jews underlined the grotesqueness of the accusation. The empty defense offered by the communists here was most tersely expressed by Mike Gold in the Daily Worker. "These men were guilty or they would not have been executed," he wrote in what must surely stand as the least verbose analysis of the Soviet judicial system ever presented.

Despite the monstrousness of the crime and the world-wide eminence of the victims, there were men of distinction in the United States and elsewhere who sought to discourage public protest. This was not the time, they said, for divisive debate; the argument could imperil "Allied unity"; it would "play into the hands of the fascists." All these are the ageless excuses for condoning injustice; to one who has ever been a communist, the cry has a peculiarly specious and offensive sound. If there is one thing all of us should have learned, it is that the time to fight any wrong is when it occurs; once you have capitulated to the proposition that there is some "larger" reason for condoning the immediate infamy, a fatal corruption of spirit sets in. Each new compromise seems cheaper and more defensible until finally every judgment becomes an exercise in *Realpolitik* rather than a search for honest conviction.

Amid the entreaties for silence there were public declarations. It is to the everlasting honor of David Dubinsky, the wise and warm-spirited president of the International Ladies Garment Workers Union, that he refused to heed the insistent counsels of caution. He insisted upon speaking out and organizing public memorials. The CIO's Jim Carey, who had been ousted from the presidency of the Electrical Workers Union a year earlier because he refused to come to terms with the communist faction after the Nazi attack on Russia, was equally outspoken despite ugly left-wing threats to drive him from his remaining post as CIO secretary.

While even non-communist CIO leaders were joining in the widespread call for silence, Carey went up to New York to address a memorial rally sponsored by Dubinsky. I worked with him in the preparation of his speech and traveled to New York for the demonstration. There had been advance intimations that the communists would try to disrupt the meeting, but it went off without violent incident; at the last moment the communists decided that any disturbance might merely call more attention to the case. And silence was the keynote; the communists wanted to make the world forget the two dead men.

In his speech, which was primarily aimed at the contention that now was the time for all good men to stand mute, Carey said: "To us in the labor movement, this war is not merely a negative crusade against the evils of fascism. It is a struggle to affirm those principles of justice, and the dignity of individual human life, which have been the symbols of the labor movement in all times past. . . . We have been aware that some of our words will be parroted and broadcast by our enemies; but we have not remained silent. We spoke because we knew that the ultimate strength of our cause would be increased, not lessened, by our open determination to wipe out injustice behind our own lines as well as in the lands that nazism has conquered. . . . The execution of Alter and Ehrlich has been a grave blow to our vision of world labor unity. While recognizing the debt all people owe the Soviet workers for their heroic resistance to nazism, we believe there can be no true unity achieved unless the Soviet Government acknowledges its responsibility to the workers of other countries. . . . It cannot dismiss the questions and the fears stirring in the minds of millions of workers all over the world who knew the record of Alter and Ehrlich."

Ten years afterward I was to try to recreate the circumstances of that meeting for a bored Wisconsin Senator who had obviously never heard of Alter and Ehrlich. When the session ended the stenographer asked me to spell the names of "the two murderers" whom I had mentioned. That perfectly innocent query seemed to epitomize the futility of reciting such ancient history in the setting of 1953.

PM's coverage of the Alter-Ehrlich story was respectable, if phlegmatic. In view of the communist attempt to bury the bodies without notice and other efforts to hush the incident, PM's interest in the affair was noteworthy. Along with other things, it indicated that the communists were in retreat in the PM battle, and their vexation with John P. Lewis was mounting. But they never stopped fighting while awaiting Ingersoll's return. In the interim they were suffering real rebuffs: Arnold Beichman was installed as city editor, Lavine in effect acted as news editor and Lewis was working closely with Max Lerner, whose editorials gave the paper a degree of intellectual variety and spontaneity that had been sadly missing. Whatever retroactive criticism might be made of some of his words, Lerner was never a mechanical mind and, with Lewis, made a real effort to establish *PM*'s independence. But the heat was unrelenting. Lewis, moreover, was admittedly unversed in the esoterics of left-wing politics. He was frequently deceived by men who loudly professed their political integrity even though they were drawn almost magnetically to the communist position on major issues. The phenomenon of the practicing fellow-traveler genuinely bewildered him for a long time; he constantly underestimated the pressure for orthodoxy that permeated New York's left-wing set. A rugged character with an expression of simple rectitude befitting a small-town preacher, Lewis found himself constantly pulled and pushed in obscure political struggles. Sometimes he blundered, as when he sanctioned drastic foreign-desk censorship of Ken Crawford's dispatches from North Africa, which failed to meet the ideological specifications of the left wing—among other things Crawford refused to view the State Department's Robert Murphy as a fascist. The row led to Ken's resignation, and Lewis placed me in charge of the Washington bureau. For many months thereafter all the copy filed by the bureau was handled on the national desk in New York by a politically adroit party liner who frequently found that space limitations prevented the publication of stories uncongenial to the prevailing communist view of things. This led to a long and bitter succession of inter-office communiqués, the agitated tone of which seems a little quaint in retrospect; I often wonder how we found time to cover anything amid all the feuding.

After Ingersoll's departure the communists pictured Crawford, Lavine and me as the evil spirits lurking behind the "red-baiting" remarks that found their way into *PM* with increasing frequency. In December, 1942, we were the objects of a full-dress attack in the *Daily Worker*. Crawford had written a piece suggesting that it might be a helpful contribution to Allied unity for the American Communist Party to dissolve itself; I had published an article in *The Guild Reporter* criticizing the communist "second-front"

campaign and pointing out that the invasion of North Africa
fairly effectively refuted the communist charge that the Allies
weren't doing enough to take the pressure off the Soviet front.
The *Daily Worker* thereupon published an extensive critique of
*PM* by Milton Howard which began this way:

> The nervous self-consciousness of certain *PM* writers
> about the Communist Party is interfering with that paper's
> accuracy in sheer news reporting. Anti-communist prejudice
> is warping the facts with growing frequency.

Then he chided PM for failing to recognize that Jan Valtin—
whose best-seller, *Out of the Night,* had just been published and
was under furious communist attack—was really a playmate of the
Gestapo, a characteristic communist way of saying that he had become a critic of the Soviet Union. Having disposed of that matter,
Howard continued:

> That this is no isolated incident, but springs from some deep
> well-spring of political prejudice, is indicated by the loony
> demand of *PM's* Washington bureau chief that the Commu-
> nist Party "dissolve itself.". . .
> Then there is the case of James Wechsler, an ex-commu-
> nist, who, in his work in *PM's* Washington bureau, displays
> the typical jitters of an "ex" since he is never quite sure that
> the Dies Committee or the influential people he wants to im-
> press will accept his conversion at its face value.
> Wechsler suffers especially since the Dies Committee
> launched the cry that some "communists" announce their de-
> sertion of "communism" only the better to propagate their
> communism.
> Such chronic suspicion of "ex-communists" is of course an
> occupational hazard of that tribe which would have only a
> private clinical interest were it not for the fact that Wechsler,
> apparently, is a determining voice in *PM's* political policies.
> For example both Wechsler and Crawford spread the view-
> point that the landing of American troops in Africa consti-

tuted a rebuke to the popular movement for a second front in Europe and, from now on, the people had better keep quiet and refuse to be organized into any other movements concerning the war. . . .

Asserting that I had been engaged in a mischievous attempt to create a rift between CIO President Murray and the CIO's left wing, Howard denounced the "jittery group in *PM's* staff which warps news to conform to its desire to conciliate Martin Dies." And he concluded:

> But is it fair to *PM's* readers that Wechsler's private worries as a renegade communist should produce inaccurate reporting? It is due to Wechsler's influence that *PM*, alone of all the New York newspapers, suppressed from its news report Premier Sikorski's warning: "The Germans will try to frighten the democracies by the threat of Bolshevism."

This essay is quoted at some length both as a clue to the temper of the communist attack and as a curious prelude to my meeting with McCarthy ten years later. Certain of the *Worker's* comments are hard to follow; I haven't the faintest idea, for example, who did what to the story dealing with Premier Sikorski's orations. Howard's version of my influence on *PM's* policies was unhappily exaggerated. Possibly more important, both Crawford and I happened to be vociferous critics of the Dies Committee and it is true that Mr. Dies—long before Senator McCarthy—had announced that ex-communists critical of his work could not, by definition, have ceased to be communists. Then as now it did not seem to me that criticism of congressional committees was inconsistent with hostility to communism. To the best of my ability I was fighting both Dies and the communists; perhaps this is as good a point as any to note that not long afterward I drafted a statement for Walter Winchell decrying the excesses and extravagances of Martin Dies and asking Dies to explain why he chose only to "expose" the Left and displayed no interest in subversion on the Right. Winchell's statement appeared in *PM* in the form of an exclusive interview with me, which may lend a certain ludicrous undertone to his recent discovery that the real test of an American is the fulsomeness of his respect for investigating committees.

After Crawford's resignation, the communists tended to give me exclusive recognition for any sinister stuff in *PM* that failed to reflect what every "good progressive" should have been thinking in that time of alliance with the Soviets.

In 1940, when Britain was fighting alone and its survival seemed to hinge on the steady flow of American supplies, the communists exploited all of labor's grievances, and manufactured them where none existed. They had denounced Walter Reuther for his interest in promoting arms production; after June, 1941, they dedicated themselves to the task of keeping labor quiescent, no matter how serious the inequity that may have produced unrest, and they angrily assailed Reuther for quarreling with the auto corporations over working conditions in the plants. Such conduct, they cried, amounted to nothing less than sabotage. As for John L. Lewis, the savior of 1940 was the traitor of 1943. No epithet was too vile to describe the man who called a coal strike while America and Russia were fighting nazism.

Although *PM* remained strongly critical of Lewis, it did try to give labor's side of the argument in many of the home-front battles. The underlying issue was "equality of sacrifice." Having accepted a no-strike pledge for the duration, AFL and CIO leaders found their bargaining power drastically reduced. As a lone wolf unbound by any such accord and untroubled by any overwhelming sense of responsibility, Lewis felt free to lead the legions of militant insurgence. He was a constant harassment to his fellow labor chiefs; to the communists he was the devil incarnate.

In the spring of 1943 I wrote a number of pieces describing the complexity of the problems confronting the AFL's William Green and the CIO's Phil Murray in their efforts to protect labor's stake in the stabilization program. I noted that they were engaged in an incredibly difficult operation since there were points at which labor's immediate goals collided with the broader, if shaky, framework of the anti-inflation program. The *Daily Worker* promptly construed these comments as further evidence of my deficient patriotism:

> We consider it our duty [the *Worker* wrote on April 21, 1943] to call attention to the fact that *PM's* labor expert, Mr. James Wechsler, is currently helping to insinuate into the trade-union movement the John L. Lewis notion that the war against Hitler and labor's economic interests are contradictory to each other. . . .
>
> This could be the viewpoint only of one for whom the war unity of the nation is a secondary matter, and for whom "labor interests" are considered as being hostile to or in contradiction to the nation's war against Hitler. *PM's* labor expert has become bearer of this subversive, wrecking viewpoint in the pages of a paper asking the support and confidence of patriotic labor.

Beneath this gobbledygook there was, of course, a real clash. With the exaggeration that always characterizes their shift to a new position, the communists now excelled the National Association of Manufacturers in their demands for model labor behavior. They hunted out "troublemakers" with the zeal of the old Pinkertons.

In 1943 I spent many weeks in the coal fields, covering the strikes that Lewis had called in his strange, morose guerilla war against the White House. Then, as in the auto and steel strikes I had covered earlier, I was reminded that labor editorials should rarely be written in newspaper offices. To most Americans the coal strikes were pictured as involuntary demonstrations in which honest, patriotic workingmen were coerced into insurrectionary action by a despotic old labor boss. This version of the walkouts was offered by conservative commentators and duplicated in the communist press; both portrayed the coal miners as reluctant warriors dragged into a conflict they abhorred. The coal miners I saw neither talked nor acted that way. They believed in Lewis and they trusted him with almost pathetic simplicity; they trusted no one else. They felt there was a great gulf between themselves and the rest of American society, and that whatever measure of improvement they had won in life had been won through their union, fighting against corporate and institutional power. They loathed "the enemy"—whichever one it was they worked for. They were delighted to tell you what had happened to convince them that the company was the personification of avarice and heartlessness. They despised the press, and they could remember a thousand things it had done to them in past battles. They dwelt in the memory of misery and they were sure that only their union stood between them and a return to the past. Lewis was their leader, and they had no faith in "politicians," except one—Franklin D. Roosevelt. It was a source of continuing anguish to them that Lewis and Roosevelt had fallen out; they still couldn't quite believe it.

What they resented most fiercely were aspersions on their patriotism. Many of them had sons in service; they were sure their sons would want them to heed the union's call. They were generally unimpressed by the argument that it was improper to strike when other Americans were risking their lives at the front. To the coal miners danger was the daily business of living, and a deep fatalism surrounded their homes. Each mining town had its saga of the last disaster, and the weeping wives and the orphaned children; the casualty lists were old stuff here. Sure, the soldiers were fighting at army wages; but did anyone notice the companies turning back their war profits? "Look at Joe, here, he lost two fingers down there; you know anybody who wants to be a miner?"

They had endured all the denunciations, by land and air, and they had the answers, and they would sit it out until Lewis told them what to do next, regardless of what the columnists or communists said. If someone reminded them that John L. Lewis was drawing a pretty big salary, they replied defiantly that he earned it. When they saw pictures of his Cadillac, they derived vicarious pleasure out of the sense that their leader was just as big a man as the company president. As free Americans they would still vote as they pleased on election day. Union business was a different matter.

Like so many other American dramas, the coal strikes had to be seen on two levels. There were the private intrigues of an embittered labor leader making a desperate bid to recapture his power in the labor movement, and there were his followers, convinced they were American stepchildren and that they had to fight for their lives against an unfriendly world. I tried to write both sides of that story in the book on Lewis published the following year. It was denounced with equal fervor by both Lewis's spokesmen and the communists, a point which seemed lost on the senatorial literary critic I met in Washington nine years later.

By 1944 I was pretty firmly established in the official communist analyses as the leading ideological villain in PM's house, with Lavine and Beichman identified as co-conspirators. Acting editor Lewis and Max Lerner were suspected of clear collaboration with us in what was solemnly denounced as a craven effort to affirm PM's independence of the communists.

# 8

It was a rough fight and, it seemed to us then, a momentous one. *PM* was making circulation progress under Lewis; it had begun to overcome the handicaps of its unhappy infancy. But we knew its rehabilitation would take a long time. The issues were again being clouded. The Red Army's resistance had stirred the world, and more and more people seemed to feel that its achievements warranted uncritical reverence for the Soviet dictatorship and a renewal of comradeship with the local communists. The fellow-traveling set on *PM* assiduously exploited these emotions. Nevertheless Lewis stood up to them and under his editorship the paper achieved its peak circulation (never quite 200,000) and its finest financial hours. This is not a self-serving remark, since I was in the Army at the time its circulation was highest. When I returned Ingersoll was back at the helm and Lewis was again "number two."

I was originally scheduled for induction in late 1943; after I had passed my physical and a week before I was to leave, the ban on induction of "over-26's" was announced. So I spent a large part of 1944 covering Tom Dewey's campaign; then, one week after Franklin D. Roosevelt's funeral, I arrived at Camp Meade.

I was sent to Camp Lee for basic training. There I heard the news of Germany's surrender and of the Labor Government's triumph in Britain. Everybody was talking about how many of us would be killed in the approaching invasion of Japan for which we were presumably being prepared. Nobody, of course, knew anything about an atom bomb, and it is a little appalling to think how enthusiastic we might have been if we had known that a weapon was in the making which would make that invasion unnecessary.

My military memoirs would serve to demonstrate beyond dispute that the only weapon I should be allowed to play with is a typewriter, and there may be argument on that point. Arriving late on the scene, I had the same defensive feeling as other inductees of those months, and the noncoms under whom I served made clear their relief that the country was winning the war in advance of my arrival. I had never joined the Boy Scouts as a youth because my capacity for dealing with such mechanical problems as the tying of knots was simply nonexistent; the Army gave me a chance to prove my lack of progress in that sphere. The process of cleaning a rifle tantalized me; as countless others had no doubt done before me, I found a barracks-mate who was willing to perform that chore in return for literary guidance in what must have been one of the most extensive romantic correspondences of the war.

To many anonymous men of that era I owe innumerable debts. There was the afternoon of latrine digging when it became horribly clear to my partner that he was doing all the fruitful digging. A husky, taciturn fellow who had obviously done a lot of work for a living, he suddenly dropped his shovel and stared at me sadly.

"Hey, what were you before you got here—an actor?" he asked with mingled curiosity and contempt.

I humbly explained I had been a newspaperman.

"Oh, same thing," he grunted. "Drop your shovel, I'll do it."

The only time I imperiled my life or anyone else's was in grenade training. It was explained to us time and again that, if you didn't throw the thing swiftly after releasing the pin, it would blow up in your face. Aware of my ineptitude with such gadgets, I thought about that a lot, which no doubt explains why I almost waited a second too long before releasing the first one ever placed in my hands. Each recruit did his throwing from a trench shared by a noncom; my companion was a veteran of heavy Pacific fighting who was now relaxing at Lee. When he saw me freeze, he turned white. He was still shaking a little when I got it off in whatever fraction of overtime destiny had miraculously allotted to me.

"Boy," he said, trying not to shout, "it would've been sure funny if I got killed here after all those Japs I saw."

One thing I learned at Lee was the difference between officers and noncoms who had served in combat overseas and those who had been spared such duty. With rare exceptions the returning veterans were quite gentle and pitying toward the new recruits, as if aware that we hadn't seen anything yet and that these were probably our last tolerable days on earth. Those who had spent the war at Lee were far more severe and exacting. The men who had fought bore the least resemblance to what we had feared might be the post-war military caste; they had had enough, and they wanted to shed their uniforms as soon as possible. In all the ensuing charges of American "imperialism," I thought often of those prematurely aged veterans who had fought in so many distant places and now revealed not the slightest desire to establish American hegemony where they had been.

The crowning humiliation of my Lee adventures came at the end of basic training. I had survived the physical maneuvers, somewhat to my own surprise, but I still faced the written test designed to discover whether we had absorbed the incidental military knowledge. This was regarded as a mere formality, since anyone who had paid the slightest attention and was able to read and write was presumed certain to pass this exam. A couple of days after the test about a dozen of us were informed we had flunked it. The CO assembled the failures and began by asking the disconsolate group whether any of us had been graduated from elementary school. Several had. Then he asked if any had attended high school. Two of us miserably identified ourselves. Then he asked if there was a college man in the crowd, and it was I. Columbia will be relieved to know that he did not ask the name of the college; he just gaped at me.

At this juncture Joe Lash probably saved my life. We were informed that we would be given a re-examination, particularly for the benefit of those who could not read or write; instead of a written test, we would be asked to perform a variety of operations reflecting the knowledge we had allegedly acquired in the previous weeks. The exam was to be the next day. Anyone who failed, we were told, would have to repeat basic training, which at that point seemed to me a more hideous prospect than walking into Tokyo unarmed.

Lash, who had recently returned from the Pacific and was now an officer at Lee, came to my rescue. His wife was visiting him in Petersburg at the time; we went down to the boarding house for dinner, had several big drinks and then, while Trude watched and tried hard not to laugh, Joe taught me everything about basic training that I had neglected to learn, or at least enough to permit me to pass the test designed for illiterates.

Camp Lee was remote from the battle of *PM*. After finishing basic training I was assigned to Special Services and spent many quiet weeks raking leaves, typing copies of the company newspaper and reading books. For the first time in years it looked as if I had really gotten away from it all, and I rather enjoyed the respite from political combat.

When I quit the Young Communist League I had resolved to put that experience behind me and not allow it to become the determining factor in my future existence. I wanted to function affirmatively as a liberal journalist rather than become entrapped in retroactive quarrels.

But I had reckoned without history. What had been the sectarian feuds of the thirties had actually become the universal dilemmas of the forties. The American Communist Party still remained small, clumsy and chaotic, but communism was one of the central dynamisms of the age, given new momentum by the Russian military triumphs. For the thousands who had fled the "locomotive of history" at the end of the earlier decade, there were younger replacements being recruited here and abroad to crowd the train anew. In the months after the Nazi-Soviet Pact many of us had assumed that Stalinism could never again be taken seriously in the American intellectual world, but under the spiritual cover of advancing Soviet guns, the communists had retrieved much of the lost ground. Within the area of my own activity they had been able to keep up a fight for control of the paper that I regarded as the hope of journalism.

And so, though I tried to walk ahead, the shadow of the earlier communist involvement always seemed in pursuit, and at the crucial corners it was there.

On *PM* there was the face of the man I had last seen on the Ninth Floor, now masked as a liberal journalist; there were the tedious deceits practiced by Stalinists in a manner that I recognized from the days of the Student Union; there was the bland hypocrisy of men pretending to be inquiring reporters in search of truth when they knew they had all the answers in the back of a book.

When I was abruptly transferred from Camp Lee to Germany in August, just a few days after V-J Day, I thought again that this might be a fresh universe. But again, as they say in the trailers, the false faces came out of the past. Perhaps rather belatedly it dawned on me that as long as communism remained one of the most powerful world movements, there would be no escape from the entanglement; all humanity is involved in the issues communism has created. Unless he chooses to abandon politics, an ex-communist cannot bury the dead recollections along with the withered hopes, or find an island where the past ceases to confront the present.

That quickly became plain in Germany.

My transfer was arranged by Colonel Bernard Bernstein, a former Treasury Department official. He was then in charge of the Finance Division of Military Government, entrusted, among other assignments, with the final destruction of the German cartels. His unit, for example, was ostensibly empowered to break up the notorious I. G. Farben trust and make certain that no such fabulous political-economic combine should reappear. Long one of the bright New Dealers in Henry Morgenthau's Treasury entourage, Bernstein had been to the wars for several years and distinguished himself in a lot of places. He was a burly, effervescent, energetic citizen with a contagious warmth and limitless capacity for bureaucratic in-fighting. He was also a devout believer in the Morgenthau Plan, which provided in primitive terms for the transformation of Germany into a permanently helpless agricultural nation. A liberal Rooseveltian, he had no very complicated or abstruse opinions. He had a general belief that the Russians were determined to crush the Germans—which he considered a good idea—and that the Americans, British and French could not quite decide what to do about the Germans, which he thought was a dangerous kind of indecision. In short, he thought the Russians saw more merit in Morgenthau's plan than the Allies did and he said so quite loudly to anyone who would listen. There was never anything veiled or furtive about his views, and he was probably the most outspoken colonel in the ETO, or any other theatre.

He wanted me to work for him because he thought he needed public-relations help. He had known my brother in Washington and, when he heard I was raking leaves at Lee, he started moving through channels. Many weeks later I landed in Frankfurt. By the time I got there he was deeply involved in top-level battles, losing most of them and beginning to look forward to an early homeward journey, which would have been understandable· even if he had been winning; he had fought a long war.

Although I had only the dimmest guess as to what I was headed into when I received my travel orders, I was glad to be going. I had tried for many months to get John P. Lewis to send me abroad for *PM* and, though the military show was now over, it was already indicated that the political drama was just beginning.

Like most Americans in post-war Germany, I arrived with ambivalent feelings; I never resolved them in the months I remained there. On the one hand I remembered the days when Paul Hagen had labored for a democratic rising against nazism. When Americans impatiently expostulated that "the only good German is a dead German," I thought of the German anti-Nazis who had voluntarily risked so much more than so many Americans in the fight to overthrow Hitler. But I also knew that Hagen had been denied a chance to participate in the post-war German reconstruction. How many others like him had been the victims of Allied idiocy, and what were the human materials we had selected in their place?

In my first hours in Frankfurt, before I could even locate Bernstein, I wandered around the ruins of the city. It was rather late in the decade to be stunned by the sight, but this was my first visit to the twentieth century's grotesque monuments. Looking at the blasted apartment houses, where one could see the remnants of rooms in which life had obviously been interrupted in its most casual phases, I had no trace of exultation, or even any sense that it was "they" whom "we" had hit. At the moment "they" were the dispossessed, and it was a little difficult to believe that planes flying above the city had been able to select their victims with the precision historically associated with Anglo-Saxon justice. This was the image of civilization desolated that we had talked of so often in an earlier decade, and the fact that it was Germany —rather than France or England or some other place on our side— did not render the view any lovelier.

I peered at the faces that so often seemed blank and dazed, as if belonging to sleepwalkers, and began trying to decide—as I kept doing almost every day for months—whether I could read anything in those countenances: Which belonged to the bedraggled ex-storm trooper and which to the anti-fascist just liberated from a concentration camp? Which had been the murderer and which the bystander? It was easy to say that this was simply the mass face of the enemy, but somewhere in any crowd was the lonely man who had resisted nazism as Hagen and Ernst Reuter had, and it was almost more important to recognize him than to unmask the beaten killers.

Within a few days I had other things to think about. I finally established contact with Bernstein and, after a genial, three-minute briefing, he told me I would live with Neil Naiden, a young Treasury Department public-relations man recently released from the Air Corps for service with Bernstein's Finance Division. So, although an enlisted man, I moved into officer-civilian quarters in a house that had obviously belonged to some solid middle-class Frankfurt family. The night I moved in I received my first premonition of trouble; living in the house, along with Naiden and a couple of other Treasury men, was Russ Nixon, an active figure in the left-wing CIO bloc which had engineered the ouster of Jim Carey as President of the United Electrical Workers; in both magazine and newspaper pieces I had written caustically of this political execution. In Frankfurt I got the impression that Nixon was as disturbed to see me as I was to encounter him; without explanation he moved to another house the next day. That may have been pure coincidence, but it seemed a rather grim prelude to my Frankfurt sojourn. Nixon was a veteran who, like many others in the Finance Division, had been "civilianized" for service in Military Government. He had not been previously employed in Government and I do not know who initiated the transfer. But he was very much there and had apparently wangled the post of chief deputy to Bernstein. It soon became apparent that he wasn't the only man of good standing in communist circles who had found his way into this sector of the ETO. But it also included many sophisticated anti-communists and some comparatively non-political men who were solely interested in preventing a revival of German militarism.

History has taken many sharp turns since then. In the revised alignments of 1953, past sympathy for Morgenthau's position is widely construed as some form of treachery to America and those who were eager to get Germany back into business overnight are labeled far-sighted statesmen. But it was not that simple in 1945 and it may not even be that simple now.

In the house we occupied at 41 Stettenstrasse there were long and lively arguments about what seemed to be very genuine issues. The crux of the controversy was the old debate: Was a strong Germany necessarily an aggressive Germany? Conversely, how could we hope to nourish democracy in Germany if we thwarted the national instinct for revival? Twice in our century Germany had unleashed aggressive wars, but there was also a time when we had been convinced that the harshness of Versailles had paved the way for the collapse of German parliamentarianism. Now America was confronting a comparable problem, and the only thing that seemed clear was that the answer wasn't easy. The communists were clamoring for a rigorously punitive policy in accordance with what appeared to be the Russian line in the Soviet zone; later, of course, everything changed and the Russians excelled the Allies in extending forgiveness to former Nazis, wooing the German military and frantically competing for the affection of the most extreme nationalists. But even in 1945 it was absurd to contend that only communists opposed the resurrection of a powerful Germany and that "Morgenthauism" was just a nefarious Moscow plot. Then, as in other times, the communist clique was able to make headway because its position catered to the emotions of many non-communists.

Several of the former directors of I. G. Farben, that colossus of German economic imperialism, were in the custody of Bernstein's division when I arrived. They were being interrogated at length about their relationships to the Hitler regime, their war roles—including the use of slave labor—and other phases of their activity in the era when it looked as though Hitler were invincible. What I saw of them gave me a real foreboding about the future. Their empire had crumbled, yet many of them seemed jaunty, urbane and implacably confident that in the end they would somehow extricate themselves from this embarrassment. Most of them were candidly unrepentant; they seemed to have persuaded themselves that they had simply conducted certain business transactions and that they bore no responsibility for the "political" acts of the regime they served. Perhaps with reason, they were quite sure they would ultimately be rescued by the influence of businessmen in other countries; they even seemed a little puzzled at the delay. They were, I think, completely amoral men, bitter at Hitler because his diplomatic blunders were responsible (in their opinion) for Germany's defeat but seemingly untroubled by any nightmares over the mass murders committed during the glorious days of Nazi conquest. Literature is full of the prison meditations of radicals who remain serenely certain that their day of vindication will come; the Farben directors seemed to have some of the same patient conviction that this incarceration was just a passing phase and that they would one day be back at their old stands. Possibly this bravado masked panic but it was nevertheless disconcerting.

Whether one favored a tough or moderate policy toward German economic reconstruction, it seemed plain that Germany's industrial and financial oligarchy had to be broken up. But one heard mutterings about the need for German "know-how" and there were frequent suggestions that no real economic stability could be restored without the co-operation of the industrial geniuses who, after all, had merely produced the tools with which Hitler marched across Europe. The more one heard that talk, the more merit there seemed in the Morgenthau contention that the only safe Germany was a weak, de-industrialized Germany. Before I reached Frankfurt I had believed that a democratic Germany could be built under the leadership of the anti-Nazis who had resisted Hitlerism when it was most perilous to do so; now I wondered whether we were really looking for such men, or whether enough of them had survived.

From Frankfurt I wrote Nancy in early October:

"Last night several of us tried to figure out why the mood of many Americans here—including ourselves—is so cheerless. . . . The best explanation, I think, is one I've suggested before: we came over here believing there are decent, hopeful elements in Germany and that they must be encouraged, and that the world can only make sense if an authentic democratic structure emerges here; but ever since arrival we have been full of fears—fear that the Nazis won't be rooted out of business, that Nazi youth won't be re-educated, that Nazi leaders won't be punished, that most of the 'good Germans' are dead and that in twenty years Mike and other kids will inherit the same problem. It is really fear of ourselves as a nation—not of individuals, but of our ability to do anything here. Distrusting ourselves, we may exaggerate the perils; what we really question is our capacity to govern and to teach, and to make wise decisions. So, as individuals, we begin to fear our 'softness' because we think the Germans are shrewd enough to exploit it; and so a lot of the liberals become 'hard peace' advocates, even though that program may fatally conflict with the initial goal—the creation of a democratic society."

This was the attitude of the non-communists in Frankfurt who were pressing the fight for more vigorous decartelization and more sweeping "denazification" statutes.

But when I went up to Berlin, where I was to be "civilianized" so that I could perform the functions of a public-relations man in the style to which ETO press agents were accustomed, the picture was altered. There, for one thing, I learned that men like Newman Jeffrey, a staunch anti-communist trade unionist, were working with German labor and socialist forces along the lines that I had envisaged. In Frankfurt the word had been spread that Military Government was being overrun by big-business conservatives concerned only with the restoration of the German status quo, and William Draper, Chief of the Economic Division of Military Government, was pictured as Wall Street's agent. But in Berlin I discovered that Dave Ginsburg, one of the ablest of the young New Dealers I had known in Washington, was Draper's top adviser and that Carl Auerbach, who belonged to the same New Deal school, was another prominent planner in the top echelons of Military Government. In Frankfurt this battle of the ETO had been depicted as a clear-cut alignment between reactionaries whose hearts belonged to the German industrial-financial bloc, and liberals who were idealistically striving to make certain that those who had died fighting nazism had not died in vain. I had suspected this was a gross oversimplification, and my trip to Berlin confirmed the suspicion.

The struggles inside Military Government involved bureaucratic bids for power as well as competing ideas; it was rarely possible to decide where "empire building" ended and authentic clashes of policy began. I had come into the story late and the fight was nearing its end by the time I got there. The State Department was steadily edging the Treasury out of the ETO. The scope of Bernstein's Finance Division was drastically reduced and he went home a couple of months after I arrived; the Morgenthau program was being quietly pigeonholed—if indeed it had ever been officially embraced—and relations between the quadripartite commanders of Berlin were becoming steadily cooler.

With Bernstein's departure there remained one more act in the play into which I had been thrust. Nixon was appointed to succeed Bernstein in the now curtailed division to which I was assigned. It would henceforth deal exclusively with the cartel cases. The remainder of the table of organization remained largely unchanged; Naiden, a lively, inquisitive Iowa liberal, and I were to continue to serve as the division's public-relations men.

I think Nixon, a lean, rather cold-visaged young man who had been a college instructor before becoming one of the articulate spokesmen of the CIO's left wing, appreciated the irony of my working for him as a publicist. He had not been an admirer of my writing and I had been less than respectful of his left-wing activities in the CIO. But he had apparently captivated some of the brass in General Clay's headquarters and no great dispute was stirred by his succession to Bernstein's post. Possibly that was because this phase of the operation was disintegrating anyway.

Our relationship was strained, polite and brief. We had somewhat sharp exchanges about CIO politics which confirmed our previous views of each other. But within a matter of weeks he had become involved in a battle of high policy and announced that he was resigning in protest against America's course in Germany.

Nixon's political history had hardly been a secret, and I knew neither more nor less about it than any Intelligence officer could have ascertained by reading the newspapers. I had resigned from the YCL long before he appeared on the left-wing scene; I met him when I was a labor reporter, and his allegiances and identifications were a matter of record. All this had been discussed and debated in the ETO long before my arrival, and it was still being talked about at press headquarters when I was there. Yet somehow he had survived, and eight years later a Senator was to suggest that I was somehow responsible for his survival.

With Nixon headed homeward, the Treasury began recalling personnel; the Justice Department was about to take over what remained of the decartelization program. By January, 1946, I was back in Washington.

Ingersoll had resumed command and *PM* had relapsed into its old grooves. I returned to work as head of the Washington bureau, but it was soon clear that I was not long for that world. Most of the advances John P. Lewis had made in giving *PM* a measure of political integrity were being nullified. The Stalinist bloc reemerged as soon as Ingersoll got back.

The office was full of rumors, the most persistent being that Ingersoll was dissatisfied with some of the "red-baiting" that had occurred in his absence. I had been designated by the communists as the source of this vile tendency and Ingersoll appeared less than jubilant to see me back.

He came down to Washington soon after I had resumed my *PM* post and summoned me to an audience at the Carlton Hotel. There I received a stern lecture. He began by saying he found it necessary to remind me that he expected unequivocal loyalty from every executive in realms of the spirit as well as in organizational affairs. I had become widely known, he said reprovingly, as a "red-baiter" and he did not regard such a viewpoint as constructive. He said *PM* no longer had any communist problem and, I gathered, neither did civilization. I was henceforth expected to abandon my juvenile anxiety. I almost felt as if I were being called upon to sign a non-anti-communist affidavit. It was a depressing argument in which I tried to convince him that there still were communists in the world; it ended in an unfriendly truce. I left him with the gloomy sense that all the early scenes were about to be repeated and that all the ground gained would quickly be lost.

Much later John P. Lewis confided to me that Ingersoll seemed obsessed with my political insubordination. He had told Lewis he was certain there was no longer any problem of staff communists but that a new peril confronted *PM*—the menace of a "socialist conspiracy" to seize control of the paper. He was convinced that such a conspiracy existed, he told Lewis, and that I was leading it. Whether he had invented this fantasy on his own or whether the communists around him had thought it up for him I have never discovered.

After our hotel-room session I was pretty sure my days on *PM* were numbered. I was now thirty years old, and the prospect of another five-year battle, with Ingersoll leaning to the Stalinists more self-righteously than before, was entirely gruesome. It seemed unlikely *PM* could survive another siege of its early political ailment.

As a matter of fact the recurrence proved worse than the original affliction. When Wilbur Baldinger covered the auto workers' convention early that spring, Ingersoll personally edited all the dispatches Baldinger filed, striking out or rewriting any passages which intimated that the communists were using R. J. Thomas as front man in their crusade against Walter Reuther. Not even the *Daily Worker* concealed that point, but *PM*'s reports, as revised by Ingersoll, gave the impression that Thomas was a simple proletarian combating a socialist schemer. When Harold Laski opposed the readmission of the communists to the British Labor Party, *PM* quoted only his assertion that British Labor should remain independent of both Washington and Moscow, ignoring the main point of his remarks. When Emil Rieve, in a speech to the textile workers' convention, criticized the bellicose course of Soviet policy, *PM*'s account of his speech omitted his foreign-policy utterances. The distortions and suppressions were big and little, usually crude, occasionally clever. Hal Lavine was still in the Army and Beichman had resigned; after the unhappy years the communists had endured under Lewis, they were entrenched again.

There were interminable long-distance quarrels between the
Washington bureau and the New York desk, but the fighting was
futile. I stuck around for a few more months; Lewis and Lerner
kept voicing the wistful hope that Ingersoll would shift his course
again. Instead he seemed to become more and more committed
to the notion that the Russians could do no wrong and that only
wicked men in Washington were responsible for the growing rift
among the wartime Allies.

Possibly encouraged by news of what was happening inside
PM, the communist press became even more violent in its attacks
on any heresies that slipped into the paper. In April Earl Browder,
who had recently been deposed as communist chieftain as "an
unreconstructed revisionist, social imperialist and enemy of the
working class," announced that he was making a trip to Moscow,
and had received assurances that he would be admitted. I wrote
a Washington dispatch suggesting this might mean that the
Soviet leaders were contemplating a new shift in the communist
line and holding Browder in reserve as the man whose reinstatement would herald the change. The *Worker*, after an approving
reference to an editorial by Ingersoll decrying Allied treatment
of Russia, angrily denounced me for implying that there was
any link between the Kremlin and the communist parties of other
countries:

> That busy little red-baiter and ex-member of the commu-
> nist movement, James Wechsler, gave himself a real send-off
> with musings on the course of American communist views,
> attempting to "link" those views with some "shift" in Soviet
> foreign policy.
>
> The Wechsler imputation of a "shift" merely echoes the
> current warmongering propaganda of the reactionaries that
> it is the Soviet Union's actions and not the violations of
> the Yalta agreements by the Bevin-Churchill-Byrnes-Vanden-
> berg lineup which have caused the recent tensions. . . .
>
> It is not the communists who get their "line" in disregard
> of obvious developments; it is the professional red-baiters

like James Wechsler who must seek to make his readers forget what is actually happening in the world. . . . For it is the Wechslers and the red-baiters of this world who have their "line" remorselessly handed down to them.

In the same month Ingersoll told me there would have to be a substantial cut in the Washington bureau; at least three of the eight staff members there would have to go. He badly needed economies, and since the Washington office had become a kind of citadel of the anti-communist thinking he now deplored, it was the obvious place to begin saving money. For exactly the opposite reasons, Nate Robertson and I argued that the bureau was worth keeping intact; it was the one department which still had some reputation for independence and produced a high proportion of the "exposé" news and inside stories that made *PM* something more than an editor's handbill.

I told Ingersoll I thought the dismissals were a reprisal for political disagreement and that I would not execute them. It was agreed that I would step down as bureau chief and remain as a correspondent, pending arbitration of the cases. As in most arbitrations, the underlying issues were pretty well obscured and Ingersoll was quite rightly sustained on the principle that he had the authority to reduce his staff in a time of economic emergency. When we received the verdict, Robertson, Baldinger, Charley Michie and I agreed that we had long outstayed our welcome. The dream newspaper had become a dead end. We resigned on June 18, 1946, just six years after the first edition had hit the streets. In explaining our resignation, we said we could not in good conscience work any longer for Ingersoll who, "though clearly not a communist, continuously yielded to communist pressure." We added that

he has destroyed the confidence of those who believe that *PM* should be as realistic and critical in its coverage and examination of Russian foreign policy as in its evaluation of the foreign policy of our own government.

We also expressed regret for "any embarrassment our action may cause to Marshall Field, an honest and courageous American."

When it became known that we were about to resign, Ernest Lindley, *Newsweek's* Washington bureau chief, generously offered me a job; it was to *Newsweek* that Ken Crawford had gone some years earlier after leaving *PM*. I was on the verge of accepting when the late Edward P. Flynn, then executive editor of the New York *Post*, telephoned me and said I could go to work in the *Post's* Washington bureau. The *Post* had been a staunchly liberal New Deal newspaper, exhibiting none of *PM's* reluctance to differentiate liberals from communists. Although I had known Flynn only slightly, he had previously talked to me about the shift and I felt very lucky to be able to make it. I still thought of myself as a functioning liberal newspaperman, and the *Post* was one of the few places where I could function. Charles Van Devander, a widely respected correspondent, was head of the *Post* bureau; I went to work for him forty-eight hours after resigning from *PM*.

Even after we had left *PM*, we looked back over our shoulders often, with affectionate concern. It was a little difficult to believe that the adventure was over. The last months had been full of bitterness, but there had also been great days of excitement and innovation when we seemed to be fighting journalism's noblest battles. *PM's* technical flaws were many, from the start to the finish. It rejected a lot of old techniques without perfecting new ones; in the constant struggle for survival, it was never afforded the luxury of a calm moment and, under both Ingersoll and Lewis, its scream was often so loud that one could not quite make out what it was saying. But despite all the absurdity and frustration, we knew it beat working for Hearst; when *PM* died some months later (to be replaced by the less flamboyant but listless and short-lived New York *Star*) we all joined in the mourning, not primarily for what it had been but for what we never gave up believing it might have been.

# 9

American liberalism has had its good and bad years, its times of hope and eras of retreat. By almost any standard 1946 looked dismal. It may be said that the curve of liberal emotion has often fluctuated too violently from giddy optimism to nerveless despair. Yet in that first full year of peace after the century's Second World War, there seemed solid reason for pessimism. The world was witnessing the beginning of the cold war. In the United States Harry S. Truman was still unpretentiously and, as far as the observer could detect, uninspiredly grappling with the heartbreaking problems of an office he had never sought. Some years earlier Franklin D. Roosevelt had announced that "Dr. Win-the-War" had replaced "Dr. New Deal"; now even the last New Dealers were leaving, to be replaced, for a time at least, by more conventional political types who could never have been mistaken for intellectuals. The change was symbolized by the substitution of Tom Clark for Francis Biddle as Attorney General, and there was comparable reshuffling all along the line. Everywhere, it seemed, the New Dealers, now middle-aged if not mellow, hung out signs announcing they would henceforth engage in the private practice of law.

In those months there appeared to be only two animated political movements in the United States. One was the comeback of Old Guard Republicanism, climaxed by the election of the

GOP-ruled 80th Congress in November; the other was the renascence of the communist United Front.

Remote as these movements may have appeared from each other, there were vital points at which they joined hands. Both were isolationist. Both were dedicated to the destruction of the liberal center. Stirred as they were by quite different impulses and loyalties, they were alike in their repugnance for that pragmatic progressivism to which the country had so long adhered; the Republicans saw in it the hobgoblin of "socialism" and the communists detected in it a determination to resist post-war Soviet expansion. The right-wing Republicans increasingly exhibited the symptoms of a modern political know-nothingism; the new participants in the communist-front enterprises were described by Arthur Schlesinger, Jr., as the heirs of the Civil War Doughfaces—the "Northern men with Southern principles" were now the "democratic men with totalitarian principles." The responsible conservative and the anti-totalitarian liberal were the targets of the strafing.

In the State of Wisconsin that autumn these two forces cynically united for a political killing. They did not formally proclaim their alliance; each would have been embarrassed by such an announcement. But their joint objective was to eliminate Bob La Follette. To reactionary Republicans, La Follette was an interloper, an incorrigible progressive wearing false political colors. To the communists he was a dangerous "anti-Soviet" voice. In fact he was a gifted, conscientious man who, having renounced isolationism, became—like Arthur Vandenberg—an eloquent spokesman of American responsibility. He was one of the first legislators to warn the country that the peace was not secured by military victory. He saw the scope of the Russian design early and he spoke of it bluntly; what rendered his performances especially distasteful to the communists was the difficulty of labeling this son of Midwestern progressivism a "lackey of Wall Street imperialism."

La Follette was seeking renomination on the Republican ticket, which was considered tantamount to election. The CIO in Wisconsin was then under communist domination; it quietly encouraged its members to help defeat La Follette by voting in the Republican primary—Wisconsin's primaries are open and no previous party enrollment is required. With that curious assist, the Old Guard prevailed. Bob La Follette was driven from public life.

The nominee who defeated La Follette and eventually took his Senate seat was Joseph Raymond McCarthy, an ambitious ex-Democrat with a modest reputation for political cunning and no demonstrated convictions of any passionate sort beyond a very real belief in his own political destiny. When, a few days before the primary, he was asked to comment on the communists' unusual display of interest in a Republican primary, he replied: "Communists have the same right to vote as anyone else."

The final vote was McCarthy, 207,935, La Follette, 202,557, a narrow margin which surely entitled the communists to feel their intervention had carried the day. They must have felt even more triumphant when McCarthy announced that "Stalin's proposal for world disarmament is a great thing, and he must be given credit for being sincere."

We knew little about the man who had beaten La Follette. The fact of La Follette's defeat and the circumstances under which it occurred seemed sufficient to underline the sadness of the year, the strangeness of the times and the loneliness of the liberals who resisted any reunion with the communists.

The Popular Front had reached its heyday a decade earlier, when Franco attacked the Spanish Republic. To one who had been a communist as a young man in the 1930's and had escaped at the age of twenty-two, the communist revival of 1946 was particularly disconcerting. One saw some of one's elders who had avoided the earlier communist entanglement reliving what seemed to be one's own childhood. Henry Wallace was perhaps the most stubborn example of a man who refused to respect what his youngers were telling him.

But there was also a new generation yielding to the old blandishments and this was a good deal more painful to watch. For here, to some extent, were all the ideological props of an earlier stage set—the collapse of hope that another war to end war had really ended war, the befuddlement of our own post-war society, the already mounting pressures for political orthodoxy. To a youth in 1946 the New Deal probably seemed as distant as the New Freedom once had seemed to us. And a new Russian illusion had arisen—not necessarily the view that Soviet society contained the solution to all problems, but admiration for the military valor of the Russian armies, not of the October Revolution but of the defense of Stalingrad. In 1946 a young man who became a communist at, say, the age of eighteen had been eleven years old when the Nazi-Soviet Pact was signed; to him the memorable thing about the Russians might well be the Soviet military legends rather than Molotov's handshake with Ribbentrop. Proust said "the facts of life do not penetrate to the sphere in which our beliefs are cherished."

So, while political reaction scored at the polls, a new age of innocence appeared to be dawning on the American Left—an age in which men and boys of reasonably upright intentions were again being drawn into the communist network. It was comfortable for them to believe that the devils were all in Washington (with perhaps some intimate relatives in London) and that these devils alone were fomenting the crisis. When Henry Wallace was exiled from the Truman cabinet, what further proof was needed—so the story went—that the "warmongers" were in command in Washington? Wallace had been the invention of non-communist liberals; he alone seemed to remember "Dr. New Deal" while "Dr. Win-the-War" was operating. Now those of us who questioned the communist analysis of the international estrangement were the prisoners of a myth we had created. For Wallace, in the deepening bitterness created by his ouster from the cabinet, became convinced that he had been the victim of a plot manufactured by "the war makers," and more responsive to the overtures of the communist politicians who had not lost their capacity for recognizing a potential captive when they saw one.

In that year of my thirty-first birthday there were times, if I may say so, when I felt dismally old. This was the re-enactment of a story I had seen before, and much of which I had personally experienced; there was all the frantic idealism and the earnest single-mindedness mingled with sullen indifference to knowledge; there were the hardened, cynical communist operatives who believed in nothing except the doctrine of Kremlin infallibility. How did one recreate the meaning of the Moscow trials and the Russian slave-labor camps and the persecution of dissidents and the Soviet embrace with nazism for an eighteen-year-old or an ex-cabinet member who were convinced that anti-communism was no more than a witchcraft practiced by Dr. Goebbels?

In Europe men were talking of new beginnings for the non-communist Left and the initials NCL were being used in official State Department memoranda. Whatever his failures on the home front, Harry Truman had early glimpsed the nature of the international struggle; it is one of the unceasing wonders of democracy that this modest, seemingly provincial man from Missouri was blessed with an instinctive wisdom—and with competent advisors—in the realm where error could have been so calamitous. Regardless of what finally happens, the European Recovery Program initiated by his Administration will stand as one of the landmarks of United States foreign policy. It reflected awareness that poverty was communism's secret weapon; that any long-run hope for stability hinged on the reconstruction of Europe's battered economy. It was the irrefutable answer to the communist charge that America was greedily inciting war and callously indifferent to Europe's human welfare.

The post-war communist world line had been plainly fore-shadowed in the celebrated Duclos article, published in the April, 1945, issue of *Cahiers du Communisme*. In that article Jacques Duclos, the French communist chieftain, began to break the news that the Kremlin's policy of wartime collaboration was nearing its end. His composition took the form of an angry assault on Earl Browder, then the American communist leader, who had been particularly loquacious in spelling out the notion that wartime unity had laid the basis for permanent rapprochement between Moscow and the Western democracies. Duclos specifically rejected Browder's thesis that communists might live happily ever after with the Roosevelt Administration (the article was written some weeks before FDR's death) and upheld William Z. Foster's view that the communists ought to be planning a "militant" third party.

In fact the gulf between Moscow and Washington had been widening before Roosevelt's death. Within weeks after the signing of the Yalta agreement, the Soviets had ruthlessly ignored the treaty's guarantees of political freedom in Poland and Rumania.

With the ouster of Browder in February, 1946, the American communists formally signalized the end of a honeymoon which had been going badly for quite a while. Now they were creating a new United Front movement chiefly dedicated to undermining and discrediting American foreign policy. And again they were finding allies in the strangest places. In February, 1946, Eugene Dennis, the new communist leader, declared that henceforth the communists must concentrate on the establishment of "a national third party—a broad peoples' anti-monopoly, anti-imperialist party . . . If possible—and it is preferable—steps toward forming a third party should be taken early in 1947." The National Citizens Political Action Committee and the Independent Citizens Committee for the Arts, Sciences and Professions were to constitute the public base for creation of such a party.

The timetable was meticulously followed. A merger of NCPAC and ICCASP was effected in December, 1946, resulting in the formation of the Progressive Citizens of America (PCA) which became, in 1947, the foundation on which the Progressive Party was built.

What the communists were doing in 1946 was what they had done so often before in the USA and other countries; they were filling a vacuum on the Left, and filling it with some of the most energetic spirits, if not the most informed minds, of the day. For a brief period they even captured Harold Ickes, who allowed himself to be employed for several months as chairman of the Independent Citizens Committee. His association abruptly ended when, at a big Chicago "peace" conference in the autumn of '46, the mimeograph machine mysteriously broke down and prevented circulation of the text of his speech to the press, a speech in which he had strongly suggested that Moscow's tactics had aggravated the growing international disorder.

At that point Ickes decided there was something strange about the enterprise and not long afterward he announced the result of his researches. "Communism is a nonassimilable political ideology," he said. "A true progressive movement has no chance of success unless it rigidly excludes communists." This was twenty-two years after the elder Bob La Follette had pronounced exactly the same conclusion at the start of his campaign for the presidency; it was the verdict countless other men had rendered after engaging in trial marriages or feverish romances with the communists. But it was a lesson that still seemed unlearned by a large fragment of the 1946 liberal class. When the communists engineered a "Win the Peace" conference in Washington that year, it attracted a substantial representation of dignified innocents who lent their names to manifestoes that *Pravda* could warmly endorse; like all well-managed communist shows, the conference reviewed the world scene with simulated detachment and reached the conclusion, carefully prepared in advance by the communist caucus, that Moscow sought only peace and quiet while fellows in places like Washington were trying to stir things up.

The communist thrust was being fiercely contested in some places. Inside the American Veterans Committee Charles Bolté, Gil Harrison and others were challenging the communists, and winning, but the battle was long and costly. A development of great significance was Walter Reuther's final emergence as president of the powerful United Auto Workers in the face of last-ditch communist opposition. Few leaders of labor possessed Reuther's imaginative awareness of the new crisis confronting freedom; few cared as much about the outcome. Long before the phrase had become a cliché, Reuther was pleading for a democratic counter-offensive against communism and warning that it must be conducted by men who understood the deceptive appeal of the communist mystique for the underfed multitudes of Europe and Asia. Reuther combined his socialist heritage with a Rooseveltian realism; the blend produced an extraordinarily effective political man. Socialist heredity immunized him against the corruptions of success, and New Deal environment gave him a shrewd sense of the possible.

But for Reuther and Bolté and the others like them, there was no real center of political operation in 1946 America. The communists were busily creating new fronts and diversions, discarding their disillusioned dummies and stuffing new ones. They still lived on Russia's wartime reputation and the illusions it had rekindled, and on the absence of competition. The New Dealers now constituted what was being called a "government in exile," but they had no real refuge and they were scattered all over the landscape. The best instincts of some young people were being squandered in the lost week-ends of communist endeavor; we who were in our early thirties were in danger of becoming prematurely tired radicals or politically displaced persons.

Neither then nor at any other point did the communists constitute anything resembling an imminent revolutionary threat to the republic. They were a small battalion hardly capable of staging an abortive insurrection in even a few precincts. Their mission was to create confusion, not revolt. They knew they could hardly hope to seize power themselves; they could only seek to divide and disorganize the non-communist Left and, if that meant the victory of reaction here, so much the better for communism's world chances. It was not the first time that the communists had tacitly collaborated with the Right to create the turmoil in which democracy may be most easily undermined.

So they sought to convince the world that American foreign policy was the creature of "Wall Street imperialism" and that all true progressive souls were up in arms against it. In Europe there was a growing "Third Force"; in America, so it seemed, there was rising Republican reaction, a pro-communist Left and nothing in between except the still inept, bumbling presidency of a man who wished he wasn't there.

In that year Americans for Democratic Action was conceived. American liberalism was about to find a new beginning and, for many of us, a long and often lonely migration was ending. None of us, I trust, found in ADA a fanatic faith comparable to the dogmas of the simple days. We did find a home and fellowship and a place where we could fight for the things we believed in without imitating the inhabitants of the totalitarian political jungles.

The story of ADA actually goes back to May, 1941, when an organization called the Union for Democratic Action was formed. It had been in the making for several months; its sponsors were strongly anti-isolationist liberals who wanted to create a group that would press for liberal domestic policies while vigorously supporting the Allied cause abroad. Their call was for "A Two-Front Fight for Democracy—at Home and Abroad." They issued it at a time when some conservative interventionists were deploring any excessive interest in democracy's problems at home and the communists were insisting America had no stake in democracy's struggle in Europe. The first Chairman was Reinhold Niebuhr, the gallant theologian whose rational pessimism about man's nature has never diminished his concern about man's fate. The Executive Secretary was Jim Loeb, a lean, youthful former teacher of Romance Languages who has never permitted his ulcers to weaken his intestinal fortitude. If there is any veteran of the liberal wars who merits decoration for devotion above and beyond the call of duty, it is Loeb; he devoted more than a decade of full-time labor to the effort and, even now, as the new co-publisher of the Adirondack *Daily Enterprise,* he remains one of ADA's most conscientious volunteers.

One month after the UDA was established, Hitler broke his pact of eternal friendship with Stalin and hurled his armies against Russia. The UDA immediately urged full aid to the Russians but cautioned American liberals against any revival of the United Front which was always, in Loeb's phrase, more front than united. During the ensuing five years, the UDA was subjected to savage assault from the communists and from others who resented any reminders that cast doubt on the glorious military partnership.

"During those years," Loeb has recalled, "we became almost the pariahs of the liberal movement. We were sometimes called 'the hang-back boys' because we refused to participate in so many 'worthy causes' that we knew were run by the communists. They were the things to do and we refused to do them. We fought at meetings, we pleaded, we warned, and we were damned unpopular. We fought in the Teachers' Union, the labor unions, and all over the place. Tragically for the world, we were right about the way it would turn out, but nobody ever loved Cassandra."

Then, as now, demagogues demonstrated their inability or unwillingness to differentiate anti-communist liberals from communists; even while the UDA was conducting its lonely battle against communist infiltration in the liberal movement, Martin Dies issued a "special report" accusing the UDA of subversion. Among those assailed by Dies as "a significant part of the interlocking directorate of the communist movement in the United States" were such notable anti-communists as Reinhold Niebuhr, A. Philip Randolph, George Counts and Ken Crawford. The communists roared with delight.

Only selfless and dogged effort kept the UDA alive during the war. Its annual budget rarely reached $40,000. It had only a handful of chapters. Its membership consisted almost exclusively of a select portion of that group one day destined to become known as egg-heads.

By the spring of 1946 Loeb and his colleagues agreed the time had come to expand or give up. At a meeting of the UDA board he was authorized to try to organize a conference of leading liberals and laborites at which some program of expansion might be mapped. If that venture failed, it would probably be the last try.

In the ensuing months Loeb patiently talked to countless people and held a series of small meetings, most of which I attended. Possibly the most important thing that happened was that he met Joe Rauh, who had recently returned from prolonged Army duty in the Pacific and was now Wilson Wyatt's deputy in the housing administration. A great-hearted, battling New Deal attorney whose identification with the underdog began when he toiled on the hapless Harvard basketball teams in the early thirties, Rauh brought immense resources of tenacity, drive and conviction to the undertaking. Uninvolved in the past internal wars on the Left and never beguiled by the communists, Rauh infused a buoyant tough-mindedness into the enterprise; he had clear-headedness, great moral character and a freshness of spirit that was totally infectious. The third moving force was Arthur Schlesinger, Jr., the brilliant and animated young Harvard historian who has somehow managed to become a passionate participant in history without losing detachment about it. He almost seems to occupy two points in time as he rushes from the platform of an ADA rally to the archives of the Roosevelt Memorial Library at Hyde Park, with time out for classes at Harvard along the way. He never quite resembles a prodigy because he always sounds a little older than most people in the room.

There were others, including Dave Ginsburg, Boris Shishkin of the AFL, George Weaver of the CIO, Carl Auerbach, John Edelman and Gardner Jackson, who had served as conscience and confidant for a generation of Washington liberals. The problem was to get a sufficiently eminent group of sponsors. Loeb talked to Mrs. Eleanor Roosevelt, Reuther, and innumerable others; the rest of us made other approaches.

I was asked to talk to Averell Harriman, with whom I had spent several long evenings at Stewart Alsop's house. This lean, handsome, soft-spoken man was then the object of furious communist attack. The communists pictured him as one of the dangerous master-minds behind American foreign policy, and it was sufficient to cite his polo-playing career as proof of his servitude to finance capital. Actually Harriman was one of the most sophisticated and thoughtful men around. He had been deeply skeptical of ultimate Soviet intentions for several years; he was Ambassador and later Lend-Lease Expediter in Moscow during the war, and he had, in the phrase he used so often, "met the issue." That issue was the capacity of democratic man to abandon his illusions about the Soviet system; until he did so, he would be totally confused by each new turn and bewitched by each new phrase. To "meet the issue" did not mean to relinquish all hope for stability in our century; it meant understanding that there could be no accommodation through weakness or wistfulness. But Harriman perceived more than the implacable nature of the enemy; he also understood the nature of the fascination. It was not the know-nothing reactionary and the comfortable exponent of laissez-faire capitalism whom the communists feared; the decisive battle in Europe in 1947 was between the communist legions and the non-communist Left. Europe was too old, too war-weary and too skeptical to be enthralled by any vision of an American century based on the economics of the National Association of Manufacturers or its spiritual brethren. Nearly everywhere abroad the great divide was between those who had succumbed to the communist mirage and those who saw, in some form of democratic socialism, the chance to achieve, without imprisoning the human spirit, the economic justice which the communists proclaimed as their goal. If there was to be an effective challenge to the post-war communist advance, America would have to recognize socialists as allies. The issue was not the preservation of a particular economic blueprint, but the defense of free institutions. The American fallacy, Harriman believed, was to view communism and socialism as equivalents and fail to recognize that they were mortal enemies; the great lack in American political life was the absence of a non-communist Left that could uphold this distinction. Almost before I could begin soliciting his support, he was explaining the need for an organization that would fill this gap. He became one of ADA's earliest and most devoted sponsors.

It is a clue to the American atmosphere in those months that there was great disagreement as to whether the founding conference of what became known as Americans for Democratic Action should be held in public or in private, and that the most serious opposition to its creation was communist, not conservative. There were some active liberal politicians who were reluctant to identify themselves with the movement lest it offend those of their constituents who were enrolled in communist fronts and whose political god of the moment was Henry Wallace. There were intimations that the tone of the new group, descended as it was from the UDA, was too "anti-Soviet" and too permeated with "red-baiting." There were murmurs of doubt as to whether any truly progressive group should identify itself with the foreign policy of an administration committed to the Truman Doctrine in Greece and Turkey; it was still considered in some liberal circles little short of warmongering to support active opposition to Soviet expansion. The merger which established the Progressive Citizens of America had just been completed, and it was suggested that the ADA conclave might be construed as a merely negative response to that development.

Nevertheless, after some postponements and defections, the first conference took place on January 4, 1947, in Washington. Niebuhr and Elmer Davis, the droll voice of America's best instincts, presided at the opening session. An organizing committee was formed with Leon Henderson and Wilson Wyatt as Co-Chairmen and Loeb as Secretary-Treasurer. A press committee, headed by Barry Bingham, publisher of the Louisville *Courier-Journal* and including Marquis Childs and me, drafted the first general statement, which included a provision for screening members to prevent communist infiltration.

ADA's debates and decisions on foreign-policy issues in those first meetings were a major episode in the maturing of American liberalism. The liberals had come to grips with the reality of Soviet power and discarded the naïvetés that had so often led many of them into the blind alley of international wishful thinking. In supporting the Truman Doctrine ADA helped to bury the notion that Soviet expansion could be met by hoping for the best.

And so it was under way. Mrs. Roosevelt volunteered the first contribution—$100—and pledged to raise $500 more in a week, which she did. One of the most important gains in this organizational period was the enlistment of a powerful contingent of Minnesota liberal Democrats who were then engaged in a battle for control of the Democratic Party in that state. Back in May, 1946, Loeb had published a letter in the *New Republic* discussing the irreconcilable cleavage between liberals and communists. The letter evoked considerable correspondence, including a missive from a housewife in Red Wing, Minnesota. Her name was Eugenie Anderson. She told Loeb she agreed with his view and invited him to come to Minneapolis to talk to the insurgents there. When he arrived, she introduced him to the Mayor of Minneapolis— Hubert Humphrey—and it was out of that association that the Minnesota bloc joined ADA.

Although an intellectual by profession, Loeb has repeatedly exhibited a remarkable talent for political scouting; he is always spotting stars before they reach the major leagues. I remember his telling us about Humphrey in the fall of 1946, and being unmoved when our glances reminded him that we had never heard the name. In the late fall of 1951 he similarly began talking about the Governor of Illinois as a man who would make a distinguished Democratic candidate for the presidency.

The first official national conference of ADA was held in late March of 1947. There were roughly four groups in the assemblage: members of the "government in exile," like Henderson, Wyatt, Paul A. Porter and Rauh; some influential labor leaders, notably Reuther, Jim Carey, David Dubinsky, Emil Rieve and Hugo Ernst; younger liberal politicos, such as Humphrey, Franklin D. Roosevelt, Jr., Richardson Dilworth and George Edwards; and the intellectuals who had formed the core of UDA, led by Niebuhr.

I covered the conference for the *Post* and helped to write the words for ADA's first program. In that declaration the founding fathers and mothers of ADA declared:

> Liberalism is a demanding faith. It rests neither on a set of dogmas nor on a blueprint, but is rather a spirit which each generation of liberals must learn to apply to the needs of its own time. The spirit itself is unchanging—a deep belief in

the dignity of man and an awareness of human frailty, a faith in human reason and the power of free inquiry, a high sense of individual responsibility for oneself and one's neighbor, a conviction that the best society is a brotherhood that enables the great numbers of its members to develop their potentialities to the utmost.

Opposed to this spirit have always been the wealth and power of the organized forces of reaction which today find their most virulent expression at home and abroad in fascism. In our time the democratic idea is also threatened by the communist forces that reject democratic values of truth, justice and freedom in the interests of a police state. Those who believe in the democratic spirit must devote their energies to the creation of an organization of their own and must work through it. . . .

Thus began the organization which Fulton Lewis, Jr., was to call a galaxy of "OPA, long-haired, left-wing, star-gazing, mouths hanging open, fair-haired boys" and the communist *Daily Worker* was to describe as "the imperialist fifth column inside the liberal and labor movement."

# 10

Early in 1948 Henry Agar Wallace began his campaign for the presidency as the leader of a movement which he likened to Gideon's Army but which, as he acknowledged later, turned out to be a division of Stalin's foreign legion. For most of ten months he journeyed up and down the country pleading for converts to his cause, and when he had finished it was generally agreed that he had many fewer supporters than when he began; but though the result was ridiculous, the ride was indisputably record-breaking. Through nearly all of that time I was one of two newspaper correspondents regularly assigned to follow him. My companion was Howard Norton of the Baltimore *Sun*, an able, genial newspaperman who had the good fortune to feel no personal involvement in the story and therefore suffered only the physical discomforts of an improvised journey on a breakneck schedule.

We estimated afterward that we flew more than fifty thousand miles with Wallace in the course of that merry-go-round; we also rode trains, busses and autos over uncounted distances. We heard Wallace deliver an infinity of words, recordings of which would undoubtedly sound as painful to him now as they did to me then. It was a pathetic expedition, covering nearly every state in the Union and proving beyond dispute that a candidate can travel almost indefinitely without getting anywhere.

For Wallace it must have been a heartbreaking voyage and,

despite my bitter disagreement with most of what he was saying, there were moments when I suffered vicariously. It is almost impossible to spend that much time in such close proximity to any man who seems to believe in what he is doing without detecting some poignancy in his ordeal. But my sadness about what he was doing was mingled with outrage over what the communists were doing to him. Perhaps I sentimentalized the case. Wallace was a shy, self-conscious, withdrawn man who seemed strangely unsuited to the elementary political routines. He was almost a caricature of an innocent, murmuring the sentences which left-wing ghosts had usually written for him and denying that ghosts existed, parroting the oldest communist clichés as if they were rare insights he had just acquired on his way to a press conference. Yet there were times when I wondered whether he was as blind as he seemed to be, or whether, once he had committed himself to the endeavor, he simply put on blinders and refused to take them off.

I took the assignment voluntarily. I could have gotten out of it. But though I anticipated some of the ensuing unpleasantness, I knew it would give me a chance to see some varieties of the liberal and left-wing movement in areas I had never visited, and a better chance to see America than one got on the usual campaign train. At intervals during the journey I nostalgically recalled the *de luxe* days on the Dewey campaign special back in 1944 when we wrote most of our dispatches in a club car and frequently listened to Dewey's orations over a radio conveniently installed in the train for non-ambulatory correspondents. But I did not regret the Wallace trip. Traveling as we did without benefit of a protective curtain, I glimpsed more clearly than ever before the diversity of the American landscape, which is probably the basic wisdom any newspaperman should possess.

It was also, however, a special kind of trip for me because it took me back into the left-wing precincts I had left a decade earlier and I saw close up the revival of the communist operation.

And before it was over I also saw confirmed what I had long suspected: that the answer to communist confusionism could be given most effectively by liberals with an affirmative program of their own, rather than by scatterbrained patrioteers who thought they served the republic by hurling eggs at Henry Wallace or enacting a local ordinance to prevent him from being heard by defenseless children.

The recurrence of eggs as instruments of political warfare fascinated me. I had first seen them splatter the supporters of Reed Harris back in 1931, and there they were again as Wallace traveled through hostile Southern communities in 1948. Possibly it is in throwing off the yolk that egg-heads are born. I have no doubt that some of Wallace's youthful supporters were as perversely influenced by the know-nothing attacks to which he was subjected as I had been by the egg-throwers of Morningside Heights. What is most difficult for many of us to learn is that a man may be cruelly martyred without necessarily being right.

To be a member of this small entourage created keen embarrassments for me. As a Washington correspondent I had known Wallace for several years. In 1944 I wrote many sympathetic words about him when he was seeking renomination for the vice-presidency and when he seemed to be carrying the banner of liberalism against the compromisers and conservatives inside the Democratic Party. I had had several personal conversations with him during his subsequent years in the Cabinet and we got along well. Like almost everyone who has seen him often I was nonplussed by his intermittently vague glance, which seemed to convey the suggestion that he was in the room alone. One of his colleagues once remarked that it would never be possible to understand Wallace until one knew what was going on in his head when he thus appeared to have left this world. But later it occurred to me that he was perhaps thinking of some new formula for the cross-breeding of chickens and that the thought was far more important to him than the birth of a political idea. I still believe he had a more genuine passion for poultry than for politics, which may explain why he was so often regarded as a politically queer duck.

But having known him and having been counted as one of his adherents when he was fighting for second place on the Democratic ticket four years earlier, I occupied an anomalous position in his fellow-traveling road show. With the exception of Norton, who was primarily concerned with producing a story that warranted page one, I was the only hostile character in the cast. The ADA had vigorously denounced Wallace's candidacy and it was known that I had been active in forming ADA; moreover, almost as soon as the trip began, I was filing copy that must have displeased him. Each day I wrote a dead-pan news dispatch describing what he had said and done and then, about twice a week, I contributed a column of comment on his performances which described the latest evidences of communist inspiration in the venture.

Though he never took me to task for what I had written, I knew he was puzzled and hurt. Gradually I got the impression that he regarded me as the field representative of all the New Dealers who had once been on his side and were now, for reasons that he refused to comprehend, appalled by his alliance with the communists. The defection was so unanimous that it might have shaken another man, but Wallace seemed confident that his aloneness was irrefutable proof of his virtue and that it was everyone else, rather than himself, who had fallen out of step with the ideals of the departed Franklin D. Roosevelt. In much of what I wrote I tried to spell out the obvious facts about the men behind Wallace's campaign, but, as the months passed, Wallace grew increasingly irritable at any reference to facts. He publicly prided himself on his lack of knowledge of the communist movement; each time he was reminded of the real allegiances of the leaders of his party, he would insist that the informant was suffering from an obsession and that only a man with his own vast absence of information could render objective judgment. The communists have taken a lot of credulous men for a ride; Wallace seemed anxious to step on the accelerator himself.

What disturbed me most was the reappearance of familiar faces I had known in an earlier setting; I might add that they appeared even more pained to see me. They were all efficient, articulate young men whom I had last seen at fraction meetings of the Young Communist League; now they were pillars of the so-called Progressive Party and it was apparent that Wallace regarded each one as a symbol of the indigenous grass-roots soldiers who had spontaneously sprung up to join Gideon. I have no way of knowing whether they had all maintained their association with communism through the intervening years, but I could hardly share Wallace's view that the presence of such bright, earnest and comparatively youthful faces demonstrated the amateur standing of his party. At the very least they knew what this project was all about and it seemed equally clear that they were not disposed to let the candidate in on the ill-kept secret.

Actually Wallace had begun his campaign under circumstances that might have confounded a less stubborn man. Only a few weeks after he had started his gullible travels, the communists staged their coup in Czechoslovakia, destroying overnight one of the model democratic governments of the world. Up till that moment Wallace himself had been contending that the moderate men in Benes' regime might serve as the bridge between East and West, and he depicted himself as their American counterpart. At a press conference on a wintry morning in Minneapolis he faced the news that the bridge had blown up. He explained that the death of Czech democracy was lamentable but that one must not discount the degree to which American deeds had "provoked" the Russians. The whole unfortunate episode, he said, was a result of the cold war, which he was determined to end. A little later in New York, however, he had seemingly received a different briefing; there he took the Russians out of the picture and explained that it was United States Ambassador Steinhardt who had precipitated the crisis which led to the disaster. When it was demonstrated that Steinhardt was not even on the scene at the time of his alleged plotting, Wallace shifted his ground. As for Jan Masaryk's suicide, he was unwilling to accept the view that it had any connection with the communist putsch. When a reporter questioned him about it, he replied, "I live in the house that John G. Winant lived in, and I've heard rumors why he committed suicide. Maybe Winant had cancer. Maybe Masaryk had cancer. Maybe Winant was unhappy about the fate of the world. Who knows?"

I doubt that Wallace read the *Daily Worker*, but undoubtedly others did his reading for him. As Dwight Macdonald noted in *Politics* at the time, Wallace's curious observation came four days after Joe Starobin had offered this comment on Masaryk's suicide in the communist daily: "Let Americans remember another suicide—that of John Winant, who found that post-war America was not what he hoped and expected it to be, and could not endure the strain of it."

In subsequent days, Wallace's justifications for the communist overthrow of Czech democracy became more glib. He grew petulantly scornful of the suggestion that there was any real link between the native communists in any country and the Kremlin. As his associations with communists, some of whom I had known from way back, became closer, he seemed to know less and less about them—and to want to know nothing. Within a few months he was advancing the quaint view that "there is just as much variation among communists as there is among Democrats and Republicans"—a viewpoint he defended quite literally despite the communists' own boasts of the monolithic nature of their party; thus he sought to convey the idea that "some" communists might be working for him while others were against him.

His refusal to acknowledge the most elementary facts of communist life was almost unwavering, perhaps because he had no other source of organized strength. Before he formally announced his candidacy he was warned by many old friends that he would become a prisoner of the communists; he ignored such counsels and plunged ahead. For a while he clung to the view that his critics would see the light. When he dimly discerned that they would not, he had only the alternatives of giving up the battle or letting the communists run it for him.

The American communists were his all-out supporters, in their own inimitable, inelastic manner, but the Russians, it must be conceded, were less than helpful. They kept committing diplomatic atrocities that undermined his most roseate speeches about the mellowness of Russian intentions. The Czech coup occurred against the background of the mounting Soviet attacks on the Marshall Plan, and this too accentuated Wallace's predicament. Initially he had hailed the program, as had most other liberals, as the beginning of a great reconstruction effort that would give new vitality to European democracy, as a rejection of post-war isolationism and the epitome of generous statesmanship. But now, with the Soviets aligned against the plan and the communists everywhere called on to take up arms against it, Wallace revised his line. The Marshall Plan, he shouted, was nothing more than the latest attempt of American imperialism to foist itself upon the defenseless peoples of Europe. All the banalities of the communist polemics against the program and the man whose name was identified with it found their way into Wallace's texts, most of which were prepared for him by a bright young man well versed in communist doctrine. Wallace had known George Marshall for a long time; he had hailed his appointment as Secretary of State many months earlier. Now he was drawing an unrecognizable cartoon of him.

In the early stages of his campaign Wallace seemed to be trying awkwardly to fix responsibility on both Washington and Moscow for the development of the cold war, but gradually he was weaned away from even this somewhat synthetic neutrality; all his big speeches were aimed at Washington. "Wherever Brown Brothers, Harriman and Dillon Read and Co., operating through the Trojan-horse cabinet, have extended their intrigues, there you will find crisis," he cried at one point. An Iowan, he still sought to define himself as the spokesman of America's grass roots, but one had the inescapable impression that the rhetorical roots were transplanted from Union Square.

Nevertheless, and especially in the early months, there were good and gracious people enlisted under his banner; that was the sadness of the project. In many communities men were risking their economic lives in his behalf, and there were real casualties. Often they were the historic mavericks of the town; often they were simply frightened inhabitants of the atomic age who thought they detected in his presence the modern apostle of peace on earth; perhaps most often they were comparative youngsters flushed with their first true political passion and, as in all first love, determined not to hear or read and certainly not to believe an unkind thought about the object of their affections. In 1933 I had been one of those who stubbornly refused to find out the truth about the communist role in paving the way for Hitler's seizure of power. These children of a new generation seemed no less resistant to any information about the coup in Czechoslovakia. They preferred to believe that all the wickedness was in Washington, as we had believed once before. They eagerly devoured any evidence of real or alleged American mischief and stonily ignored the record of Russian belligerence. They became justly aroused about a violation of academic freedom on a Midwestern campus and remained apathetic to the mass enslavement of minds and bodies in the Soviet empire.

It was a long springtime for Henry Wallace; what kept his candidacy alive throughout that unprecedented barnstorming which preceded his formal nomination was the behavior of some of his enemies rather than the astuteness of his friends. In Evansville, Indiana, a hostile throng stormed the hall where he was speaking and slugged C. B. "Beany" Baldwin, his campaign manager. Finally the police intervened and the meeting went on; one could not avoid a feeling of sympathy for the serious-looking men and women who walked through the mob to hear Wallace speak and thus probably branded themselves as eccentrics in the community. During the fracas I found myself using a press card to summon the dilatory police. When it was over William Gailmore, who was traveling with Wallace to deliver the fund-raising pep talks, thanked me for my help and asked me whether I didn't now realize that I ought to join up with Gideon. I declined the invitation without inflicting upon him my mature judgment that the foolishness of the mob gave no belated merit to Wallace's sermons.

In late spring Wallace made his stormy Southern trip. It was probably the only occasion in American presidential history when a candidate traveled so many miles in the South in order to win votes in the North. Nobody in the Wallace high command believed he could get any votes in deepest Dixie, but it was expected the journey would stir enough tumult to command sympathetic attention in the Northern liberal and Negro communities. Possibly the commissars also believed a reasonable amount of disorder, sharply focused on the anti-segregation issue, might provide valuable propaganda for the Soviet microphones. At the start of the trip it appeared that such hopes would be fulfilled; at the first stop in Raleigh, North Carolina, another mob scene was enacted, which stopped just short of being a major riot. Back at the hotel where we were staying, Newbold Noyes, Jr., of the Washington *Star* and I rode up in the elevator with one of Wallace's managers, who remarked with agitated indiscretion that the riot was "the best thing that could have happened for us." At other stops along the way in the same state there were more demonstrations of varied degrees of ugliness, with the egg invariably the symbol of attempted repression. Since North Carolina was deemed to be the center of Southern enlightenment, there was a good deal of ominous talk about what might happen when this political medicine show invaded the deeper Southland. Nevertheless, in a gesture for which General MacArthur might have provided more ringing lines, Wallace announced that he would go on to Alabama, Mississippi and other hot spots. There were increasingly melodramatic rumors, including the suggestion that the train carrying us into Alabama would be dynamited, and I remember thinking that it would have been grotesque to be blown to bits because of physical proximity to a cause in which I so thoroughly disbelieved.

Then a strange and wonderful thing happened, and it is worth pondering by those who still insist that American life is ever predictable. The deeper we went into the South, the quieter things became; except for a couple of minor incidents and a certain amount of unhysterical heckling, Wallace was unmolested as he completed his tour. There was a flurry of eggs in Houston, but they were thrown wildly, and most of the meetings were un-marred by even such episodes. Wallace himself was at his best during some of those Southern interludes. He threw away the scripts which others had prepared for him. Most of the time he appeared to be preaching the Sermon on the Mount rather than the gospel according to William Z. Foster; he said a good many things that needed to be said about the brotherhood of man. He may even have jolted the complacency of a few citizens who had never doubted that the Lord preferred them to those born with darker skins. He established in at least a dozen places that unsegregated meetings could be held without civil war. In his improvised performances Wallace was always far more impressive than in the great, stage-managed productions. This Jekyll-and-Hyde quality was visible throughout the long campaign. In an afternoon he might talk informally to a group of college students under a tree on a quiet campus, and in that setting he seemed almost the personification of reasonable man. There he would avoid derogatory analyses of the motivations of other men, the method he so bitterly deplored when others applied it to him; he would even admit the magnitude of the problems confronting Mr. Truman and the fallibility of his own conclusions. But by evening of the same day, appearing on the platform of a public rally carefully staged by the local left-wing stalwarts, he would be a changed man, sanctimoniously intoning the bitter words that had been written for him, beaming at the adulation of the crowd, reaffirming without humility the certitude that he and Joseph Stalin could work everything out if people would let them alone.

During and after the campaign I wrote pretty severe condemnations of the great exercise in double-talk in which I felt Wallace was engaged. Yet these were not always easy to write. They were clouded by the image of the reticent, white-haired man so incredibly unsuited for the baby-kissing ordeals of campaigning; the inarticulate, awkward, sixty-year-old man enduring all sorts of minor indignities and committing incredible political gaucheries; a lonely, withdrawn man who must have sometimes wondered late at night whether it was worth the effort and yet who bridled angrily when anyone suggested that he might be afflicted with doubts; and who carried on to the end even as his army dwindled and the nature of his entrapment on a left-wing island became so perfectly clear.

There was the night in Topeka when we wearily waited in a railroad station until 2 A.M. for a coach train to Kansas City. When a train limped into the station, we all leaped hopefully forward, but the conductor bellowed that the train was full, so the ex-Vice President of the United States was coldly pushed back with the rest of us to spend another hour in the crowded, dreary waiting room where almost no one paid any attention to him.

There was the day in Detroit when Wallace addressed the strikers on a Chrysler picket line. The strike had begun that morning and many of the workers had dropped into the nearest saloon to bolster their spirits for the long siege. Oblivious to the alcoholic level of the audience, Wallace delivered a serious speech; he was like the one sober character at a far-gone, ribald cocktail party. When he was through one of the strikers grabbed the microphone; the candidate seemed to expect a hearty endorsement of what he had just finished saying, but instead the ebullient volunteer shouted: "All right, men, now let's all sing 'I Had a Dream, Dear.' "

Wallace was one of the country's drabbest platform orators, especially when reading a speech. There were agonizing letdowns at the large public rallies when, after frenzied receptions, his monotonous delivery acted as a sedative. There were occasions when he frankly acknowledged his oratorical limitations and mumbled, "Perhaps I wasn't cut out for this kind of work." There were the enfeebled jokes with which he tried to liven his style, the ad libs that trailed away into the nothingness of unfinished thoughts, the fumbled greetings and ill-at-ease ripostes with local admirers who kept hoping that his remoteness was Lincolnesque.

So it was difficult to keep writing that all his weary words, all the long journeys, the sleepless nights and the daily frustrations, the continuing grapple with the machinery of campaign life, the forced handshakes and the moody milkshakes, the desperate small talk, the nerve-racking, infuriating minutiae of a lost cause—that all these were wasted, or wrong, or both. It was especially difficult to sum it up that way because a lot of decent citizens were taken for the same ride, and risked prestige, profit and position in his behalf. And there were some who really believed they had seen the Messiah. There was the earnest woman in Birmingham who drove a carload of newspapermen around during that phase of the trip; after several of the journalists made facetious remarks about the status of the Wallace expedition, she turned to them with hurt eyes and said, "You talk as if you don't believe Mr. Wallace has a chance of being elected."

There were more sophisticated people who resented the preeminent role of the communists but clung to the simple faith that any third party was better than none at all. So they averted their eyes and tried to stick with this one. But as Election Day neared the non-communists fell away from the Progressive Party in mounting numbers. Once again the communists had demonstrated their seemingly limitless propensity for destroying the thing they pretend to love.

It may be useful to tell ourselves at all times that no good cause is a lost cause; but it is essential to learn that a lost cause is not necessarily a good one. By midsummer it was apparent to most independent spirits in the Wallace adventure that this project was not only doomed, but deserved to be. The Philadelphia convention of the Progressive Party dispelled any ambiguity on this point. It was a crudely contrived communist production. As Alistair Cook wrote in the *Manchester Guardian*, "The convention roared along the single track and thundered through its automatic signals."

Sitting in that press box was like watching a Youth Congress or Student Union convention of the thirties. The most interesting and depressing fact about the assemblage was that more than 40 per cent of the delegates were under forty, and a large percentage of those a good deal younger. The youngsters were vociferous, ardent and outwardly unshaken by the rehearsed and rigid pattern of the proceedings.

Nevertheless there was some discord beneath the surface. Much of it may have been crystallized by the challenge to the convention issued by Americans for Democratic Action. Attacks from reactionary sources could be discounted or turned to advantage by the convention's left-wing manipulators, but ADA represented influential sectors of the liberal and labor movement. Its galaxy of sponsors—led by Mrs. Roosevelt—could not be written off as war profiteers, relatives of Jim Crow and tools of fascist reaction.

The ADA's stand was presented by Jim Loeb to the Platform Committee of the Progressive Party convention. In his statement Loeb called the Progressive Party a communist front, but he suggested that those who questioned that description could confound the party's critics and prove their independence by taking these steps in the framing of the platform:

1) Repudiation of the communist drive against the Marshall Plan.

2) A declaration of support for the American proposals on the control of atomic energy which had then been accepted by every nation outside the Soviet sphere.

3) Renunciation of the "double standard of political morality" and a clear statement that the new party condemned dictatorship everywhere—"whether in Mississippi or the Soviet Union."

4) Withdrawal of the Progressive Party candidates who were running for the Senate against such anti-communist liberals as Hubert Humphrey of Minnesota and Paul Douglas of Illinois and thereby threatening to swing the elections in those states to isolationist Republicans. (The GOP nominee in Illinois, for example, was C. Wayland "Curly" Brooks, otherwise known as Colonel McCormick's private Senator. When the Progressive Party entered its own candidate in that race, liberals appealed to Wallace to intercede; he replied that he really wasn't familiar with Brooks's record—although, as Vice President, Wallace had presided over the Senate for several years while Brooks was rolling up his fabulous record of isolationist votes.)

The platform committee swiftly brushed off Loeb's challenge; its chairman was Lee Pressman, the long-time communist promoter in the CIO who finally split with the communists a few years after that convention. He ruled the committee firmly, with considerable aid, of course, from other carefully placed brethren, and it was in the shaping of the platform that the so-called Progressive Party ineptly dropped the flimsy guise it had been wearing. Two preposterous incidents completed the strip tease. The first involved, of all places, Macedonia. In the original draft platform, prepared many weeks before the convention with the aid of the highest theoretical talent in the communist stable, there appeared a declaration of support for the Macedonian quest for national freedom and independence. This was an old war cry at communist conclaves and hardly calculated to stir dispute. But between the time that Pressman and his comrades had written the original draft and the afternoon he pulled a copy out of his pocket at Philadelphia, the Macedonians had indicated they might turn to Tito for guidance, and Tito was then becoming the leading *bête-noire* of international Stalinism because of his insurrection against Moscow rule. Apparently some valiant communist theologian noticed this point at the eleventh hour; as a result, when the platform draft was submitted to the delegates, the Macedonians were uncordially stricken from the mimeographed document.

All this might have gone unnoticed except for the vigilance of an irredeemably querulous soul from Minnesota who got up on the floor of the convention and demanded an explanation: he was still pro-Macedonian. Albert J. Fitzgerald, the genial unionist and perennial front man for the communists who was presiding at that convention session, turned helplessly to Dr. Rexford Tugwell, who had suppressed his own liberal deviations in the interest of third-party unity, and he turned to Pressman, who for once also seemed stricken mute. Finally Louis Adamic made a speech which no one could quite follow and in the ensuing confusion the Macedonians were efficiently eliminated. At that point Bill Lawrence, who was covering the convention for the New York *Times*, leaned over to me and murmured: "What in God's name are these people trying to·do—hang themselves?"

At times it seemed that way. By the last hours of the convention we thought we had seen everything. But we hadn't. As the meeting was adopting its foreign-policy statement, which incorporated every thesis in the communist book on such matters as the Marshall Plan and atomic-energy control, a delegate from Vermont rose to speak on behalf of a brief amendment. It was indeed a modest suggestion. In the light of the controversy sure to be created by resolutions previously adopted, he asked the delegates to join with him in this simple affirmation of honorable intent: "It is not our intention to give blanket endorsement to the foreign policy of any nation." To the undialectical boys in the press box this seemed a gentle request and they found the ensuing tumult incredible. In rapid succession American communist dignitaries and others who were trying to imitate the accents of earnest, idealistic liberals rose to announce that they were shocked by these words. "They will be interpreted as an insinuation against a foreign ally," one speaker cried, and I am quoting him literally. Thus, while it was deemed the height of political propriety to accuse the American Government of every form of sin from fratricide to genocide, it was intolerable to state in explicit form the possibility that Moscow might deserve criticism: this was, as other orators emphasized, a weak-kneed concession to the forces of reaction. The discussion reminded me of Dr. Niebuhr's remark that it was always a pity to see a man proclaiming "my country right or wrong," and especially when it wasn't his own country.

The Vermont rebellion was thereupon crushed. The convention roared on to nominate Wallace, who had already campaigned for six months as the choice of the party which now selected him. It chose as his running mate Senator Glenn Taylor, Idaho's cowboy intellectual, who was fond of boasting that all he knew about communists was that they were in favor of three meals a day, and so was he.

They were a pathetic pair in many ways because some of their protestations of innocence were undoubtedly authentic and because, as so often happens to participants in a communist front, they had to become steadily more disingenuous as their knowledge increased. It was widely held at the time that, whatever else might be said about them, Wallace and Taylor were exhibiting a rare kind of political valor. But in fact their ultimate submission to the communist machine was a craven surrender to political bossism.

As Dwight Macdonald observed in *Politics*, Wallace invented what might be called "Utopian *Realpolitik*." When Wallace was taken to task for failure to criticize the Russians, he emphasized that he was just a practical man trying to work things out in a difficult world; when he was charged with excessive severity toward his own government, he rose to his full moral height and said that nothing, no nothing, would prevent him from speaking the truth about any situation, and damn the consequences.

There had been times in the early months of the campaign when I wanted to reach out to Wallace and try single-handedly to persuade him to abandon the vicious nonsense being fed to him; but by fall he was thriving on the diet, and beyond communication. He acted like a man who was perfectly certain that anyone who was against him had been bribed, which was probably a measure of the extent to which he had absorbed the outlook of the communists around him without knowing where he got it.

During that long summer there was another reminder of an earlier age of innocence. It was provided by those alumni of the Popular Front of the thirties who proclaimed without hesitation —and with much fury—that Alger Hiss could not conceivably have been the man Whittaker Chambers said he was. To have been a communist in that contested era, and to remember communists no less respectable in their bearing than Alger Hiss, made me feel quite aged at thirty-two. Throughout the quarreling stirred by the case, I always seemed to be telling my elders, in probably insufferable tones, that they just didn't know what things had been like when I was a boy.

The lines of division were not always clear. But in the liberal community the sharpest split seemed to be between those who had once been identified with various Popular Front causes, without ever becoming communists, and those who had actually signed up. The first group seemed compulsively moved to declare that Hiss could not conceivably be guilty and must be the victim of a vicious tale told by a demon; while those who had been communists at least tended to reserve judgment, and saw no inherent implausibility in Chambers' story.

The difference in approach had, I think, certain obvious origins. Many liberals had flirted with the communist movement in the previous decade without formally enlisting in it; to believe that Hiss was guilty required a confrontation of their own pasts. They had not been communists, but they had been foolish and credulous, and it was hard for them to face the disclosure that the movement they had once helped, however remotely, promoted such operations as espionage. If Hiss had gone as far as was now alleged, so might other men. The one-time Popular Fronter was now being compelled, as the former communist had been, to re-examine his own delusions, which is never a pleasant pursuit.

To anyone who had ever been a communist there was a ring of inescapable authenticity in the script. The great majority of us were spared any involvement with the bleak espionage regions of the movement, and we all like to believe we would have recoiled if an attempt had been made to draw us into them. The trouble is that we could imagine the rationalizations which led Hiss to disaster. In the decade that Chambers was testifying about, many men had become communists because they believed Russia was the great barrier to the fascist advance and, in particular, the only true ally of the Spanish Republic. To help the Russians was not in their view an act of treason to America, but an affirmative service to embattled democratic mankind; if one occupied a position in which government papers were available that might be helpful to what was then regarded as the citadel of anti-fascism, was it "inconceivable" or "fantastic" or "out of this world" to pass the papers? In the Soviet mystique of the thirties, Stalin, unlike the diplomats of Downing Street and Pennsylvania Avenue, had no goal except to save the world from fascism. On this premise there could be no conflict between Russian national inter-

est and the cause of peace and freedom; and—as the simple corollary—there could be no fatal hesitation about aiding the Russians
through whatever means were available. Hiss's generation had
grown up with savage contempt for the ancient symbols of na-
tionalism; its tragic fallacy was to identify Russia with the vision
of internationalism.

For all these reasons it seemed to me disastrous for so many liberals to invest so heavily in the proposition that Hiss "can't be
guilty." A presumption of innocence pending trial and conviction
is inherent in our law, but nothing requires us to confuse the presumption with certitude. By staking so much on Hiss's defense,
the liberals were walking into a trap. For their bitter right-wing
opponents were contending—especially after the documents were
produced—that the Hiss affair was judgment day for the New
Deal and its works; that Hiss's conviction would finally expose
and establish the "communist conspiracy" that lurked behind the
New Deal era; that Franklin D. Roosevelt, not Alger Hiss, was on
trial. This was as absurd as the notion that communism was just
another variety of indigenous American radicalism, but it seemed
to be sustained by the emotional character of the drawing-room
defense. So the argument dragged on, with some liberals stubbornly refusing to concede that there could have been communist
espionage in real life and some voices on the far Right crying
that it all proved that the Fair Labor Standards Act had been devised by communists.

For those who had been communists, there was another note
in the tone of the Hiss defenders that undoubtedly intensified our
preoccupation with the case. In conservative as well as liberal
salons the theory was being widely advanced that it was ridiculous
to take Chambers seriously since he was an admitted former communist, therefore a confessed liar and probably out of his mind.
This was accompanied by the spread of a loathsome whispering
campaign, encouraged with peculiarly ill grace by men who were
then engaged in decrying the phenomenon of character assassina-
tion in other areas of American life.

There was a final absurdity in the controversy; it was the "Ivy

League" analysis of the case. American conservatives are often the victims of their own stereotypes; to some of them the trial became something of a national beauty contest in which Hiss, resembling as he did every man's conception of a bright-eyed Princeton man—he went to Johns Hopkins and Harvard Law School—was assumed to be on the side of virtue against the shabby, morose character who surely personified communism.

In the unending battle of the Potomac precipitated by the case, Hiss's adherents often triumphantly asked: "Why did Chambers wait so long to bring out the documents?" This was the key to the puzzle, and I think the answer was damaging rather than helpful to Hiss's cause. It seemed to me that Chambers, in his original testimony, had tacitly invited Hiss to acknowledge the limited charge—membership in the Communist Party—so that it would be unnecessary to reveal the papers which finally injured both men, transforming the case from a matter of communist affiliation to the grimmer domain of espionage. Hiss, I conjectured, construed Chambers' initial failure to offer the documents as final assurance that he never would; and Chambers was equally confident that Hiss, correctly understanding his gesture, would never sue for libel. I suggested this possibility in an article published in the *Progressive* before the first trial in which, among other things, I urged pro-Hiss liberals to modify their view that Hiss's innocence was one of the certainties of the century.

None of us yet knows whether every chapter of the story has been told; while I accept Chambers' basic account of events, I feel the narrative will be incomplete unless Hiss finally chooses to unfold his own version of the same events with his own time perspective, and an inventory of his own motivations. But in that summer of 1948 some liberals joined the Hiss defense society with desperate eagerness, indignantly banishing the thought that the former law secretary of Oliver Wendell Holmes could ever have been a communist. It was a dreary episode in the recurrent confusion which communism had inflicted on American liberalism.

In mid-winter Henry Wallace had talked of getting at least

ten million votes and astute politicians had taken him seriously; by autumn Gideon's Army was on the run.

There was an unhappy personal sidelight in what was happening on the *Post* while I followed Wallace to the end of his long ride. In the preceding months, under Ted Thackrey's editorship, the paper had sharply assailed the State Department's equivocal role in the Arab-Israel conflict; now Thackrey was veering toward the Wallace camp even as most non-communist liberals were aligning themselves against it and Dorothy Schiff, then his wife, and owner of the *Post*, was actively supporting ADA's anti-Wallace legions.

When I was initially assigned to cover the Wallace caravan, it was my impression that Thackrey simply felt that news interest in the third party warranted such a step, and I thought he was right. With the passage of months, however, he drew increasingly close to Wallace personally and found himself in the communist circle which vigilantly surrounded the candidate to protect him from ideologically bad companions. After the Progressive Party convention in Philadelphia, I spoke to Thackrey briefly and asked him what he thought of the proceedings. He replied, "Terrific." I am sure he meant it.

And suddenly it was clear to me that, like some other middle-aged men I knew who had never had the faintest youthful identification with the communists or any of their operations, he was getting huge delight out of the organized excitement. A lively, imaginative newspaperman who had once been known as the boy wonder of the Scripps-Howard chain, Thackrey, like Wallace, was impressed by the ardor of the young left-wingers and resolutely indifferent to the cynical mechanics of the enterprise. Like Wallace, he was given the full treatment by the communist attendants and he seemed to revel in it and in the general enthusiasm; there were times when he seemed to have all the fervor and lack of discernment of an editor of the Columbia *Spectator* I had known.

In the end Thackrey personally endorsed Wallace, though the paper did not. Despite his feelings about the campaign, he never reproached me for the harsh words I had written about his candi-

238

date or censored any of my copy, and I kept wishing I could have a long fatherly talk with him.

On election night I drove down to Wallace headquarters with him. When we got there, I was somehow separated from Thackrey in the throng. By the time I got to Wallace's office, Ted was already inside and a husky young zealot was guarding the door. When I disclosed my identity, he was either unimpressed or displeased; when I persisted in seeking admission, he would not budge. I finally shouted something to the general effect that it was time the communists let Wallace see someone other than themselves, and the youth promptly punched me in the nose. At that moment the door opened and Wallace benignly invited me in.

His wounds were more serious than mine; enough returns had already come in to indicate that he would be lucky to get a million votes, rather than the ten million of which he had dreamed, and that—in spite of the third-party defection—Mr. Truman might be staging the political miracle of the century. And there Wallace and Thackrey sat amid the ruins, heroes to the clamorous youngsters outside the door but strangely removed from the real political currents of America, two tired men after a long night out with the communists.*

The crushing setback suffered by the Progressive Party marked the turning point in American communist fortunes in the decade of the forties. They never recovered from the blow; their biggest attempt to seize command of the liberal-labor movement by amassing a huge "rank-and-file" vote had been thwarted, and the newly born Americans for Democratic Action, which had campaigned for Mr. Truman, emerged from the campaign as a far more significant political force than the stillborn Progressive Party.

In the spring some of ADA's leaders had frantically joined the movement to substitute Dwight D. Eisenhower as the Democratic

* Like Wallace, Thackrey eventually despaired of his Progressive Party associates; in 1952, as editor of the New York *Compass*, he rejected the Progressive ticket and supported Adlai Stevenson.

nominee; he alone, they said, could rescue liberal congressional candidates in the unfriendly political climate of 1948. When nothing came of that desperate project, ADA finally endorsed Mr. Truman; perhaps more important than the endorsement was its victorious fight for a strong civil-rights plank at the Democratic convention. This plank helped revive Democratic prestige in vital Northern areas. It grieved the Wallace followers, who had heretofore claimed the issue as their own, and seriously undercut Wallace's bid for a major share of the Negro vote.

Thackrey, however, was not ready to abandon his newly found crusade and, for a brief period after election day, I thought I was reliving an old nightmare. When the New York *Star* (*PM*'s successor) closed up shop, Thackrey immediately hired as *Post* columnists two men who had been Wallace adherents and had generally sided with the communists during *PM*'s long internal struggles. His continued entanglement with the so-called Progressives reached its peak with his appearance as a featured player at the celebrated Waldorf Conference—the international conclave staged by the communist intellectuals early in 1949 in an effort to rebuild their fading political dynasty.

His separation from Dorothy Schiff was now both personal and political and his resignation was announced in April, 1949. Shortly afterward I was called to New York to act as chief editorial writer of the *Post* in the reshuffled staff and on May 29th I was appointed editor with Mrs. Schiff as publisher.

The first editorial published after my appointment said:

## THE THINGS WE BELIEVE

The men and women who are putting out this newspaper have done a lot of soul-searching in recent days about the function and character of a liberal newspaper. All of us are newspaper people who respect the techniques of our craft; and all of us regard ourselves as independent liberals with strong convictions about the kind of world we want to live in. What we have come up with is the deep belief that there is no conflict between our craft responsibilities and our social idealism, if we may be permitted a lofty phrase. In fact, we are convinced we will be better newspapermen because we are liberals; and—in the most profound sense—better liberals because we are newspapermen.

Which means we have a transcending allegiance to printing the truth, even if it confounds our most cherished premises (or prejudices); that we believe the heart of the liberal tradition is tolerance for contrary opinions; and that in our angriest hour we will try to remember that those who disagree with us are not necessarily thieves and villains. We shall even concede the possibility of our own error.

There are those who believe that a newspaper cannot fight hard unless its dogmas are inflexible. It is often suggested that the great strength of both the fascists and communists is their denial of the principle of doubt. They profess to know all the answers and they are equally certain that those who do not accept their answers are fools or knaves. This doctrine may bring private solace but it bears no relation to the essential values of American life.

We believe an independent liberal newspaper can fight harder, more effectively and more resolutely than a journal committed to an absolutist party line. For what we are saying and doing represents not what we have been told to believe by an all-wise leader or what we have read in a political text (which may be reinterpreted to mean something else next week). It represents the intensity of conviction arrived at with the use of our own minds and the exercise of our best judgment.

When we take our stand we will do so with the awareness that we are not God—but with the certainty that there are things for which men are willing to fight and even die. We will not equivocate in the defense of civil liberty. We will not differentiate between "good" dictators and evil ones. We will not accept a moral double standard under which tyranny and exploitation are defensible in one area of the world and intolerable in another. We despise repression and cruelty in

Greece or in Georgia, in Moscow, Madrid or Manhattan. We believe millions of people in our own country and abroad deserve a better break; that too many children are still born into this world without a fighting chance for human happiness; and we hope this institution will never grow so old or so smug that it becomes indifferent to suffering or tries to discover elaborate reasons why nothing can be done about it.

It was said long ago that the function of a newspaper is to "comfort the afflicted and to afflict the comfortable." Too many newspapers have forgotten the words or grown so fat and comfortable themselves that they view the phrase as inflammatory. We like it and we propose to remember it, not because we regard success as subversive but because success too often means the complacent loss of conscience.

We know where we are going and only a final explanatory word is needed. It has often seemed as if liberal journalism must be dull journalism on the theory that any interest in the variety of human experience is somewhat irreverent or irresponsible. We don't accept this grim view. A newspaper is the first draft of history; it is the record of how people lived, exulted and suffered in every phase of their existence.

We know that all of you will not agree with us all of the time, but we vow that you will never be bored.

This is not a book about the New York *Post*, and perhaps somewhere it should even contain the disclaimer that the opinions expressed herein are those of the editor and not necessarily those of anyone who works with him. But in view of the circumstances that led to the writing of the book, a few things ought to be noted about what the newspaper has been saying in the four years since I became its editor.

Whatever its journalistic sins or virtues in that period, the *Post* has editorially reflected the attitudes of anti-communist liberals in America. Within the general framework of that position, there have been differences on particular issues as on individual candidates; if liberals accepted a rigid party line, they would repudiate the essence of their political being. But on the great issues of this four-year period there has been comparatively little discord in the ranks of the American "Third Force." In this interval the *Post* has vigorously backed the European Recovery Program against the combined attacks of isolationists and communists; it has supported the effort to create an Atlantic defense community militarily strong enough to meet external aggression and economically resilient enough to withstand internal disruption. When the communist aggression began in Korea, the *Post* warmly upheld the UN's decision to resist aggression while both the communist *Daily Worker* and Colonel McCormick's Chicago *Tribune* steadily disparaged the effort, for somewhat diverse reasons but with equal fury. At the same time we waged what I hope were many good fights on the home front, consistent with a general premise that the defense of democracy must be simultaneously waged at home and abroad.

I like to believe that the *Post* has been equally militant on both fronts. This is not, of course, a point that can be measured in column inches. In the months immediately after I assumed the editorship I felt that communist confusionism was still seriously effective in some places, and especially in the New York area where the Wallace vote had been heaviest; perhaps a preponderance of editorial attention was devoted to meeting that issue at that time. Subsequently, as the disintegration of the local communist battalion became apparent, the danger of what has come to be known as McCarthyism took precedence. It is one of the signal ironies of modern American history that McCarthy's great crusade, rather inadvertently begun at Wheeling, West Virginia, in 1950, started after the communist tide had plainly receded. The decisive rebuff to the communists had occurred in the election of November, 1948, and in the months immediately thereafter when the anti-communist liberals mobilized in ADA steadily gained strength. Then the CIO, under Phil Murray, declared open war on the surviving communist-led unions and broke their political power. There was a time when the communists could boast that they owned such trade-union stalwarts as Joe Curran and Mike

Quill. But both men had begun battling the communists long before it occurred to Joe McCarthy that anti-communism might be
a fruitful realm of political endeavor.

The *Post* has been the target of far more virulent communist
attack than has the Hearst press or its imitators, and with good
reason. For if the often desolate record of our times signifies anything, it is that the communists would rather compete with know-
nothing conservatism than with principled liberalism on almost
any day of any week. I am humble about many things but I should
be glad to argue in any public place that *Post* writers like Murray
Kempton, Max Lerner and Arthur Schlesinger, Jr., have done far
more to undermine the fading communist legions than have
George Sokolsky, Fulton Lewis, Jr., and Cholly Knickerbocker, or
any comparable triumvirate, and for the reasons indicated at some
length earlier in these pages.

There have been moments when the *Post* has served as a sort of
Finland station for those who were on their way out of the communist camp. Bella Dodd could testify that one of her first stops
after resigning from the communists was at our office. Paul Sann,
executive editor, and I spent many hours with her imploring her
to write her experiences for the *Post* and assuring her we would
print anything she cared to say. She demurred; she was fearful of
being called a "red-baiter"; she was still unready for the total separation. When Henry Julian Wadleigh offered the decisive cor-
roborative testimony at the second Hiss trial, we asked him to
write his memoirs for us and he did. He, too, was reluctant to
exploit his past in the gaudy Hearst fashion but eager to publish
a first-person narrative in a paper which did not demand that he
embroider the story or draw the conclusion that his experience
with communism proved that the New Deal was a communist
plot.

We published Eleanor Lipper's story of her ordeal in a Russian
slave-labor camp and Joy Davidman's recollections of her adventures in the Young Communist League. But we published these
and similar articles in the context of an affirmative, continuing
fight for that measure of social and economic justice which the

communists had long proclaimed as their goals. What we kept trying to say to young men and women whose best impulses led them to some degree of radicalism was that one not only did not have to become a communist to pursue those goals, but that in the real world the communists were fundamentally hostile to all treasured humanist values. In a way, I suppose, the *Post* was trying to say what I felt liberals had failed to say with adequate persuasiveness to me in a time that seemed very long ago, yet not totally unlike the present. For now there was an atom bomb, a war in Korea and the prospect of more trouble to come, and there was no guarantee of peace or tranquillity in our time—all the sources of a despair which keeps the communists in business.

We tried to say something else that seemed no less important, and on which we did not often have much company in the press. While pointing out that grown men could not treat the peril of communist espionage and sabotage as a fable we maintained that free trade in ideas was the free enterprise most worthy of defense; that what communist orators said in public constituted no clear and present danger to the republic; that the moment we lost confidence in our capacity to answer the open communist argument— as distinct from the subterranean communist operation—we had lost a major battle in the war for freedom. We condemned the Smith Act prosecutions of communist leaders on that ground; the inescapable implication in any prosecution directed against a conspiracy to *advocate* ideas was that we somehow feared to engage in combat with those ideas. And such a fear was the negation of everything that had given greatness to the republic. It could justly be said that the Communist Party differed from other political parties in its slavish obedience to a foreign power, but that was what ultimately rendered it so futile as a propaganda force. To prosecute for "advocacy" the pale and servile revolutionists who led this party was an announcement of democratic weakness.

Our stand in support of the general outlines of United States foreign policy won us incessant denunciation from the communist press; the feverishness of the attack was undoubtedly intensified by the incontestably liberal ground we occupied on so many issues traditionally exploited by the communists. On April 12, 1950, the *Daily Worker* devoted a column to me because the *Post* had suggested the possibility of a deal between Stalin and Franco. The essay, entitled: "The Frightened Child Who Edits the New York *Post*," was signed by Joe Clark, whom I had known many years earlier when he was a leader of the National Student League. In this manifesto he maintained, with the solemnity he employed many years earlier in discounting any chance of a Nazi-Soviet Pact, that a rapprochement between Moscow and Madrid was beyond the bounds of imagination. A few months later Clark again dedicated a piece to me, this time because I had editorially intimated that the so-called Stockholm peace petition was made in Moscow; on this occasion his dissertation was entitled: "Wechsler's Lies Can't Halt Struggle for Peace."

But our battle, as I hope I have made clear, was not with the communists alone; as their strength perceptibly dwindled, we got into what appeared to be a no less formidable fight. In September, 1951, we published our seventeen-part series on Senator McCarthy. It was called "Smear, Inc.: Joe McCarthy's One-Man Mob" and it heralded a long campaign of exposure against a man whom we identified as the foremost demagogue of the day.

The series described McCarthy as "the hoax of the century." It pointed out that he had obtained his Senate seat with the help of the communists, that many of those he now branded "procommunist" had been battling communism long before he stumbled onto the issue, and that all his bombast had failed to uncover "a single spy or anything remotely resembling an espionage operator." It noted that the man who had set himself up as a tireless servant of his country had three times been called to account for irregularities in his income-tax payments; that he had accepted $10,000 as a "literary fee" from a corporation deeply concerned with pending Senate legislation; and that, by the standard of guilt by association he so freely employed, his own associations with characters on the pro-fascist fringe were damning. His role in the investigation of the Malmédy massacre was also explored, and we noted that the Senator who seemed disposed to convict countless of his fellow Americans without a trial had labored long and hard to reverse the convictions of Nazis found guilty—after extensive trial—of slaughtering Americans taken prisoner during the Battle of the Bulge. Most of all, the series suggested that McCarthy possessed neither the wisdom nor the background to serve as an expert on communism and that "McCarthyism" could in fact be defined as a kind of "Political Murder, Inc." It had already succeeded in creating "an atmosphere of distrust and suspicion in which men become willing to sacrifice traditional constitutional safeguards."

The man who emerged from this portrait was not an unprecedented political figure. America had known and survived other demagogues. McCarthy's advantage was the peculiar depth and intensity of the crisis he was exploiting; the atomic bomb gave a new dimension to our fears. While he pretended to be waging single-handed war against the enemy, his activities seemed far more likely to create panic on our side.

We said these and other things about him, and much of what we said is now being repeated in many places; but at the time there were few newspapers arguing with Joe McCarthy and we had reason to assume that he would not forgive us.

This, then, is what had gone before April 23, 1953. Much of it was admittedly inconsequential, by contrast with the grander dramas of the age; the essential fact about the communist experience in America in the 1930's was that for many of us nothing truly cataclysmic ever happened; we joined exultantly, we suffered silently and we departed quietly. Others might write of barricades in Berlin; we recall the endless tedium. Even the subsequent phase of our conflict with local Stalinism lacks an epic quality; it was often like a fight conducted in a side street while history's main parade moved on a broader avenue.

What finally made it all seem worth setting down was not what had gone before but what happened afterward.

# III

# The Age of Suspicion

# 11

In journalism, as in politics, America has been lately overrun by men who have converted anti-communism from a matter of conviction into a flourishing business. They are not serious men; they have neither the wisdom nor the desire to make real distinctions: they are working what they regard as the profitable side of the street.

They may have spent most of their previous lives recording café gossip. But they have found anti-communism a new and bigger industry. They cannot admit anyone was opposing communism before they arrived on the scene. Neither can they admit that the American Communist Party was sharply reduced in power and influence before they sounded the alarm; indeed, they can never concede the threat is diminishing because that might reduce the value of their labors. When they cannot find new menaces in the heart of Broadway, they must invent them; they capriciously identify thoughtful anti-communists with the communists, thereby reviving the dwindling prestige of the communists. They are not seriously concerned with the massive and complicated challenge of Soviet power; they are businessmen, plying a local trade.

In the spring of 1952 the *Post* began preparing a series of articles on the lives and works of Jack Lait and Lee Mortimer, two Hearst performers whose *Confidential* books tended to create the impression that America was a large brothel presided over jointly by subversive madams and Dean Acheson.

Several weeks before our series was to appear, I received a letter from Lait and Mortimer warning that they would sue for libel if the articles contained any "inaccurate and defamatory statements." They professed to have inside information that we would make such statements. I told them I shared their fastidious respect for facts, expressed regret that they had declined to be interviewed and again asked them to see a *Post* reporter. They refused. Just before we published the articles, Lait and Mortimer filed libel suits against the *Post*, Dorothy Schiff, Murray Kempton and me, all based on a critical review of *U.S.A. Confidential* that Kempton had previously written. We proceeded to publish the series.

In mid-July I was called to testify at a pre-trial examination in this case. The nature of the interrogation indicated that Lait and Mortimer would contend that the unfavorable treatment accorded them by the *Post* reflected our lack of patriotism. They depicted themselves as the peers of anti-communist journalism mischievously maligned by a newspaper which could not match their devotion to the flag. This lament was a trifle ludicrous since the theme of our articles was that the dreary picture of a corrupt, decadent America which their books unfolded was immensely valuable to communist propagandists abroad. Nevertheless, they pursued their point with some vigor at the hearing. During the afternoon I was invited to rehearse the details of my youthful communist associations. I was also compelled to confess that I had been a long-time critic of Senator Joseph McCarthy.

By ordinary standards my testimony scarcely constituted big news; my communist past was as much a matter of record as my anti-communist—and anti-McCarthy—present. But there were commercial reasons which made this testimony newsworthy for the New York *Journal-American*, the Hearst afternoon paper in New York. The *Journal-American* has had advertising trouble for years. Despite a circulation of sizable proportions, it has been unable to attract an amount of advertising commensurate with its newsstand sales, and in the spring of 1952 things seemed to be getting worse rather than better. The *Post*, on the other hand, had been gaining in both circulation and national advertising and, if I may say so, was viewed by the *Journal-American* as an increasingly rugged competitor. Ours being a rough profession, some Hearst advertising salesmen were not above using whatever weapons seemed handy; they were feverishly trying to spread the word in New York advertising circles that the *Post* was an inflammatory radical gazette. Though I have long ago rejected the oversimplifications of economic determinism, I am reasonably confident that the *Journal's* advertising woes explained the page-one prominence which the paper gave my testimony the day after the Lait-Mortimer hearing. The headline read: "Post Editor Admits He Was Young Red; Wechsler Ties Bared." The story, like the headline, was written as though this were secret stuff belatedly revealed.

It was at this point, I think, that Howard Rushmore began to assume an obsessive interest in my career. He covered the libel hearing for the *Journal-American*, and he has stayed with the story. Rushmore is a tall, husky ex-communist with the sulky countenance of an ageing left tackle. A former member of the *Daily Worker* staff, he had remained with it through the incredible days of the Nazi-Soviet Pact and for some months afterwards when the communist organ was discovering merit in an alliance with nazism. When he quit it was not, according to his public announcement, over such mundane matters as the pact, but over the party's refusal to allow him to write a favorable review of the movie *Gone with the Wind*. This piece of bit-playing earned him an invitation to work on the Hearst paper where he first unfolded his reminiscences and then gradually established himself as that newspaper's "communist expert." He is a rather classic instance of a journalist whose solitary claim to distinction lies in his having had the foresight to be a communist.

The *Journal-American* splash was a one-day wonder. I took it rather lightly at the time. After years of communist attacks on me, I could not believe at that moment that a large storm was developing. One of the oddities of daily editorial writing is that one never quite believes that the calamities of which one writes may have any personal significance; thus, though I had written for many months that the essence of the McCarthy disorder was the victimization of the innocent, I assumed rather overconfidently that my own status was beyond serious question. Though I had long anticipated that the issue would be raised, I hardly imagined it could be transformed into a large argument after all the intervening years.

Less than three weeks later, I had reason to wonder at my optimism.

I was appearing at that time on a television show called "Starring the Editors," a program on which executives of metropolitan newspapers discussed and debated the news. The program's sponsor was the Grand Union grocery chain.

Not long after the *Journal-American*'s story appeared, Robert Hersey, whose advertising agency had thought up the program and found the sponsor, telephoned me and asked if he could come down to my office. I had a strange presentiment that I knew what he was going to say. When he arrived, he told me, with obvious embarrassment and pain, that Grand Union had ordered him to drop me from the program, apparently as a result of the *Journal-American* "revelations." Hersey was a decent, conscientious man in a spot, obviously upset by what had happened. His problem was intensified by the fact that the contract with Grand Union was about to expire and its renewal was hanging fire. At that point the worst development, he emphasized, would be public controversy. For 1952 was a year when nervous television and radio officialdom believed that, although "controversy" might be the life of democracy, it was the death of trade. Neither pressuring nor pleading, Hersey asked me if I would agree to step off the program temporarily, at least until the new contract was signed; then an effort might be renewed to "work things out." He pointed out that I was due to go on vacation shortly anyway and that the passage of time might ease the tension.

I asked for time to think it over and talk to the *Post*'s publisher about it. I also asked Hersey to see whether he could arrange an appointment for me with the Grand Union official who handed down the exclusion edict. With excessive confidence I said I was sure I could clear up any questions that might have been naïvely raised.

I never obtained the audience. When it became clear that the sponsor was determined to bar me from the air without a hearing, I knew there was no way of avoiding a public blow-up. We had been fighting what we called McCarthyism for a long time; we had been imploring men to stand up to it and fight back, even if doing so involved some personal inconvenience. Now this was it and I happened to be the target. I was a good deal more fortunately located than many other victims. Dorothy Schiff is a courageous liberal who has demonstrated on many occasions that she cannot be intimidated, and her reaction in this instance was as firm as it proved to be in the larger upheavals that were to follow. I told Hersey I would have to make the incident public unless I was reinstated on the program in time for my next scheduled appearance.

And so the story broke on August 6th, and for much of the ensuing twelve months I found myself in the grotesque position of reaffirming that I had really left the Young Communist League nearly fifteen years earlier, and that, for better or for worse, I was the man I pretended to be, and had been all along.

After the Grand Union episode was aired, TV-radio columnist Jack Gould wrote in the New York *Times*:

> As he has publicly acknowledged many times both in print and on the air, Mr. Wechsler was a member of the Young Communist League and quit the Red group fifteen years ago. Since that time he has been militantly anti-communist, a fact acknowledged, if it matters, by Ted Kirkpatrick, who published *Red Channels*.
>
> Particularly disturbing is the company's refusal to discuss Mr. Wechsler's dismissal. How many people objected to Mr. Wechsler? No one knows. Who did the objecting? No one knows. Were the objections spontaneous or organized? No one knows . . . under the vicious credo of "controversiality"

one of the most articulate voices speaking out against communism has been silenced on a television program.

On the program that followed the announcement that I had been banned, Erwin Canham, editor of the *Christian Science Monitor*, Alicia Patterson, publisher of *Newsday*, and Lloyd Felmley of the Newark *News* spoke out against the decision. So did Edward P. Doyle, news editor of the *Journal-American*, whose paper had started it all. Grand Union did not renew its contract. After a further flurry, the Du Mont network invited me to return to the program which was then briefly tried as a sustaining feature. But it was abandoned fairly soon when it became apparent that no sponsor could be found to lend his name to this "controversial" venture.

We never did establish conclusively how the ban had been brought about. There were some later intimations that it had been promoted by an upstate New York grocer who has entrenched himself as a kind of one-man censor of TV and radio and managed to exert a degree of influence almost as remarkable as his carelessness with facts. Others told me that an influential Grand Union stockholder had insisted on my departure.

The disturbing thing about the episode was the mystery in which it was cloaked, the anonymity of the accuser and my inability to secure a meeting with the man who handed down the decision. Such furtive pressure was operating all over the TV-radio world. An accuser did not feel morally obligated to prove a case; by merely bringing any charge, he made his victim "controversial" and this was sufficient ground for exclusion.

In my own case, the incident was not ruinous because I earned my living as an editor, not as a commentator. What would I have done if I had been dependent on the mercies of TV? How many men had quietly "disappeared" when asked to do so rather than risk a public dispute which would indelibly label them "controversial personalities"? This dread of controversy was a disease; it had spread quietly, without open recognition or effective challenge.

I never found out, as I have said, whether Grand Union's action represented one man's whim or whether it was induced by the pressure of a dozen self-designated vigilantes of the air. The uncertainty in some ways remains the most terrifying aspect of all. In a *Journal-American* essay published at the time, Rushmore, jubilantly saluting the company's decision, attributed it to "the roar of anger from the hinterlands" stirred by my presence on the program. But that roar was never audible to the rest of us. If this was a lynching, the mob never showed up.

Now it was clear to me anyway, as it probably should have been before, that the story of my days in the YCL would be endlessly reopened. There was a certain luxury in knowing that there had never been any concealment about it. I could not avoid thinking then of the suspense which must harass anyone who slipped in and out of the YCL without discussing the experience, and who always faces the possibility that the past may be resurrected and given darker meanings against the altered backdrop of a later decade. The books are never closed.

Shortly after the Grand Union episode, Walter Winchell rediscovered me. Like some other things that happened, this was predictable. Back in January of 1952 the *Post* had published a critical twenty-four-part analysis of the evolution of a gossip columnist into a statesman, and the transformation of that statesman from ardent champion of the New Deal into militant crusader for Republicanism, from bitter foe of Martin Dies into friend of Joe McCarthy. The series fully conceded Winchell's eminence as a gossip columnist but questioned his fitness to offer political counsel to the country as if he were the poor man's Bernard Baruch. We particularly noted Winchell's violent sensitivity to criticism. It had become an established rule of American journalism that any publication which displayed disrespect for him was certain to be the target of unending reprisal. After the *New Yorker* published an entertaining profile of Winchell in the early forties, he opened fire on editor Harold Ross and had the misfortune, ten years later, on the eve of Ross's death, to announce that Ross's sickness was a spurious attempt to evade a personal entanglement. Winchell has similarly engaged in a frenetic feud with *Time* magazine because it too failed to appreciate him. Those who are discreet enough to avoid any quarrels with him are permitted to live in peace and those who violate his rules can expect to be set upon from behind in the journalistic dark alley known as "Walter Winchell on Broadway."

This seemed to me reason in itself to publish the series. Whatever else might be said about him, it had to be acknowledged that Winchell had achieved a frightening power to bully and browbeat.

Dorothy Schiff and I assumed that we would be accorded the usual treatment once the series appeared and that my early political history would form the basis for his attack on me. That is how it turned out, but I must add that I had underestimated the man's capacity for invention. Our series had recognized his modest talent in that sphere; in his counterattack on the *Post*, he surpassed himself.

Actually he exhibited almost unprecedented self-restraint for several months; although we had completed our articles about him in March, he did not take cognizance of them until September. Up till that time, he may have been persuaded that a campaign of retribution could only serve to call attention to the series in many places where the *Post* did not circulate. But eventually he could not keep still. Possibly the Grand Union incident convinced him that the moment was at hand to finish me; if I could be excluded from television as the result of a *Journal-American* story, surely Winchell could administer the coup de grâce.

Anyway, he started in September and, as this is written almost a year later, I am still a recurrent topic of agitated comment in his column and truly extravagant notice on his television-radio shows. In the beginning he seemed to be partly using me as a whipping boy for the purpose of belaboring Adlai Stevenson. The *Post* was one of the small company of newspapers supporting Stevenson; we had, in fact, urged his nomination early in March, immediately after Mr. Truman announced he would not be a candidate. Further, it was publicly known that, largely through my friendship with Arthur Schlesinger, Jr., I was one of those sending memoranda of speech suggestions to Springfield. I had met Stevenson exactly twice before the campaign, once at a large luncheon in New York and the second time when Dorothy Schiff and I went out to see him in May to ascertain whether his refusal to run was final. Nevertheless, it was obviously useful to some Republican strategists to picture me as sinister and influential.

So Winchell, furiously campaigning against Stevenson, spread the word that the Governor of Illinois was the creature of dangerous men like me. One day he announced in all solemnity that I was slated for the post of Secretary of Defense if a Stevenson triumph occurred. Thinking back to my hapless days of basic training at Camp Lee, I found this item far funnier than its author could have intended it.

In his early columns Winchell referred to me as "Jake" Wechsler, a nickname no one had previously bestowed on me and an unusual selection for one who had himself been the target of intolerance as often as Winchell. But perhaps he felt the designation would give flavor to the attack in some backward areas. One of the intriguing aspects of a full-scale Winchell offensive is his apparent need to believe that it is achieving immediate results. Thus, one day late in the presidential campaign, he announced that I had not attended a Madison Square Garden Stevenson rally because I was afraid of the public wrath stirred by Winchell's "exposure" of me. On the evening in question I was on a platform in Yonkers debating August Heckscher of the New York *Herald Tribune* in full view of several hundred people. Any Winchell fans in the audience must have been a trifle startled by what they read in his column the next day about my supposed flight into darkness. On another occasion he happily announced that Nancy and I had canceled plans to go out on our anniversary because we could not face the angry glances of the aroused populace; the only errors in the item were that we went to the theatre on our anniversary and to Sardi's afterwards and nobody, as far as I noticed, gazed at us. Despite Winchell's promotion campaign, I was less of a celebrity than a utility infielder on the Giants.

Winchell's work on me was chiefly assisted by Rushmore. Winchell was not content simply to rehearse the well-worn details of my early political activity; with increasing frenzy he suggested that the story of my severance of communist ties fifteen years earlier was not to be believed and that I was plainly still a communist. The accusation came strangely from a man who had, through a large part of the forties, been so credulous a dupe of communist propagandists as Winchell; for several years his column had been full of items planted by communist historians, including fierce attacks on anyone who questioned the benevolence of the Russian judicial system or doubted the peacefulness of Russia's post-war intentions. Winchell has never betrayed any self-consciousness about such inconsistency.

His columns about me were long and dull. In some cities editors began to eliminate them; the dispute was clearly not of profound interest to a citizen in the far West who turned to Winchell for news of Eva Gabor. But television was a different matter. For one thing, here we had literally no chance to answer back; for another, Winchell's use of the visual technique was far more effective than his use of the written word. Thus on one night Winchell would flash a picture of Gil Green on the screen, noting that he was a fugitive hunted by the FBI, and follow it with a peculiarly grim-looking photograph of me, with a hurried reference to the fact that I had once been associated with Green; the impression created was that of two rogues from the same gallery. Obviously pleased by the trick of juxtaposition, he tried to link me to Julius and Ethel Rosenberg; with a jumble of almost incoherent words, he sought to convince the casual viewer that we were lifelong companions.* The fact was that I had never met either of them, and Winchell did not even allege that I had, but he operated on the undoubtedly justifiable assumption that the audience would miss the details and remember the succession of faces.

It was after such a broadcast that we decided to sue for libel.

* Incidentally, the *Post* had published an extensive series exposing the communist manipulation of the Rosenberg case and debunking their charge of "frame-up."

Up to a certain point the argument involved simply free competition, but the air introduced a new dimension in which we lacked the resources to fight back, and where failure to sue might finally be construed as an admission of guilt. Since the network and the sponsors seemed perfectly prepared to let Winchell imitate Dr. Goebbels' methods, we decided we had no recourse except the courts. That is where we are at this writing.

Everything that has happened has convinced me that the series on Winchell constituted a form of public service. It may be said that we have given excessively serious status to the man, but any barker who reaches several million Americans on Sunday night is worthy of attention. Let me add, for whatever satisfaction it may afford him, that he has created unpleasant moments; both Michael and Holly Wechsler have a habit of walking into the room when Winchell is exhibiting their father with all the overtones of criminality on a TV screen. Possibly, when they are a little older, this book will give them some idea of what all the screaming was about, and why the commentator whom Holly calls "the jumping man" seemed so intense.

# 12

In the final weeks of the 1952 Republican campaign, Senator McCarthy twice delivered nationally televised addresses in behalf of the GOP ticket. I am sure his orations are recalled with as much pain by thoughtful and responsible Republicans as by their political opponents. As things turned out, these performances were as unnecessary as they were vile; in Wisconsin General Eisenhower ran ahead of McCarthy and his national margin was so great that not even McCarthy could publicly claim that he had decisively affected the outcome. In both speeches McCarthy attempted to describe Adlai Stevenson as the pawn of communism; he even said that the *Daily Worker* had instructed its readers to support Stevenson. This was a lie (the communists loudly backed Hallinan) and McCarthy knew it.

In both speeches McCarthy proclaimed as well that Governor Stevenson was the tool of Americans for Democratic Action, which was, he said, closely related to the communist conspiracy, as exemplified by the presence in it of such men as Wilson Wyatt, Arthur Schlesinger, Jr., and me. It might be contended charitably that since the Senator was still unaware of the communist problem when ADA was formed in 1947, he was now merely naïvely displaying his ignorance. But this explanation would not stand much scrutiny. I think McCarthy knew what he was doing and so did many of those who encouraged him to do it. His description of Governor Stevenson's proximity to ADA was exaggerated; his description of ADA was a lie. Those who defended him by saying that his intentions were noble even though his methods were unscrupulous reminded me of those fellow-travelers who long defended the communists with exactly the same argument. The McCarthy apologists have shown remarkably little shame about using the contention that the end justifies the means.

In his mid-October speech McCarthy made one reference to me that still arouses my curiosity. Waving a slip of paper before the television audience, he shouted that this was the documented record of my continuous telephonic communication with Governor Stevenson's Springfield headquarters. When reporters attempted to see the evidence after the program, he swiftly eluded them. I did talk to Schlesinger several times when he was at Springfield and I also spoke to another of the Governor's aides in connection with the campaign fund that the *Post* was publicly raising. The question that intrigues me is whether McCarthy's private agents freely tap telephone wires in violation of the law or whether some friendly spirit in the telephone company made its records available to him, to be distorted as he chose. Possibly the paper he waved was blank.

The campaign speeches were not McCarthy's first notice of me. Many months earlier, during the course of a Senate Foreign Relations Committee hearing, Senator Fulbright had cited certain material from the *Post* series on McCarthy. The following colloquy ensued:

FULBRIGHT (to McCarthy): Are you familiar with an article that was written in the New York *Post* which quoted your own campaign in Wisconsin? If you care to, I will read this excerpt which is in the New York *Post*.

MC CARTHY: If it has something to do with Philip Jessup, I will be glad to hear it; otherwise let me say this, that Wechsler, who is editor of the *Post*, and his wife have both admitted membership in the Communist Party. So what they say about McCarthy doesn't concern me. I don't read their tripe. I understand they claim they have reformed since that time. However, I have seen no indication of the reform in the New York *Post*. So if the Senator is going to read some of the smear on McCarthy from the New York *Post*, he is welcome to read it.

That was on October 2, 1951, a few months after our series about McCarthy had appeared. When I learned of McCarthy's comment, I sent a wire to Senator Sparkman, Chairman of the committee, reciting the well-known facts of my early communist ties and my subsequent anti-communist activities. I volunteered to appear and make the statement under oath, but Sparkman replied that my statement would be incorporated in the record of the hearing without further ado. Then, on May 26, 1952, on the privileged floor of the Senate, McCarthy renewed his attack, including these words:

"This is the same Wechsler, incidentally, who is now editor of the New York *Post* and who admits that he was a communist some time in the late thirties. He claims to have reformed but has never, so far as we know, shown any evidence of his reformation."

At this time I asked Senator Lehman to insert in the *Congressional Record* the text of the statement I had previously sent to Sparkman. He did so at once. Thus, the *Record* of June 9, 1952, carries on page 6928 this statement, published at my request:

The New York *Post* recently published a documented series of seventeen articles on Senator McCarthy. These articles critically evaluated his record both before and after his election to the Senate. Senator McCarthy has not taken issue with a single fact published in them. A newspaper, as you know, has no immunity; it assumes full responsibility for anything it publishes. Instead of challenging the articles Senator McCarthy has chosen to make a personal attack on the editor of the *Post* and to imply that only a subversive newspaper could have published this series.

I am sure that Senator McCarthy knows the *Post* is a militantly anti-communist newspaper. I am sure he knows that the communist *Daily Worker* has frequently denounced both the *Post* and its editor. I am sure that he knows that the *Post* and its editor warmly support the efforts of the United States Government to resist communist aggression through military action in Korea, through the organization of the North Atlantic defense forces and through economic aid to nations menaced by communist imperialism. Nevertheless Senator McCarthy chose to tell your committee that "their [the *Post's*] editorials parallel the *Daily Worker's* editorials." He has further attempted to discredit factual material published about him in the *Post* by questioning the loyalty of the *Post's* editor.

I have never made any secret of my youthful communistic associations. They were ended in 1937 when I was twenty-two years old; may I add that I ended those associations before Whittaker Chambers, Elizabeth Bentley and Louis Budenz did so. I have actively and publicly opposed communistic totalitarianism since that time. It is a matter of public record that in 1946 I resigned from the newspaper *PM* with a public statement explaining that I felt compelled to leave because the newspaper was communist dominated. Prior to that time I was known to be one of those engaged in a long effort to eliminate communist influence on the paper and in the American Newspaper Guild. In 1948 I was one of the founders of Americans for Democratic Action, which, as you know, is an actively anti-communist liberal organization and specifically excludes communists as well as other totalitarians from membership. I am a member of the National Executive Committee of ADA.

Since Senator McCarthy has also seen fit to denounce my wife, may I add that she resigned from the Young Communist League at the age of twenty-one and has similarly engaged in public anti-communist activity since that time.

. . . Much of my answer to Senator McCarthy is on the public record—both in my own writings and public statements and the attacks which the communists have leveled against me for more than a decade. . . . Any professed expert on communism—such as Senator McCarthy—must know that the communist *Daily Worker*'s attacks on the *Post* and me have grown even more intense in recent months because of the *Post*'s continued support of the efforts of the free nations to resist communist aggression.

All this was thus officially set down in the *Congressional Record* many weeks before the *Journal-American*'s front-page report of my "confession" at the Lait-Mortimer libel hearing and nearly ten months before I was summoned to testify before McCarthy's investigating committee.

Nevertheless, as Winchell stepped up his attack, there were growing rumors that I would get a summons from McCarthy. It was well known in newspaper circles that Roy Cohn, the ambitious young prosecutor who had joined McCarthy's staff after the Republican triumph, was a Stork Club confidant of Winchell's and a source of stories for him. Many weeks before I was actually called, Winchell reported that my name was on the list of prospective witnesses. When I learned that Rushmore had also joined McCarthy's staff as another "expert," I was even surer my invitation would come soon, on some pretext that I could not quite imagine.

It finally came just a few days after Cohn and G. David Schine returned from their jaunt abroad.

I have said that in a way I looked forward to the encounter. That is true. I have enough newspaper instinct to be able to achieve some degree of excitement and detachment about such a meeting; indeed, there were moments during the hearings when I caught myself watching McCarthy with a kind of fascination, trying hard to look behind the masks he wears and almost forgetting that it was my life he was playing with.

But let me add that neither in anticipation nor in actuality can the role of witness at such a hearing be described as sport, or anything approaching it. For McCarthy has very successfully managed to create an atmosphere of ominous suspense about anything he undertakes.

This is, in a sense, McCarthy's triumph. I had no doubt of my own innocence and I was sure I had enough documentation to establish it; yet flying to Washington that bright April morning I kept trying to visualize what surprise he might spring, what hoax he might invent, what fragments of events he might fraudulently seek to reconstruct to conform to his own revision of history. It has been an axiom of our national life that an innocent man has nothing to fear, but McCarthy has helped to undermine that tenet. I had been given no hint of what the nature of the hearing would be. But what reason did I have to assume that he would hesitate to call me subversive? He was, after all, the man who had questioned the patriotism of General George Marshall. It would be surely less ridiculous for him to try to do the same thing to a newspaper editor who was an admitted former communist.

Joe Rauh and Bill Shannon, the *Post's* brilliant young Washington correspondent, met me at the airport. We lunched together at the Congressional Hotel where Joe said that it was his considered opinion as an attorney that a citizen might legitimately have a martini before confronting McCarthy. It was a gay luncheon and we tried to avoid giving it the tone of the condemned man's last meal. Yet I must confess that by then I was rather grim and angry. Quite possibly this was the chance I had awaited to settle my accounts with the past once and for all. That would require, among other things, keeping my temper, refusing to be taunted into irrelevant argument and, if possible, making a record that would be readable and conclusive. It might be that one only got one such chance in a lifetime, and that this was it, and that the way it turned out might one day mean a great deal to my wife and children. But there seemed to be an absurd indignity in having to plead this case before so biased a judge.

# 13

The hearing had been scheduled to begin at 3 o'clock, but it did not actually get under way until seventy minutes later. I spent the interval pacing the corridor of the Senate Office Building with Shannon and wondering whether the delay was a stratagem designed to try the nerves of the witness. That suspicion proved unfounded: the delay was a result of Wayne Morse's refusal to permit unanimous consent for a committee hearing while the Senate was in session.

This was an executive session, and the press and public were barred. When I walked into the spacious hearing room McCarthy was seated at the head of the table. At his side was Roy Cohn, looking like a precocious college sophomore visiting Washington during spring recess. Nearby was Rushmore, slouched uncomfortably in a chair that, like most chairs, was too small to hold him. My seat was at the opposite end of the table, facing McCarthy. On my left, a few feet back, as if keeping at a respectful distance from McCarthy, were G. David Schine and Don Surine, neither of whom uttered a word throughout the proceedings. On my right was the only conceivably friendly face in the room—Senator Henry Jackson, a former Representative just elected to the Senate from the State of Washington.

When I entered McCarthy stood up stiffly and motioned me to the witness chair. Disarmingly, he asked me how I pronounced my last name. I was tempted to respond that he had pronounced it correctly on television but I resolved to fight such temptation. I answered the question.

Then McCarthy began in his low, unprovocative voice: "Mr. Wechsler, we are sorry we kept you waiting but there originally was an objection to this committee sitting this afternoon by Senator Morse, and we had to wait for permission to sit." *

I replied that I understood.

"I may say," he continued, speaking quite swiftly and softly so that I almost had difficulty hearing him, "the reason for your being called today is that you are one of the many authors of books whose books have been used in the Information Program in various libraries, and we would like to check into a number of matters. Mr. Cohn will do the questioning."

Cohn took over briefly for a review of the names and dates of my published works. He elicited the fact that two of the books—*Revolt on the Campus* and *War Our Heritage*—were written when I was a member of the YCL. Then he jumped quickly to nonliterary fields and, during most of the remainder of the two hearings, little attention was devoted to the ostensible subject of the hearings—the books I had written. First he established that I had used the name "Arthur Lawson" on my YCL membership card.

"Let me add," I said, "that it was a name I was given when I joined and that I never used it again."

Cohn dropped the subject. Now he wanted to know how long I had been a member of the YCL. I gave him the answer and added that the whole chronology had already been published in the *Congressional Record* in the statement that Senator Lehman had inserted at my request.

The committee's researchers were apparently unaware of the existence of the document and wanted to know the date.

McCarthy seemed only mildly interested in Cohn's question-

---

* All quotations from the hearings are taken from the official transcript of the Hearings of the Committee on Government Operations of the United States Senate.

ing; he was getting ready to take over himself. After another moment, he jumped in.

"May I interrupt, Mr. Cohn?" McCarthy asked and, without waiting for an answer, he interrupted at length, while Cohn maintained a sulky silence, like a star pupil whom teacher has pushed aside.

"Mr. Wechsler, do you have any other people who are members of the Young Communist League, who were or are members of the Young Communist League, working for you on your newspaper?"

The fight was beginning rather sooner than I had expected, and on ground I had hardly expected him to invade so casually.

This was the first of many questions that I answered fully despite my belief that they were far beyond the scope of the committee's authorized inquiry. I had resolved much earlier that silence was suicidal in dealing with McCarthy. I know some thoughtful people differ with me, and that there are some who believe I should have refused to answer any questions dealing with the policies and personnel of the newspaper I edit. But I was persuaded then, and I have not changed my opinion, that McCarthy was hoping I would refuse to testify so that he could use my silence to charge that I had something to hide. I was not trying to "convince" McCarthy of anything; I was trying to write a record that could be read intelligibly by bemused Americans who might still believe that McCarthy was interested in truth. To put it simply, I did not believe that my answers would tend to incriminate or degrade me but I was quite certain that silence would.

"I will say that I am going to answer that question because I believe it is a citizen's responsibility to testify before a Senate committee whether he likes the committee or not," I said.

"I know you do not like this committee," McCarthy interjected tonelessly, as if to assure me at once that he was impervious to personal offense and as if he had forgotten that he had repeatedly refused to testify before a Senate committee because he considered it hostile to him.

"I want to say that I think you are now exploring a subject

which the American Society of Newspaper Editors might want to consider at some length," I continued.

"I answer the question solely because I recognize your capacity for misinterpretation of a failure to answer. I answer it with the protest signified. To my knowledge there are no communists on the staff of the New York *Post* at this time."

What about former communists, McCarthy wanted to know. I identified them. There were four, and in each case they were men whose past affiliations were as well known as their present anti-communism.

Thus, in less than five minutes, an investigation allegedly directed at my work as an author of books in use by United States Information Service libraries had become an examination of the staff of the *Post*. There had been no indication as to what books of mine were found overseas, or any discussion of their content.

Now McCarthy got to his real point:

"You see your books, some of them, were paid for by taxpayers' money. They are being used, allegedly, to fight communism. Your record, as far as I can see it, has not been to fight communism. You have fought every man who has ever tried to fight communism, as far as I know. Your paper, in my opinion, is next to and almost paralleling the *Daily Worker*. We are curious to know, therefore, why your books were purchased. We want to know how many communists, if any, you still have working for you."

This was quite a speech; it was a summary of everything that he had to say in that hearing and the one that followed. Listening to it I had to resist the competing emotions of anger and hopelessness. But I had brought with me a document that I naïvely considered a devastating rebuttal. Since McCarthy had delivered what almost sounded like his summation before the hearing had barely begun, I decided to use it at once.

So I asked permission to insert in the record of the hearing the statement issued on December 28, 1952, by the National Committee of the Communist Party reviewing the previous election and especially the failure of the Progressive Party ticket to roll up a meaningful vote: it had in fact obtained only a small fraction of

the disappointing Wallace vote of 1948. In the course of this
analysis the communist chieftains declared:

> Support of the pro-war measures of the Truman adminis-
> tration; acceptance and propagation of the "Big Lie" of the
> external and internal "communist menace" disarmed the
> workers, blocked the path to independent political action by
> labor and its allies and paved the way for a Republican vic-
> tory.
> The major responsibility for this policy and its conse-
> quences rests squarely with the reformist and Social Demo-
> cratic trade-union officialdom. This was the content of the
> policies of the Reuthers, Dubinskys, Wechslers et al who
> paralyzed independent political action by projecting the myth
> that Stevenson was an obstacle to the advance of reaction.
> They pursued these policies despite the fact that the Demo-
> cratic Party administration, operating with bi-partisan sup-
> port, originated and unfolded the current war program in
> behalf of Wall Street.

This communist jargon was simply a way of affirming what I
had long believed—that the most effective opponents of communism in America have been the liberals and labor leaders associated with the non-communist Left. Offering the document as an
exhibit, I said: "I am rather fond of this tribute, and it may perhaps have some bearing on your comment that I have not been
active in fighting communism."

In a cold, casual voice McCarthy responded quickly:

"Did you have anything to do with the passage of that resolution? Did you take any part in promoting the passage of that
resolution?"

I thought I had expected anything, but my imagination had
been inadequate. His words registered slowly. I must have looked
baffled as well as astonished, almost incapable of trusting my own
senses.

"Is that a serious question?" I asked.

McCarthy turned briskly to the stenographer.

"Will you read the question to the witness?"

His voice was harder and tougher. In this strange proceeding he alternately played the role of prosecutor and judge, and now he was definitely the prosecutor. The stenographer read the question.

I knew I was making an obvious effort to keep my voice down as I answered, and I am sure my hands trembled a little:

"Sir, I have not been in any way affiliated with the communist movement since late 1937, as I believe your investigation will show. That resolution was adopted by the Communist Party as a tribute to the militant and vigorous anti-communism of the New York *Post* which has, in my judgment, been more effective in leading people away from communism, Senator, than those who prefer to identify liberalism with communism."

He let me finish and then, in the same flat tone, he said:

"Now will you answer the question?"

"The answer is no, Senator," I replied.

"The answer is no. Do you know whether anyone on your staff took part in promoting the passage of that resolution?"

"Senator, to the best of my knowledge, no one on my staff is a member of the Central Committee of the Communist Party or identified with it in any way."

"Now will you answer the question? Will you read the question to the witness?"

"I have answered it as best I can."

"You have said that you did not think anyone on your staff was a part of the committee. That was not the question. Read the question to the witness."

The stenographer read it. The faint smile which McCarthy had exhibited earlier was gone now. Once again, in a voice that must have sounded quite spiritless, I answered the question.

"I do not know that anyone on my staff took any part in promoting the passage of that resolution," I said. He had astounded me, and he knew it.

Thus, within ten minutes after the hearing had begun, I found myself in the preposterous position of denying under oath that I had inspired the long series of communist attacks against me, climaxed by the denunciation of the Central Committee.

With that single stroke of what Philip Graham, publisher of the Washington *Post*, later described as "brute brilliance," McCarthy thus virtually ruled out the whole structure of evidence which I had wide-eyedly assumed would resolve the issue once and for all. Here indeed was a daring new concept in which the existence of evidence of innocence becomes the damning proof of guilt. This is the way it must feel to be committed to a madhouse through some medical mistake; everything is turned upside down. What had heretofore constituted elementary reasonableness is viewed by everyone else as a quaint eccentricity; the most absurd remark becomes the commonplace.

McCarthy reverted to the same thesis several times. Each time he did so with total blandness, as though only the dullest or most subversive mind could detect anything extraordinary in his approach.

He had at last spelled out the formula under which our whole society could be transformed into a universe of suspicion. What a man had said or done could no longer be accepted as bearing the slightest relationship to what he was or what he believed. More likely, it was a disguise to conceal his hidden allegiances to exactly the reverse of what he claimed to stand for. At the second hearing he was to develop this theme even more spectacularly.

McCarthy went on to resume his study of *Post* staff members. Each one mentioned had a long record of anti-communist activity—longer, for example, than Rushmore's. Any books I had written which might have found their way into the overseas libraries were far away and forgotten. This had become an unconcealed investigation of a newspaper which had taken an uncharitable view of Joe McCarthy. When he had finished talking about personnel, he shifted at once to editorial policy.

"Have you been making attacks upon J. Edgar Hoover in the editorial columns of your paper?" he asked abruptly.

"Sir, the New York *Post* has on a couple of occasions carried editorials critical of the FBI. We do not regard any Government agency as above criticism. I assume your committee doesn't either. We have at the same time taken very strongly the position that the charge that the FBI is a Gestapo or a fascist agency was an unfounded, unwarranted charge."

McCarthy maintains a curiously ambivalent relationship to the FBI. Much of what he has done plainly implies that the Bureau is incapable of protecting the country from subversion; although a late starter, he has indicated in a variety of ways that the fight against communism did not really begin until he entered it. Yet he has simultaneously pictured himself as the FBI's truest defender. Actually, the editorials to which he called attention had dealt with the phenomenon of immunity from criticism achieved by the FBI. At the time of the attempt on Victor Reuther's life, the *Post* editorially lamented what we felt was the failure of the FBI to step into the case promptly; at the time of the escape of Gerhard Eisler and the flight of the seven convicted communist leaders, we had whimsically observed that poor Dean Acheson or some other Democratic bureaucrat would have been given a terrible beating in Congress if these events had occurred within their jurisdiction. J. Edgar Hoover has been the object of irresponsible abuse from the communists; that does not absolve him from criticism from other sources. It is certainly to his credit that the FBI has not run wild, as secret-police agencies in other countries have done, but the surest guarantee against excesses is the preservation of the public's right to examine the FBI at least as freely as the State Department. No one, to my knowledge, has advanced the contention that editorial writers should cease and desist from all criticism of a Secretary of State simply because—as in the case of both Acheson and Dulles—he is also being denounced by the Moscow radio.

Now McCarthy was asking:

"Have you always been very critical of the heads of the Un-American Activities Committee? You have always thought they were very bad men."

I confessed that I had never spoken highly of J. Parnell Thomas, who went from Congress to jail. For the record, however, I presented a letter I had received early in 1950 from a man who had been one of the Republicans on that committee. It read:

"Dear Mr. Wechsler:

"This is just a note to tell you that I thought your editorial on the Hiss case, published in your issue of January 23rd, was one of the most able and fair appraisals of a very difficult problem which I have seen.

"Since you probably have me categorized as one of the 'reactionaries' mentioned in your editorial, I thought you might be particularly interested in my reaction.

"With all good wishes,

Sincerely yours,
Richard Nixon."

"I would like to submit that," I said.

"You may put that in," McCarthy replied, betraying no more concern about this exhibit than earlier ones. "I would like to have you get back to my question, then, if you could, however."

I yielded.

"If it is a momentous issue, Senator," I said, "I am unable to present any documents suggesting that I praised a Chairman of the House Un-American Activities Committee."

McCarthy pressed the point.

"The principal villains in your book are those who have gone about the job of exposing communists. Is that correct? Or is that an unfair statement?"

"No Senator, that is not correct. I may say, since you have asked the question, that we have repeatedly taken the position that the New York *Post* is as bitterly opposed to Joe Stalin as it is to Joe McCarthy, and we believe that a free society can combat both."

Now we were off.

Q. And you are opposed to Bill Jenner, too. You think he is a dangerous man?

A. Senator, I give you a priority in that field. I have not written about Senator Jenner in recent months. With respect to the activities of the Senator's committee, I have not criticized the work of its counsel, Mr. Robert Morris.

Q. Do you think Jenner is doing a good job?

A. Senator, I assume you do not want me to make speeches here, and I am trying not to. However, when you ask me a question like that, it is difficult not to respond with a speech.

Q. You can answer that in as great length as you care to. We have a lot of time.

A. My basic position is that American society is a very strong and resilient one. I believe we have successfully resisted communist aggression in the world under the leadership of men whom you have at times deemed sinister. I believe that in the battle of ideas we can compete effectively with the communists any day of the week without resorting to methods which I regard as imitative of theirs. I see by your expression that you feel you have heard this before, so I will not pursue the point.

Q. I have. I have read it in the *Daily Worker* and in the New York *Post*.

A. You have probably read it in the New York *Times*. I can't help wonder when the editor of the *Times* is going to be down here.

Q. Will you get back to that question after a while? The question is: do you think Bill Jenner is doing a good job?

A. I am not an enthusiast of Senator Jenner's.

Cohn tried to get back into the dialogue but McCarthy brushed him aside and the young man slumped back, watching the master with what seemed to be a blend of reverence and resentment. Now McCarthy was shifting from point to point and back again so that no issue could be thoroughly disposed of before another had arisen; it was at this juncture that I realized I was beginning to watch him as though I were seated at the press table rather than in the witness chair, and that it was almost a physical effort to resume the role of participant.

Suddenly he had changed the scene. Had I known Harry Dexter White? I replied that I had met him once, for approximately two minutes, when I returned to Washington from Germany. I went to his office to obtain my formal release from the Treasury Department so that I could go back to journalism.

"Is there any doubt in your mind that Harry Dexter White was at that time a communist agent?" McCarthy asked, as if presenting the simplest question in the world.

"Senator, I haven't any personal knowledge of Harry Dexter White. If you are asking me my opinions based on hearsay and reading, that is quite a different matter. But I must confess that I hesitate to pronounce a certain answer about a dead man."

Then we got back to the *Post* staff, and there were the same insinuations and the same responses, and then back to the FBI for another attempt to prove I had been unco-operative about prosecuting communists. On McCarthy's premise my deficiency was clear; I had never described any intimacy with a single communist espionage agent, which was utterly true. Beside this great and devastating truth it seemed almost inconsequential for me to suggest that the explanation of my passivity was the drab fact that I had not known any spies.

Had I ever talked to the FBI? The answer was yes; whenever an FBI agent came to see me about someone I had known applying for a Government post, I gave as much information as I had; I always emphasized that I had no first-hand knowledge extending beyond 1937 and cautioned that others might have changed their views as decisively as I had.

I know there are some former communists who have conscientiously declined to give any information about others than themselves. I confronted that problem a long time ago and the answer I reached was that there was no justification for a vow of silence. The communist movement was not an amiable secret society to which one owed a personal loyalty after abandoning membership in it. There is abundant evidence that it is a tough, disciplined world-wide movement dedicated to the destruction of free society. I am willing to defend its right to conduct public propaganda functions because I believe there is ample margin of safety in our system and because I am convinced that communist ideas can best be met and overcome in open debate. But to defend that principle of open expression is not to argue that there is an obligation to protect communists seeking strategic positions in Government. Liberals who maintain this opinion would have been the first, I think, to rebuke a professed ex-Nazi who declined to identify his former associates in Government at a time when nazism was sweeping over Europe.

McCarthy seemed impatient as I responded:

"Where I have been asked about people I knew at that time [of my communist membership], I answered freely and fully. If I knew today that someone who had been in the Young Communist League with me was in a strategic Government post, I would certainly communicate that information. There has never been any question in my mind as to a citizen's responsibility on that point, and I do not believe the FBI would suggest that I have been unco-operative in the discussion of such cases."

But had I ever given the FBI a full list of everyone I had known?

The answer was that no such dragnet question, I am glad to say, had ever been asked me by the FBI. In 1948 I had given Louis Nichols, now the Deputy Chief of the FBI, a detailed statement of my own past connections; I had done so because of an incident involving Nancy which revealed that the FBI file on us was seriously incomplete. She had been serving as counsel for the Truman Committee on Civil Rights when a question was abruptly raised about her past membership in the YCL—a point she had fully discussed with an FBI agent after she went to work for the Government. When I heard that had been raised again, I went to see Nichols and we talked it out and the matter was cleared up.

"Do you know any of those Young Communists who are in any Government position today?" McCarthy asked.

"No, I do not."

"Do you know Bernard De Voto?"

"I trust this is not a sequitur," I replied.

"Pardon?"

"I trust this is not a sequitur."

"It is a question."

"I believe I may have met Bernard De Voto. I can't recall the occasion on which I did. I regret to say that he is not a close personal friend of mine."

"You regret to say that?"

"Yes, sir."

"You did not collaborate with him in writing the article in which he advocated that Americans not talk to the FBI?"

"No, sir, I thought that was a very bad article."

"You do not agree with that?"

"I don't agree with that."

This exchange compressed into half a minute a whole range of McCarthy devices. First there was the sudden introduction of De Voto's name into a discussion dealing with the identity of former communists; he happens to be a distinguished American scholar who never roamed into communist territory. Then there was the intimation that De Voto's article on the FBI was proof he was a traitor and that I not only sanctioned the article but had helped him write it (presumably in that spare time when I was not writing communist denunciations of myself). It was almost a case of guilt by non-association.

Then McCarthy announced:

"We are going to ask you, Mr. Wechsler, to prepare a list and submit it to the committee and consider it to be submitted under oath, of all the Young Communist Leaguers that you knew as such, or the communists."

This was the final gambit. I had characterized myself as a "responsive but not friendly witness." From the start, whether rightly or wrongly, I had believed that what McCarthy was seeking was the chance to walk out of the hearing room and tell the press that I had "balked." Once he was able to do that, I would be engaged in the hopeless pursuit of headlines describing me as just another reluctant witness. And from that point on McCarthy would proceed to discredit the *Post* because I had refused to testify freely before a Senate committee.

There may be some splendor in such a role but on the whole it

escapes me. By and large liberals have believed in giving wide scope
to congressional committees. Moreover, there is in the American
tradition a very real belief that the man who has nothing to conceal will speak up when spoken to; muteness has not often been
equated with valor. Back in 1947, in an article in the *Guild Reporter*, I had written:

> It would be nice if the world were prettier, but it isn't; espio-
> nage and sabotage are facts of modern life. I have no brief for
> anybody who refuses to testify before a congressional com-
> mittee; no matter how foolish or fierce the committee, an
> American ought to be prepared to state his case in any public
> place at any time.

Believing this, I had gone along answering everything and now
I faced what McCarthy undoubtedly regarded as the great question. I am sure that he knew enough about me to guess the reluctance with which I would give such a list to a man like him.
I am also confident that he would have felt he had finally cor-
nered me if I now refused to give it to him. Then, and for many
days after, it was a rather strange duel. For McCarthy knew I
would have been happier not to give him any list and I knew
he would have been delighted if I had taken that stand.

All this, let me add, was clearer to me after the hearing than at
that moment. The demand for the list was an almost parenthetical remark; my answer was an oblique comment about the obvious absurdity of asking a man to remember everyone whom he
had known in a different context nearly sixteen years before.

"I don't know that you would be able to do very well with a
similar list of any organization that you were connected with sixteen years ago," I said.

"Well, we are asking for the list. You say you have severed your
connection. I am not going to, at this time, try to—"

"Senator, you are raising that point," I interrupted.

He went on as if I were inaudible.

"—pass on whether that is true or not. I know that you never
testified in a case against an ex-communist. I know that none of

the men you have named here as anti-communists ever testified in a case against communists. I know that they and you have been consistently and viciously attacking anyone who does testify against communists, anyone that exposes communists—"

"Senator, that is not true."

"Let me finish. You may have all the time in the world to talk. So you cannot blame the average person who questions whether you ever did break with the party."

There it was again, and not for the last time; and each time he said it I had a feeling of rage tinged with futility. Senator Jackson was listening attentively, with manifest concern, and at various points along the way he helped me clarify the record; but how could one break through the ring of fantasy that McCarthy was constructing? If each exhibit of my anti-communism were merely additional evidence that I had led a truly gigantic political double life, what remained to be said that had any meaning?

Except for Jackson the room seemed full of the dull, smirking faces of McCarthy's staff watching their bully-boy in action and trying to show him that they were on his side and getting a big kick out of his performance. Occasionally I glanced at Rushmore, who never returned my gaze; he, of all people, knew the magnitude of the fraud and was perfectly willing to be an accomplice in it. Some years earlier we had both been active members of the anti-communist faction in the Newspaper Guild and he could not have forgotten that; as a Guild member he also knew all the details of the internal battle on *PM*. He reminded me of a communist enjoying what he knows is a demonstration trial of an alleged Trotskyist accused of being a fascist agent.

There were moments during the interrogation when I thought of the Moscow trials, and what it must have been like to be a defendant. Suppose Joe McCarthy were dictator and I had been trying to undermine his tyranny, and now he had brought me in and accused me of all sorts of heinous and implausible crimes in addition to the single offense of being against him. If there were no way of communicating the truth to the country, might not a man "confess" to the most wicked absurdities and the most fanciful charges in the hope that people would detect the burlesque?

Fortunately McCarthy was not a dictator; one could leave his hearing room and speak freely outside. So I told the truth and hoped the record would be the answer.

We had gotten now to the point where, under the friendly questioning of Senator Jackson, I was describing the editorial policy of the *Post*.

"I became editor of the *Post* in May, 1949. At that time one of the great issues which the communists were fighting in America was the Marshall Plan. I was a vigorous supporter of the Marshall Plan, and of the Truman Doctrine. These are matters that are on the record. I would be happy to submit to this committee every editorial written since I became editor."

McCarthy remarked dourly: "I do not think that I would care to read them."

For the record I suggested that anyone who rendered such harsh judgment ought to be interested in the written evidence.

McCarthy responded quickly:

"I read enough of your stuff, Mr. Wechsler, to find that your paper, so far as I know, always leads the vanguard, with the *Daily Worker* following the same line, against anyone who is willing to expose communists in Government. That may be your way of fighting communism. Now, you have a perfect right to. People have a right to buy the sheet. I do not care to read any more of it myself. I want to thank you for the invitation, however." *

That morning, before I left home, Nancy had admonished me to keep my temper, a plea I have not always heeded. Now, I must confess, I was rather impressed with my demeanor. I asked to introduce a series of additional exhibits, including the chapter from my biography of John L. Lewis dealing with his relations with the communists, my statement of resignation when I left *PM*

---

* Subsequently, in a letter to the American Society of Newspaper Editors, McCarthy denied that he had questioned me about our editorial policy toward him, which raises the curious question of whether he doesn't regard himself as one of those "willing to expose communism in Government."

and the attacks on me published by the *Daily Worker* while I was on *PM*.

The chairman admitted the exhibits and then, in a tone of simulated objectivity, as though talking about someone a thousand miles away, he said:

"Mr. Wechsler, let me ask you this. If you or I were a member of the Communist Party and we wanted to advance the communist cause, perhaps the most effective way of doing that would be to claim that we deserted the party and, if we got in control of the paper, use that paper to attack and smear anybody who actually was fighting communism. Now, without saying whether you have done it, you would agree that would be a good tactic, would you not?"

I replied that I doubted very much that this was one of the stratagems used by the communists. I questioned, for example, whether the presence of Rushmore as a staff member of his committee conclusively proved that the communists had successfully infiltrated the McCarthy operation.

At this point Senator Jackson expressed surprise that there was an ex-communist on the staff, and McCarthy hastened to explain that Rushmore was a very different breed of former communist because he had repeatedly volunteered to testify before congressional committees. Howard, in short, had won his varsity M.

"Rushmore does not spend his time, you see, trying to smear and tear down the people who are really fighting communism," McCarthy said, while Howard tried not to beam.

The chairman let me comment on the point: "Senator, let's face it. You are saying that an ex-communist who is for McCarthy is a good one and an ex-communist who is against McCarthy is a suspect. I will stand on that distinction."

That was incorrect, said McCarthy. The true test of an ex-communist was how many of his former associates he helped to expose. And so we were back there again; the yardstick of an ex-communist's virtue was how big a story he had to tell.

For the record, again, I found myself pointing out that I refused to view ex-communists as a monolithic group. I had de-

fended Whittaker Chambers against the loathsome smears directed at him during the Hiss case; but no obligation of former
comradeship required me to swear that Louis Budenz was a
scholar or a journalist.

We roved again and then McCarthy returned to what was supposed to have been the subject of the inquiry.

"Do you feel that a committee such as this has the right to and
duty to check the books by communist authors on the Information Program shelves?" he asked.

"Sir, I believe that the expedition of your associates was one of
the most absurd and fantastic wastes of taxpayers' money in history," I replied. "I do not believe that the presence of one book
on one shelf is going to be a decisive issue in the battle against
communist ideas. The New York *Post* has not been alone in
suggesting that the journey did more to enable the communists
to ridicule us than anything that has happened in years."

While I was saying this Cohn smiled fatuously, as if to prove
he was a good fellow accustomed to such unfair comment, and
Schine, whose resemblance to a vacant-eyed band leader has been
discerningly noted by Richard Rovere, seemed to be staring into
space, as though trying to recall an old tune.

"Will you get back to my question?" asked McCarthy, employing his favorite phrase.

Throughout the interrogation the grand inquisitor was by turns
truculent, contemptuous and bland. Yet I rarely had any feeling
of authentic personal animosity. He acted like the gangster in a
B-movie who faces the unpleasant necessity of rubbing out someone who has gotten in his way: he would really like the victim to
feel that there is nothing personal about it and that he rather
regrets the exorbitant demands of duty. At no time did I have the
feeling that I was confronted by a fanatic. McCarthy is a poker
player, not a zealot, a cold-blooded operator in a big game. There
were a few off-the-record asides when he almost seemed to be
saying: "Look, don't get excited, old man, we've all got our

rackets." This detachment may be his greatest strength; at moments it endows him with a certain cold charm.

When I challenged him sharply, he sometimes assumed the pose of a stern schoolmaster, but even then there seemed to be an element of play-acting. He seemed to enjoy my references to him, as though he at last found my words interesting because they concerned the only truly interesting subject on earth. I am sure some lunatics on the rightist fringe genuinely consider me subversive; at no time did I believe that McCarthy was overcome by that theory. I think he is one of the least passionate demagogues I have ever encountered. I am certain that he would have been happy to shake my hand and forget the whole thing if I had merely indicated that I had misjudged him and was prepared henceforth to write kinder things about him.

What I could not quite determine was whether Roy Cohn had achieved an equivalent cynicism at the age of twenty-six or whether he really believed he was saving the republic. He seemed rather out of things anyway.

It looked as though we were nearing the end.

"As I recall, and I may misquote this, because I do not read your sheet," McCarthy said, "I understand that you have been disturbed by the unfair treatment witnesses received before this committee. Do you feel you were unfairly treated?"

He asked the question almost clinically, like a doctor asking a patient whether the needle he had just administered was really painful.

"Senator, I question the basic nature of this proceeding, of course I do," I replied.

"You feel you were unfairly treated?"

"I regard this proceeding as the first in a long line of attempts to intimidate editors who do not equate McCarthyism with patriotism."

Again he betrayed no resentment over the use of the word "McCarthyism"; I think he is rather proud to be an ism as well as a Senator.

"You have not been intimidated, have you?" he persisted.

"Senator, I am a pretty tough guy," I responded with a certain vanity.

"I say you have not been intimidated, have you?"

"I say this is the first of a long line of attempts to do so," I answered.

"Answer my question. Have you been intimidated?"

"You are not going to win this argument, Senator. We will go back and forth all afternoon."

It was getting to be a comic colloquy, but he wasn't smiling. He seemed genuinely absorbed in the line of questioning. I think one of his true delights is the constant rediscovery of his own strength. For public purposes he may have wanted to wrest a statement that I had not been terrorized, yet I think he would have been equally happy to hear me say that I had been.

"Have you been intimidated?" he repeated in the same phlegmatically insistent voice.

"Sir, I have been taken away from my work. I have not even had a chance to write a word about Senator McCarthy today."

He smiled then; the picture of anyone writing about him could not be unattractive. He hammered back:

"You have not been intimidated at all, have you? You mean you have been inconvenienced. The question is: Have you been intimidated?"

He was provoking me into a speech.

"I am fully aware this is a proceeding designed to smear the New York *Post*," I said. "I recognize that, Senator. We are both grown up. But this is a free country and I am going to keep fighting."

"So will the *Daily Worker* and every other communist-line paper," he responded. "But have you been intimidated?"

"I am afraid that is a question we would have to discuss with doctors and get all sorts of expert testimony."

"In other words, you cannot answer that question?"

It was like being a small child and having the town bully ask you whether you have had enough. No answer you can give him is satisfactory to yourself; for if you say that you haven't been frightened, you may re-enforce his sense of virtue, and if you say that you have been he can walk away triumphant. So I clung to the evasive answer.

"I say there is no doubt that this is an attempt to intimidate me. I trust that I have the moral courage to stand up under it. I trust that other editors will."

He would not let go.

"Do you feel that you may have been intimidated? Is there a doubt in your mind as to whether you have been intimidated?"

"We will not know, Senator, until we see whether as editor of the *Post* I keep on fighting just as hard for the things I believe as I have been. I think I will."

"Do you think you have been intimidated?" he asked monotonously.

"I have great confidence in myself, so at the moment, Senator, I feel I have not been intimidated."

"Do you feel you have been abused?"

"Why of course I have been abused. The suggestion that my break with communism was not authentic is the greatest affront you could recite anywhere. I have fought this battle a long time, longer than you have, Senator, and I have taken plenty of beatings from the communists in the course of that fight. So I feel very strongly about this."

Now he spoke in the accents of a judge who, having listened to the devastating words of the prosecutor, delivers his verdict:

"I may say, so that there is no doubt in your mind, so that you need not say that Senator McCarthy intimated or insinuated that you have not broken: I have been following your record, not as closely perhaps as I would if you were in Government, but I have been following you somewhat. I am convinced that you have done exactly what you would do if you were a member of the Communist Party, if you wanted to have a phony break and then use that phony break to the advantage of the Communist Party. I feel that you have not broken with communist ideals. I feel that you are serving them very, very actively. Whether you are doing

it knowingly or not, that is in your own mind. I have no knowledge as to whether you have a card in the party."

I had vowed not to explode; I said as derisively as I could:

"I appreciate that concession."

He ignored the sarcasm; he was very much the judge now,
handing down the decision in favor of the prosecutor (who happened to be himself) and untroubled by any murmuring in the
courtroom.

"I think you are doing tremendous damage to America," he
continued, "when I find books by authors like yourself being purchased by the Information Program we are going to check into
them. I say this so you need not say that McCarthy intimated or
insinuated. McCarthy did not intimate, he said that he thinks
Wechsler is still very, very valuable to the Communist Party."

He was shuffling the papers in front of him and getting ready
to depart. My own peroration was inadequate.

"Senator, I should like to say before you leave that under the
standards you have established here this afternoon, the only way
that I could in your view prove my devotion to America and the
validity of my break with communism would be to come out in
support of Senator McCarthy. This I do not plan to do."

He was on his feet, his face preoccupied. He was a man who
had much more justice to mete out before the day was done and
who regarded the present defendant as belonging to the past.

"That I am not asking you to do," he said. "If you ever did
that, I would be worried about myself."

Then he walked out.

For the record I delivered a last statement:

"Just one further thing. The *Post* has been fighting Senator
McCarthy for a long time. Our editorial page, I am happy to say,
has never wavered on this point. It is not going to change now. . . .
I answered freely here today because I do not believe that I have
anything to hide or that the *Post* has anything to hide.

"I regard this inquiry as a clear invasion of what used to be considered the newspaper's right to act and function independently.
I am hopeful that there will be voices raised by newspapers through-

out the country in protest against this inquiry, but I repeat again that, rather than give Senator McCarthy the opportunity to distort my stand . . . I have answered all questions to the best of my knowledge and recollection."

There was a perfunctory aftermath. Senator Jackson asked me a few additional questions that enabled me to introduce the remaining exhibits I had brought with me. Roy Cohn got around to asking me about Reed Harris, and I gave the unsatisfactory answer he had anticipated; anything I had to say about Harris was favorable, and Cohn didn't labor the inquiry.

With McCarthy gone the spirit had left the hearing. To debate with Roy Cohn appeared to be the climactic foolishness of the fantastic afternoon. Senator Jackson did not need additional documentation. His problem was how to deal with Joe McCarthy.

It was all over at 5:40, ninety minutes after we had begun.

When we got outside the reporters were there. I told them as accurately as I could the substance of what had occurred and said I would ask that a transcript of the hearing be made public. I also said I would ask the American Society of Newspaper Editors to study the document, since it seemed clear that I had been questioned, not as the author of some undesignated book found in some library overseas, but as the editor of a newspaper that had been fighting Joe McCarthy.

I was dead tired; no ordeal is more exacting than the systematic suppression of one's temper. And there was also an element of despair. Often the communists had said democratic debate is a sham because reaction owns all the weapons. I was too old to believe that nonsense. But for a moment I had to fight the awful fear that this was the century of the demagogues, and that only eighteenth-century romantics could believe that truth always triumphs in the end.

# 14

It was not clear where we stood after the first hearing. McCarthy had left the room with a gesture of finality; there was no explicit indication that I was to be recalled. Still unresolved was the question of whether he would press for my submission of the list he had demanded, and whether he would try to prolong the battle.

I came back to New York on Friday evening and over that week-end I sent him a telegram, with copies to other members of the committee. The wire formally asked the release of the transcript of the hearing so that it might be presented to the American Society of Newspaper Editors.

Thus began a somewhat ludicrous struggle via Western Union. McCarthy replied at once, as follows:

SHALL BE GLAD TO RECOMMEND THAT YOUR TESTIMONY BE MADE PUBLIC IN ACCORDANCE WITH YOUR REQUEST. ASSUME THEY WILL HAVE NO OBJECTION. PROCEDURE HAS BEEN TO ALLOW WITNESS TO CORRECT RECORD FOR ERRORS BEFORE MAKING PUBLIC, IF WITNESS DESIRES TO DO SO. CUSTOMARY PROCEDURE IS TO WITHHOLD MAKING EXECUTIVE TESTIMONY PUBLIC UNTIL WITNESS HAS COMPLETED HIS TESTIMONY. WILL YOU THEREFORE PLEASE IMMEDIATELY FURNISH THE LIST OF PEOPLE KNOWN TO YOU TO BE ACTIVE IN THE COMMUNIST MOVEMENT WHILE YOU WERE AN OFFICER IN THE YOUNG COMMUNIST

LEAGUE AND SUBSEQUENT THERETO, AS ORDERED BY THE COM-
MITTEE. YOU MAY ALSO FURNISH ANY ADDITIONAL EXHIBITS, AS
YOU INDICATED WAS YOUR DESIRE.

JOE MC CARTHY *

This message indicated plainly that McCarthy was making publication of the transcript contingent on my submission of the list. Here was "brute brilliance" again. The notion of placing any names in his hands was repugnant to me, yet to refuse to do so meant to abandon the argument or let him shift it to ground most favorable to him.

I am an active anti-communist; McCarthy wanted to prove that I must be pro-communist because I am opposed to McCarthy. I did not see how I could persuade my perplexed countrymen that unwillingness to entrust such a list to McCarthy was different from the now stereotyped refusal of communists to answer questions before congressional committees. It seemed to me that any function I might serve was to establish beyond dispute that an American might be as resolutely anti-communist as anti-McCarthy, and that being anti-McCarthy did not involve any sentimentality about communists or communism. I had contended that the true issue in McCarthy's attack was freedom of the press; I believed that on that ground he might finally be challenged by editors and publishers who had been nervously pampering him, and I knew that McCarthy was hoping to obscure that issue by picturing me as just another reluctant witness in a procession of evasive communists. Having decided that silence was exactly what he was inviting, I had chosen to talk; I could not balk now.

My concern, of course, was not for anyone on the list who had remained a communist; it was for those who might have renounced communism as I had, but who might occupy positions where they were more vulnerable to attack. To protect them I could at least fight for non-publication of the list; that seemed to me a position I could vigorously, and, as things turned out, successfully defend.

* This signature is not overfamiliarity on my part. It is how the Senator signed his name.

No doubt I state the questions in terms most consistent with my own decision; but it is hard to state them any other way unless one really believes that the world communist threat is a hobgoblin invented by knaves.

I telegraphed McCarthy this reply:

I SHALL SUBMIT THE LIST BECAUSE I DO NOT PROPOSE TO LET YOU DISTORT OR OBSCURE THE CLEAR-CUT ISSUE OF FREEDOM OF THE PRESS INVOLVED IN THIS PROCEEDING.

I HAVE ALWAYS RESPONDED FREELY TO QUESTIONS ASKED OF ME BY AUTHORIZED GOVERNMENT AGENCIES AND I SHALL NOT PERMIT YOU AT THIS LATE DATE TO CREATE ANY IMPRESSION TO THE CONTRARY.

YOU ARE OBVIOUSLY TRYING TO USE A SENATE COMMITTEE TO SILENCE NEWSPAPER CRITICISM OF YOUR ACTIVITIES . . . NEVERTHELESS, SO THAT THE RECORD MAY BE PERFECTLY CLEAR, I HAVE ANSWERED ALL YOUR QUESTIONS AND INTEND TO CONTINUE TO DO SO UNTIL THE SENATE ITSELF ACTS TO CURB YOUR ABUSE OF YOUR INVESTIGATIVE FUNCTIONS.

WHEN I SUBMIT THE LIST I SHALL MAKE APPROPRIATE COMMENT WITH REGARD TO THE LIMITED TIME PERIOD MORE THAN FIFTEEN YEARS AGO IN WHICH I HAD PERSONAL KNOWLEDGE OF INDIVIDUAL COMMUNIST MEMBERSHIP AND THE INJUSTICE THAT MAY BE DONE TO INDIVIDUALS WHO, LIKE MYSELF, LONG AGO SEVERED THEIR AFFILIATIONS WITH COMMUNISM AND HAVE SUBSEQUENTLY BEEN ACTIVE OPPONENTS OF ALL FORMS OF TOTALITARIANISM.

I WILL ASK YOUR COMMITTEE AT THAT TIME TO DECIDE WHETHER THE INCLUSION OF SUCH A LIST IN THE RECORD IS PROPER OR DESIRABLE. BUT I WILL ALLOW NOTHING TO STAND IN THE WAY OF THE PUBLICATION OF A TRANSCRIPT WHICH WILL REVEAL BEYOND DISPUTE THE INVASION OF PRESS FREEDOM THAT YOU HAVE UNDERTAKEN. . . .

ONCE THE TRANSCRIPT HAS BEEN RELEASED IT WILL BE FOR THE PUBLIC, THE PRESS AND THE SENATE TO DECIDE WHETHER THIS FISHING EXPEDITION DIRECTED AT A NEWSPAPER AND ITS

EDITOR HAS ANY RELEVANCE TO A HEARING OSTENSIBLY CALLED
BECAUSE A BOOK I WROTE REPORTEDLY APPEARED ON THE
SHELVES OF AN INFORMATION SERVICE LIBRARY SOMEWHERE
OVERSEAS.

Late the same afternoon Harry Sherman, the Western Union
operator assigned to the *Post* building, walked into my office and
said a wire was coming in addressed to "Arthur Lawson, Editor
of New York *Post.*" I told him we would accept it; the drama was
getting childish, but I thought rejection of the wire would merely
further reduce the age-level. It was another communiqué from
McCarthy:

RECEIVED YOUR WIRE IN WHICH YOU STILL TAKE THE POSITION
THAT YOUR COMMUNIST ACTIVITIES ARE IMMUNE FROM INVESTI-
GATION BECAUSE YOU ARE AN EDITOR. YOU ARE ADVISED THAT
THERE IS NO PRIVILEGED PROFESSION INSOFAR AS OUR INVESTIGA-
TION IS CONCERNED. YOU REQUESTED THAT THE RECORD BE MADE
PUBLIC. THE COMMITTEE HAS AUTHORIZED ME TO MAKE IT
PUBLIC. I UNDERSTAND FROM YOUR WIRE THAT YOU NOW WANT
TO CHECK THE RECORD BEFORE IT IS MADE PUBLIC. I SHALL BE
GLAD TO EXTEND THIS COURTESY TO YOU. YOU MAY CONTACT
MR. COHN, CHIEF COUNSEL, AND ARRANGE A TIME TO INSPECT
THE RECORD AND MAKE SUCH CORRECTIONS AS YOU DESIRE.

JOE MC CARTHY

Then McCarthy thought up a new maneuver. Marvin Berger,
the *Post's* attorney, had been holding long-distance conversations
with Roy Cohn about a date on which we could inspect the transcript of the first hearing. But McCarthy, or whoever was writing
his telegraphic messages for him, abruptly sent me a telegram—
again addressed to "Arthur Lawson"—charging that I was stalling
about examining the transcript and that it would therefore be
released the following Tuesday. This was a new note since Mc-
Carthy had previously asserted that issuance of the record was
contingent upon my submitting the list.

I was still debating what to do about the list. If it had any real purpose, such information was obviously the FBI's business. I had no illustrious names to offer, and some of those I would have to name would be people I hadn't seen since I left Morningside Heights in 1935 and who might now be eminently loyal citizens leading quiet lives in Oshkosh. But McCarthy's telegram strengthened my belief that he was now eager to release the transcript swiftly and use that occasion as a pretext for charging that I had withheld vital information.

The problem was complicated by my own moral standard. I did not believe that a man had no right to remember those whom he had known as communists; my anxiety was that McCarthy would hurt helpless people if he got his hands on such a list. There would be only this comfort if I complied: McCarthy was not primarily interested in punishing anyone I might name. He was out to get me.

The date was for Tuesday. It was still uncertain whether I was to appear before the committee or whether I was simply to meet with Cohn and give him the "completion" of my testimony—the list.

Throughout this interlude the infuriating certainty was that I was on the defensive before a judge who would not listen and who had not the slightest interest in the facts of the case. I had fought the judge and this was his reprisal: it was as simple as that. But how did one tell that to one's countrymen in the age of suspicion? McCarthy deceived many Americans by pretending that he was responsible for the exposure of communist conspiracy. By now many citizens had forgotten, for example, that Alger Hiss was prosecuted long before McCarthy took note of communism, and many by now assumed that McCarthy had engineered that and every other revelation of the hidden communist past. Once McCarthy falsely attacks a man, the victim is engaged in a heartbreaking chase to catch up with the lie.

I had spent the previous week-end drawing up the list. It was not a pleasant task; it also forcibly dramatized the perils of memory. I had resolved that no name would be included unless I remembered, beyond a reasonable doubt, that an individual had been present with me at actual communist meetings over a significant period of time. In my senior year at Columbia a number of students dropped into "open" YCL meetings, took a good look and remained absent thereafter. They never joined. As far as I was concerned, they were not communists then and I would not identify them as such now. Some of the recent argument as to who was a communist has been complicated, I think, by the fact that there were many who visited a few communist meetings and retired promptly; and some witnesses, perhaps, recalling a familiar face, have failed to differentiate between those who were steady political companions and those who wanted to see what it was like.

But even making that distinction did not solve all problems. One of the names I originally put down on the list was, I thought, that of an active Young Communist Leaguer of ASU days. I remembered his face; I would recognize him anywhere. I had not the faintest doubt that he had been a committed, faithful member. But on Monday evening in Washington, going over the list again and again in an effort to be as sure as humanly possible that I had committed no errors, I suddenly realized that I had applied the wrong name to that well-remembered countenance; the name I had mistakenly used was a common one and those who go by it —there must be hundreds of Americans who do—might have been subjected to inexplicable embarrassment in future inquiries if I had not corrected myself. This is one of many reasons why the demand for such a list at so late a date was fantastic, and why I drafted it with so much foreboding and unhappiness.

Late Monday afternoon it was announced that the McCarthy committee would be assembled at the hour on which I had arranged to appear at Cohn's office the next day. I assumed then that another hearing was in prospect, and I was right.

There was even less excuse for the second show than for the first. Much of it was repetitious; McCarthy had nothing new to offer, and neither had I. I think the truth is that McCarthy had been disturbed by my insistence on publication of the transcript of the first hearing, which had at least ended in a draw; being both referee and one of the contenders, he decided to have another round.

For the first time it occurred to me that it might be he, rather than I, who was on the defensive. One must not underestimate the paranoia that afflicts the heresy hunter. Few men have shown themselves as incapable of enduring even the mildest criticism as McCarthy; few have struck out so viciously against anyone who raised even the politest question about their professed contribution. No doubt his retaliation against critics is intended to discourage other prospective opponents. But it would be a mistake, I think, to minimize his insecurity.

I began to view Joe McCarthy as a frightened man, which is perhaps the essence of all bullies. The little men around him suddenly looked even jumpier, most of all Roy Cohn, whose bluster awkwardly masks the apprehension that somebody is trying to torment him. As I thought about this, it seemed to me a fascinating and, in some ways, hopeful note about American society. Even as liberals felt that McCarthy was reaching the peak of invincibility, he was a nervous man wondering what tomorrow would bring, exploding at the slightest noise in the house and interpreting the faintest hostility as the omen of doom. Perhaps that explains more clearly than anything why he was determined to call me back into his hearing room. If one editor could quarrel with him and get away with it, others might be emboldened to do the same thing; like any uneasy autocrat, he saw the first sign of insurrection as the beginning of total upheaval.

Subsequent events have tended to bear that out. When I was in Washington Herbert Lehman was the lone and gallant Senate voice raised against McCarthy; since then others have joined him, and President Eisenhower, in the celebrated Matthews affair, appeared to throw his weight with the anti-McCarthy legions. McCarthy reacted with poorly disguised panic to these reverses.

But on May 5th nobody knew this would happen. The atmosphere in Washington was full of fear. Many old friends with whom I talked expressed concern for me. As one Senator put it, I was arousing McCarthy's "killer instinct." His obvious inference was that no man could survive if he provoked the Senator from Wisconsin.

On the eve of the hearing I stayed at the Carlton; and it seemed a wry joke that this was the same hotel where, seven years earlier, Ralph Ingersoll had rebuked me for being intemperately anti-communist.

This time Senator Symington was in the room. Senator Jackson was delayed en route by Senate business; otherwise just about the same cast was on hand. Again the doors were closed and the committee met in executive session.

In the opening moments of the first hearing McCarthy had astounded me with his suggestion that I was the author of communist statements in which I was denounced. This time he had another surprise. These were his opening remarks:

"Mr. Wechsler, the only remaining evidence we had requested was the list of those whom you either knew to be members of the Communist Party or the Young Communist League. I got the impression from your wire that you felt that that was a condition precedent to making the record public. That is not the case. I took the matter up with the committee and they voted unanimously to give me permission to make the record public at the earliest possible moment. So the order is that you give us those names and it has nothing to do with making the record public."

I had brought along a detailed statement explaining that I had decided to give him the names only because he had insisted that I submit the list before he released the transcript. I had issued the statement to the press before entering the hearing and it was already on the press-association wires. Now he had abruptly and rather shrewdly revised the rules and with this maneuver he had taken me off balance.

"May I say," he continued, "that I think you were justified in arriving at the conclusion that the record would not be made public until the list is submitted. I think my wire did indicate that we perhaps would not make the record public until your testimony was completed."

This was a remarkable concession for him to make. He might have blandly ignored the change in his own tactics. Instead he elaborated it. Then, more plainly than ever, it seemed apparent that he was still hoping I would refuse to give him the list. He had no real interest in it. He was still seeking the opportunity to tell the world that I had refused to talk, and thus to consign me to the netherworld of silent witnesses.

At that moment I was undecided what to do next. Strong impulses counseled me to leap at the chance to withhold the list from McCarthy and tell him that I would instead give it to the FBI, although the Bureau had not requested it. But equally strong instinct cautioned me to fight for time to think. My decision to give him the list had been the product of long meditation; it would be absurd to reverse that decision without further thought. To gain time I asked for the chance to read my prepared statement into the record.

Roy Cohn pompously interjected to remind the chairman that under Senate rules prepared statements were required to be submitted twenty-four hours in advance of a hearing. McCarthy benignly waived the rule. Then, after one more brief interruption, he sat there in stoic silence, gazing abstractedly out of the window, studying his notes and employing all the customary techniques of ostentatious inattention while I delivered my speech:

> In view of Senator McCarthy's insistence that the transcript of my hearing could not be released until I "completed" my testimony in this manner, I am today submitting to the Senate Investigating Committee a list of persons whom I knew to be communists in the period when I was a member of the Young Communist League—from April, 1934, through December, 1937. I was eighteen when I joined the Young Communist League.
>
> In now presenting this list, I am urging the committee to

exclude it from the record in view of the damage that might be done innocent people by its inclusion.

This sweeping inquiry addressed to me by Senator McCarthy, involving so remote a period of time, was presumably designed to create the false impression that I have resisted the inquiries of appropriate Government agencies and to obscure my long, affirmative public record of anti-communist activity and writing.

I therefore felt I had no alternative except to submit this list so that the true issue at stake in this proceeding could not be distorted.

From the moment Senator McCarthy summoned me to Washington, it has been my conviction that he has raised grave questions of freedom of the press worthy of full investigation by the American Society of Newspaper Editors. I do not propose to allow anyone to cloud that issue.

I believe Senator McCarthy instituted this whole proceeding as a reprisal against a newspaper and its editor for their opposition to the methods of this committee's Chairman.

In short, I believe I have been called here by Senator McCarthy, not because of anything I wrote or did fifteen or eighteen years ago—none of which I have ever concealed—but because of what my newspaper has said about the committee's Chairman in very recent times.

The fact that a book I wrote was reportedly found in an Information Service library overseas hardly warrants this large-scale examination—especially in view of my known hostility to communism over so many years. Incidentally, I have not yet even been told which book it was or where it was found, but Senator McCarthy has been quoted publicly as saying it was my book on John L. Lewis—a book which contains a full chapter describing the destructive operations of communists in the labor movement.

Senator McCarthy has in fact been conducting an examination of the policies and personnel of the *Post*, a newspaper which, if I may say so, has been as equally resolute in its opposition to communism as to attacks on liberty from any other high or low quarter.

Neither the *Post* nor I has anything to hide. Despite our stated opinion about the impropriety of this inquiry, I have answered all questions to the best of my ability.

But now it is being carried to a point where defenseless people may be hurt.

Many of those on the list I am submitting were young people who joined the Young Communist League out of deeply idealistic motivations in a time of uncertainty and insecurity nearly two decades ago. Even as the shadow of depression lifted, the rise of aggressive fascism created new anxieties which blinded many of them to the basic similarities between communism and fascism. They were fooled, as I was. I know that some of them have repudiated communism as decisively as I did and, where I have personal knowledge of that fact, I have so indicated on the list. But it is highly probable that numerous others with whom I have had utterly no contact in the last fifteen years or more have similarly changed their views and allegiances. The inclusion of their names in the record of this hearing could do them irreparable harm and serve no conceivable national purpose.

It could actually serve to undermine the fight against communism.

I say this in all earnestness. If not only I but others who have long ago broken with communism can be subjected at this late date to this kind of attack for the political errors of youth, young people who are now similarly realizing they have been misled by the communists may bitterly decide there is no way in which they can honorably regain their status in a democratic society.

I therefore ask the committee to recognize a deep moral responsibility to prevent the abuse of this information which its inclusion in the record would surely invite. Surely the proper disposal of this list would be its transmission to the FBI.

The bulk of those on the list were not professional, hardened communists. If I had had the misfortune to be lured into the sinister espionage underground of the communist movement, I would long ago have felt a deep obligation to identify the conspirators. I knew of no one engaged in such activity. Actually many on this list, like myself, were engaged in promoting such public propaganda activities as peace demonstrations, campaigns in defense of academic freedom and assistance to union organizing drives. I long ago became aware of the degree to which many of these activities were manipulated by the communists for their own cynical purposes; but that was not then apparent to many of the participants. I feel compelled to make this point in the light of certain insinuations by the Chairman of this committee that my statements are unsatisfactory because they are insufficiently dramatic. Unlike some other former communists who have appeared before congressional committees, my experience was comparatively brief and distinctly unhistoric. I never got any pumpkin papers.

I have spent my adult years as a journalist writing and speaking in behalf of the free institutions that one may most deeply appreciate if one has ever lived within the stifling orthodoxy of a communist organization. I broke with communism for many reasons, but certainly a major reason was my discovery that no one could breathe or speak or think or write freely as a communist. I found that communism was the enemy of freedom of thought, of justice and of tolerance.

In the ensuing years, I have tried to be more than a negative opponent of communism; I have tried to combat poverty, inequality, bigotry and oppression in all their forms—for I know these are the conditions which make young men and women in any era susceptible to the false flags of communism. It is not enough, I believe, to be an anti-communist; I have tried to establish my affirmative devotion to democratic principles—of which freedom of thought and speech and press are basic.

I have endeavored to combat those who, whether communists, fascists or any other form of totalitarian, would destroy the spirit of dissent that has given grandeur to our republic and who would enthrone the infamous doctrine that the end justified the means.

It is under this credo that I have edited the *Post*.

A grave issue of conscience was involved in my decision to make this list available to the committee in view of the danger involved to innocent individuals. I am doing so because I believe the paramount issue is the attack which Senator McCarthy is waging upon the freedom of the press.

I reiterate my belief that Senator McCarthy is engaged in a primitive fishing expedition designed to silence independent newspaper comment.

That issue I shall ask the American Society of Newspaper Editors to weigh.*

But in the interim I ask the committee to insure protection for those on the list who may be the innocent victims of this proceeding.

---

* Subsequent to the hearings, Basil Walters, Chairman of the ASNE, appointed a special eleven-man committee to study the transcript. The full committee reported that it was unable to reach a unanimous conclusion; four members of the committee, however, led by its chairman, J. R. Wiggins, of the Washington *Post*, issued a separate report, charging that McCarthy's actions constituted "a peril to American freedom." They added: "Freedom of the press in these United States . . . could not long survive the repeated exercise by Congress of unlimited inquiry into the conduct of newspapers. . . . We are compelled by every command of duty to brand this and every like threat to freedom of the press, from whatever source, as a peril to American freedom."

No member of the full committee publicly defended McCarthy's conduct, but its report said its members were divided as to whether "this single interchange constituted a clear and present danger to freedom of the press justifying a specific challenge."

Shortly after Wiggins and three of his colleagues—Herbert Brucker, editor of the Hartford *Courant*, William M. Tugman, editor of the Eugene, Oregon, *Register Guard* and Eugene S. Pulliam, Jr., managing editor of the Indianapolis *News*—released their separate statement, McCarthy issued a long denunciation of Wiggins and demanded that the ASNE investigate him. The demand was rejected.

When I had finished I added this extemporaneous comment on the new ground rules:

"If it had not been my understanding that the release of the transcript was conditional upon my submission of this list, my response to your request would have been to propose to transmit this list to the Federal Bureau of Investigation without presentation to this committee."

"I am wondering why you did not do that years ago," snapped McCarthy. "This is the first time you have made that suggestion. I wish you had done that when you say you first broke with the party or some time in the interim."

"May I comment?"

"Glad to have you do that."

"Let me say first of all that I have been interviewed on many occasions by the FBI with regard to specific individuals. I have answered questions freely. At no time did the FBI request that I submit such a list, and precisely because I believe there are people on this list who have broken just as cleanly as I have I felt no compulsion to submit such a document. Let me add that had I been aware of any of these individuals being in espionage, sabotage or any of the other activities that have been brought to light in recent years, certainly it would have been my responsibility to submit their names. But I am talking here in this list about a large number of young people who joined the Young Communist League at Columbia, people who joined for what I have suggested were high-minded if misguided purposes. I want to say in this connection, Senator, that in the inquiry the other day you took the view that I had been inadequately appreciative of the efforts of the FBI; yet I cannot help feeling that, by the question you raise, you are throwing a reflection on the functions and operations of that agency."

McCarthy's voice was peremptory and metallic:

"Will you give us the list now, Mr. Wechsler?"

"Senator, I thought I had asked a question—whether if I were, as I initially suggested, to transmit this list to the FBI, you would take the view that this was not a condition precedent."

Dorothy Schiff and discuss the new developments w
Carthy promptly granted it.

I called her and she said quite rightly that this was
personal decision "between you and your God," and it
walked up and down the corridor for several moments in a
of total irresolution. Marvin Berger, the *Post* attorney, was th
and we talked briefly; he pointed out that it might hopeless.
muddle the case if I now gave McCarthy a chance to depict me as
a balking witness.

It was a gruesome interval because I did not believe there was
a clear-cut right or wrong, and I found myself weighing rival ex-
pediencies. It was wrong to expose others to McCarthy's wickedness, but it was equally wrong, in my judgment, to embrace the
principle that a former communist should tell nothing to anyone. Whatever I did was bound to be misconstrued. If I now
withheld the list some simple-minded souls who have never seriously recognized the world communist threat to freedom as comparable to the Nazi assault would applaud me, and I would be
heroically identified with a position in which I did not believe; if
I submitted the list, I would seem to be waiving my conviction
that McCarthy was unfit to judge anyone.

Some weeks afterward this dilemma was thoughtfully defined
by Alan F. Westin in an article in *Commentary*:

> It is a wry commentary on the civil liberties scene that the
> witness who chooses not to use the fifth amendment, but to
> speak out, often finds himself caught today in a deadly cross-
> fire. If he does not actively attack the American democratic
> community, he is condemned by the McCarthys for not hav-
> ing really left communism. Yet if he holds to his faith in
> liberal values and testifies truthfully about his former asso-
> ciations, honestly abandoned, influential segments of the
> population treat him as though he were committing some
> dirty deed or selling out the very cause of freedom. The
> "forever-tarred" response of the extreme Right is understand-
> able; it is a handy way to attack the entire open-minded com-

McCarthy repeated that release of the transcript was uncondi-
onal. He added that he thought the list should probably not be
nade public at least until the names had been "very carefully
hecked by the staff."

"You are not giving the list as any reward for making the testimony public, you are giving the list because you are ordered to
give it," he said coldly. He did not sound like a man who was
fighting for possession of the list; he seemed to be trying to taunt
me into defiance.

"I may say," he added, "that I will be extremely surprised if
Mr. Wechsler submits the names of any communists other than
the well-known, well-exposed communists. I will be very surprised,
pleasantly surprised, if he does so."

He had begun to lay the groundwork for the announcement
that any list I might give him was deliberately incomplete. He
seemed to be piling up reasons why I could gain nothing by giving
it to him.

"The meditations and struggles of conscience I have had do not
involve people whom I have reason to believe—by their present
affiliations with the *Daily Worker* or other obviously communist
associations, are still communists," I said, rather gravely. "I am
deeply concerned about the fact that half of this list includes
names of people about whose political whereabouts I have no
idea."

Then I turned to Senator Symington and asked him whether, in
view of the alteration in McCarthy's position, he thought I should
turn the list over to the committee.

"Well, the Chairman has said that he would not release the list
without discussing it in executive session with the rest of the committee," Symington replied. "On that basis, based on your tele
gram to him, I would submit the list at this time."

I remarked that my telegram was in response to the statemen
that there would be no publication of the transcript until I ha
furnished the names. Yet it was a fact that I had agreed to do s
could I now change my own position without compounding t
confusion? I asked for a brief recess so that I might telephc

munity. The liberal condemnations are neither understandable nor defensible; in that they encourage silence and discourage speaking out, they do a great disservice to liberalism and civil liberties. . . .

This was essentially what I felt in those last moments of decision. To identify myself with the silent witnesses would have been to confuse beyond hope of future clàrification the position I actually held, and to become a symbol of a conspiracy I detested; I had no esteem for those who denied that free society had to fight for its life against the totalitarians of the Left as well as of the Right. I had assumed from the beginning that I might serve some purpose by clearly dramatizing the quality of McCarthy's assault on men whose only offense was opposition to him; I had insisted that freedom of the press was the issue. What would happen to those issues if I now let him shift the ground to the muddy terrain where I would be contending that a Senate committee could not be trusted with this information?

Possibly this is rationalization after the fact; possibly things had simply gone too far to permit a sudden shift of strategy. Possibly I was most influenced by my belief that Joe McCarthy wanted silence, not submission, and that I was determined not to walk into his trap.

I went back into the hearing room. There was an uglier quality in the air, perhaps because of a flare-up that had occurred just before the recess. I had pointed out that my reluctance to submit the list had been enhanced by the fact that a distorted account of the previous closed hearing had appeared in Winchell's column. I said I thought it was unfortunate that a representative of the Hearst press and a well-known Winchell aide—Howard Rushmore—was permitted to attend executive hearings while the rest of the press was barred. Once again McCarthy rallied to Rushmore's defense. In the same interval Roy Cohn suddenly jumped to his feet and announced in his deepest voice that he could not understand the delay about transmission of the list: "A very simple direction has been made to the witness." He seemed quite excited.

I said rather loudly, "Calm down," and McCarthy ordered the exchange stricken from the record.

Anyway, there was no remnant of good feeling in the room when I came back. Outside the sky had suddenly turned black, as if to provide an appropriate background for the darker mood of the hearing room.

"To avoid any suspense," I began, "let me say that it is my decision to turn over the list. I have conferred with the publisher of the *Post*, who said it was my decision to make and I have made it. I want to say that in turning this over I do so in the light of the assurance of Senator Symington that the innocent people on this list should be protected; that every effort should be made to preserve the anonymity which may surround them in the communities where they live."

I handed over the list. McCarthy, Rushmore and Cohn pored over it like village gossips who have come upon an illicit love letter. Then McCarthy said:

"I have a list from Mr. Wechsler and I have had Mr. Rushmore and Mr. Cohn check it. They tell me at this point that apparently there are no names on here except names of those who have been publicly known as communists or Young Communist Leaguers."

This was a lie; it was a monstrous lie and, though I had anticipated some such remark, it is still always startling when a man recites so vast a falsehood with so grave a face. I have no idea what Rushmore and Cohn said in the whispered colloquy, but the likelihood is that what McCarthy said was what he had planned to say all along.

After McCarthy spoke I said:

"Sir, that is not a true statement, and I do not believe Mr. Rushmore could make it under oath."

Rushmore did not request the opportunity to do so.

There was another flurry when Senator Symington observed that Rushmore had been no less identified with the communists than I had and that "it is only fair to consider the word of Mr. Wechsler to be just as good as that of Mr. Rushmore."

McCarthy disagreed; Rushmore was a good ex-communist; he had been "of great assistance."

Now the list was laid aside and McCarthy resumed the interrogation. Most of what he subsequently asked me was based on the testimony I had given in the pre-trial examination in the Lait-Mortimer case. There I had testified, for example, about "Max," the man without a name who had served as the elder statesman of the YCL National Committee. McCarthy imparted as much mystery as he could to this matter; here, as at other points, it was hard to bring myself to recite all the wearying recollections to this unresponsive audience. It occurred to me that Roy Cohn had been about ten years old when "Max" ordered a former comrade of mine to come to my house and spit in my face because I had resigned from the YCL. At the same moment Howard Rushmore was a loyal deputy to Louis Budenz on the *Daily Worker* and Joe McCarthy was an ambitious Wisconsin Democrat. What point was there in trying to relate all these things in time? Again and again during both hearings I had to prod myself into submitting exhibits and filling out the record, and to remind myself that perhaps some representative of posterity might want to read it all even if Joe McCarthy failed to listen.

Now we were talking about the trip Nancy and I had taken to Europe in 1937. I laboriously explained how the trip was arranged, how it was financed, and how the Russian phase of the journey marked the last chapter of our connection with communism. Symington helpfully drew me out on the details; I tried rather inadequately to describe the claustrophobia we experienced in the oppressive Soviet domain.

Then, abruptly, McCarthy brought up Paul Hagen.

"Did Paul Hagen urge you to leave the party?" he asked.

"Yes, Paul Hagen was a very great influence in my life."

"You said he influenced you to break with the party?"

"Yes, sir. I might say in connection with the European trip that one of those whom we saw in the summer of 1937 in Prague was

Paul Hagen. He was a refugee from nazism and he was a leader of underground anti-Nazi activities. . . ."

"You say that Paul Hagen is the man who got you to leave the party?"

I found that by looking at Symington and almost pretending that McCarthy was not in the room I could stir myself sufficiently to give more complete answers.

"He was one of the very real influences in my life," I said. "He had been a communist as a young man. When many of us were in the Young Communist League, the thing that was denounced most often was the man who left; he was called a traitor. Many people were very sensitive about that. To meet a real live 'traitor' and to discover that he was an affirmative, decent human being who had not sacrificed his original idealism was a very important thing in my life."

Intermittently I wondered whether any of this registered on Roy Cohn. Here was a "success boy," circa 1953, who had made his way as a pious figure in a negative crusade; anti-communism was his career. Did he even glimpse what I was talking about when I suggested that Hagen had proved that non-communist man could have affirmative values? Was Cohn's obsequious service to McCarthy a much worthier occupation for a young man than blind fidelity to the communist myths?

We got back to arguing about who were the true anti-communists.

"I do not believe that the fact that a man is an ex-communist makes him particularly virtuous or particularly evil," I said. "I believe that from the moment he leaves the communist movement it is his responsibility to create an affirmative existence and demonstrate a genuine dedication to democracy."

McCarthy repeated, however, that I had not spent innumerable man-hours testifying against former comrades, as had Louis Budenz. By this time it would have seemed irrelevant for me to observe that, having left the YCL at the age of twenty-two, I could not conceivably have had so many gaudy tales to tell.

Up till this point McCarthy's manner toward his Democratic

associates—Jackson at the first hearing and Symington at this one
—had been condescending but proper. At times he joked with
them companionably and at other times he lectured them with
the patient air of a man who is trying to bring a retarded pupil up
to date. But his demeanor became very severe when Symington
abruptly said to me:

"I want to say that you have been the most forthright witness
that we have had before this committee."

McCarthy promptly rebuked him:

"I may say that perhaps the only reason you say that, Senator,
is that you have not been here to hear all of the testimony."

"I have to answer," Symington said quietly, "that if you had
told me the day before he came that he was to testify I would have
been here."

For a brief moment we returned to my books, which were supposed to be the reason I was there. McCarthy maintained that
there was nothing improper about having summoned me; I was
there as an author, not as an editor. I suggested that the only possible relevance of such a call would be the content of any books
I had written which were being used overseas, and I still didn't
know which books had been found where.

"At this late date you acknowledged to me that your staff, after
a trip to Europe, is unable to tell me what books were found
there," I said.

"We know that some of your books are on the shelves, we do
not know how many," McCarthy replied.

Symington interposed with genuine amazement:

"They have not been able to tell you what books are on the
shelves?"

I explained that Senator McCarthy had told reporters he
thought *Labor Baron*, which happened to be an anti-communist
book, was in use. But counsel Cohn, perhaps aware that the content of *Labor Baron* would make a poor exhibit for the committee, had continued to insist that he didn't know which book
was being used; he simply knew that something I had written was
being made available to foreigners.

The conflict in their statements recurred.

"We have told Mr. Wechsler that the State Department has informed us that his book *Labor Baron* is definitely on the shelf," said McCarthy.

But a moment later counsel Cohn was saying:

"I think the record ought to be clear on this. The Author's Index indicates Mr. Wechsler's books are in use. That is for certain. Exactly which of them, it is a practical impossibility at this point to know."

But if this had been a serious proceeding, it would have been conceded that the issue hinged on that point. No one disputed the anti-communist character of *Labor Baron*; if that was the volume in question, what happened to the pretext for calling me in the first place?

McCarthy was impatient and annoyed. He reverted to his earlier note, introducing an even more extravagant theory.

"I may say that your purported reformation does not convince me at all," he intoned. "I know if I were head of the Communist Party and I had Jim Wechsler come to Moscow and I discovered this bright man, apparently a good writer, I would say: 'Mr. Wechsler, when you go back to the United States, you will state that you are breaking with the Communist Party, you will make general attacks against communism, and then you will be our ringleader in trying to attack and destroy any man who tries to hurt and dig out the specific traitors who are hurting our country.' You have followed that pattern."

I had begun to answer when the buzzer, signifying a quorum call in the Senate, sounded. The hearing was recessed.

Outside the storm had begun, as if in prelude to the last act; great streaks of lightning swept the sky and the thunder rumbled.

It was my turn, I reminded McCarthy soon after we resumed, and he smiled amiably. Again I was struck by the impersonality of his manner. He displayed no rancor over what I had said about him; the mention of his name in any context seemed an endless pleasure to him.

Now I attempted to describe the grotesqueness of the proceeding:

"As I understand it, you have repeated your view that in a rather elaborate and complicated world the attacks on me which have appeared in communist publications and the anti-communist articles I have written are merely conclusive proof that in some way I am a secret communist operative.

"When I get to this point it is difficult for me to keep contact with the real world. Let me put it this way: it is true that I believe that you have done serious damage to the battle against communism by confusing liberals with communists. Suppose I went on to say that you have an ex-communist on your staff and this is clear proof that you are the front for a sinister operation designed to confuse, divide and create bitterness in America. I do not state this to be a fact, as you have stated the alternative to be a fact. I state it only to indicate the nightmare world we are walking in when I come in here with an exhibit, for example, from the *Daily Worker* headlined: 'Wechsler's Lies Can't Halt Struggle for Peace.' "

Then I proceeded to offer as exhibits the long series of published communist attacks on me. McCarthy once again volunteered the opinion that these were of no material consequence since I had failed to send a single communist to jail.

Senator Jackson had arrived by now and he disputed McCarthy's yardstick of reformation.

"Wechsler's whole behavior since he left the Young Communist League has been inconsistent with anything that would be in line with the communist program," he said.

McCarthy exploded, like a schoolteacher whose pupil has just blundered unforgivably.

"Have you been reading his paper?" he demanded of Jackson.

"Sure I have," responded Jackson.

"Are you not aware of the fact that Wechsler has been the ringleader in trying to assassinate the character of anyone who deserts the party and testifies against his former comrades? . . . If, as I said before, if I were a member of the Communist Party and if I were the bright newspaperman that Wechsler apparently is, I would not stay above ground and say I was a member of the Communist Party. I would say I deserted the Communist Party and then I would do exactly as Mr. Wechsler has been doing."

I looked at Rushmore. He was staring at the storm outside. He was the one man at the table who could have most surely blasted McCarthy's fantasy, but he was otherwise engaged; he had found that shelter won by ex-communists when they join the Hearst empire.

I had to keep assuring myself that there would be a day of honorable reckoning and that I had to complete the record. I offered as an exhibit an article I had written for *Harper's* in 1947 entitled, "How to Rid the Government of Communists." In that article I challenged the thesis then popular in some liberal circles that the Government loyalty program was a senseless witch hunt. There were witches in our time, I had written, and the problem was how to banish them without hurting the innocent. I wrote that the report of the Canadian Royal Commission should have dispelled once and for all the liberal illusion that the communist movement was simply a more eccentric version of traditional American radicalism; as long as free society was under attack, it was elementary self-protection to exclude the conspirators from Government.

"The Canadian report is a fascinating and revelatory study in the pattern of communist behavior," I had written.

> It demonstrates beyond dispute the link between the Soviet intelligence networks and home-grown Communist Parties. It also depicts in detail the strange process by which men who are drawn to the communist movement by devoutly idealistic symbols become full-fledged spies in the service of a foreign power—not for monetary reward and usually with the loftiest rationalizations of their conduct. They are stirred by the concept of internationalism. They are taught to identify the welfare of humanity everywhere with Soviet national interests. They learn to regard concealment of their own political iden-

tities and transmission of official secrets as noble tricks against the pillars of society. Finally, when the political hypnosis is completed, they have resolved all inner doubt. They are agents.

In this article I also urged that stronger procedural protections be granted the objects of loyalty inquiries; McCarthy therefore ignored everything else I had said and interpreted the article as an attack on the FBI.

Then I presented exhibits growing out of my coverage of the Wallace campaign, and again McCarthy began revamping history.

"Did you think there was danger of the Wallace party winning the election or did you think there was danger of the Wallace party taking enough votes so that the old Acheson crowd would be kicked out and exposed?" McCarthy asked.

"I thought there was very grave danger of the Wallace party getting enough votes so that the world would be confused as to the nature and solemnity of American resistance to communist aggression," I replied.

McCarthy lowered his voice and addressed a history lesson to Symington and Jackson.

"Now Mr. Wechsler, let us be a little frank here," he said. "You are talking of this as a shining example of your fight against communism. Is it not the truth that you knew that the Wallace party had no possible chance of winning that election but that you were afraid if they picked up enough votes of the type that you appealed to, the left-wingers, the party-liners, that it would mean a defeat and an exposure of the old Acheson crowd that has been so thoroughly infiltrated by communists?"

"Senator, the communists up and down the line were supporting Wallace," I replied. "If you are accusing me of a subjective conspiracy to elect a Democratic president, we have certainly widened the scope of this inquiry, and that perhaps affects other Senators on this committee."

Q. We are not talking about Democrats or Republicans, but

when you get up and tell us that your attack upon Wallace proves
how anti-communist you are, that does not ring too true here.

A. Senator, it is clear to me that nothing I say will be acknowledged by you to be a valid point. I have been guilty, as I freely
acknowledge, of criticizing you pretty hard. I stand by that criticism.

Q. I have not questioned you about that criticism.

A. You have referred numerous times to my criticism of the
committee. I think it is your basic belief that the only test of
patriotism is the attitude of a newspaper editor toward the operations of your committee in this field. I cannot and do not meet that
test and do not propose, if I may say so, to try to meet it.

With the weary good humor of a judge bidding farewell to a
defendant headed for a cell, McCarthy said:

"As I have said before, Mr. Wechsler, if the New York *Post* or
Jim Wechsler started to praise McCarthy when I exposed some
of the communists, I would be right well certain that I was hanging an innocent man."

Trying to match the spirit of the remark, I replied:

"Senator, I think that the danger of praise of your activities appearing in a prominent place in the New York *Post* is one that
should not keep you awake at night."

"Thank you," said McCarthy.

There was then, as there had been at a couple of other moments
in these two grueling sessions, a strange note of amiability in the
air. At an earlier point, in an off-the-record colloquy, McCarthy
had genially observed that I was an interesting witness and that
he wished he could understand what really went on in my head;
I politely assured him that I did not find him a bore, and was just
as curious about his mental processes. These fragments strengthened my impression that he was a man of little conviction and
infinite artfulness. He was as cold-blooded about ideas as about
human beings. They were all simply elements in a great political
game. I have met men with whom I violently disagreed but whose
devotion to their beliefs inspired my respect. McCarthy's cause is

McCarthy; everything else is subsidiary, and ideas are merely weapons of the moment in an ambitious personal struggle.

The hearing was going downhill; we were all repeating ourselves. But I was determined to say one thing before it was over:

"I regard this as a very serious thing, not merely because of what I consider to be the press issue, but because I have been known as an anti-communist for many years. This proceeding against me is going to make it less likely that some young kids somewhere will break with communism. If I can be brought here fifteen years later and subjected to this brain-washing, there are going to be a lot of people who will say: 'How do you possibly win back a place in decent democratic society?' "

I had reintroduced the note on which the first hearing had ended. With almost morbid inquisitiveness, McCarthy again sought to extract an admission that I had been intimidated.

"You refer to brain-washing; you feel that the questions that have been asked you are unfair, that you have been browbeaten?" he asked in a tone of authentic curiosity.

"I have said many times, Senator, that I believe I am here because of our editorial policy."

"Do you feel that the questions are unfair, that you have been browbeaten?"

"I think that many of your comments about me, if I may speak with careful understatement, have been outrageous. With respect to the questions you have asked me, this has been a fascinating experience."

He persisted:

"Very honestly, I would like to know, do you think we have asked you any unfair questions? Let me assume that you were not a newspaperman, that you were a lawyer or something else, would you then say the questions we have asked you are unfair?"

"I think the basic unfairness is that you are repeatedly asking me to furnish proof that I have praised the operations of such Senate committees as this. I submit that is not a test."

"We never asked you about your criticism of this committee. I may say that I have no concern whatsoever about your criticism of me or this committee. . . . I would like to go back to this, do you think our questions to you have been unfair?"

"I said, and you force me to repeat myself, that the line of inquiry has been directed at a newspaper because of its policies and much of it has been far beyond any possible relevance to a man's political position."

It was getting late. There were a few listless last exchanges, as in the final moments of a bad play when, the situation resolved and the characters disposed of, the playwright is laboring the lines that tiresomely precede the lowering of the curtain. In my closing remarks I noted that I had testified fully and freely, despite my feelings about the Chairman of the committee; I suggested that McCarthy emulate me in his dealings with the Senate committee which had explored his financial operations—a committee which had repeatedly asked him to appear before it and had been met with stubborn defiance. This was one of the larger ironies of contemporary America; the grand inquisitor was the man who had himself declined to answer questions. All the majesty of the Senate was on his side when he interrogated others, but it was insufficient to bring McCarthy before the committee explicitly instructed by the Senate to question him.

When I mentioned the matter he smiled faintly but refrained from comment. It was not a subject he chose to discuss.

The hearing had begun at 2:45. It was 6:10 when we adjourned. It had been a long afternoon.

# 15

Two days after the second hearing, the transcript of both sessions was made public. The New York *Times* said editorially:

## FREEDOM AND FEAR

We have refrained from commenting on Senator McCarthy's interrogation of James A. Wechsler, editor of the New York *Post*, until the text of the transcript of the two sessions, held April 24th and May 5th, had become available. Mr. Wechsler, who testified that his youthful association with the communists ended some fifteen years ago, when he was in his early twenties, had been called before Senator McCarthy's investigating committee ostensibly because one or more of his books were to be found in American libraries of information abroad.

One of the fascinating things about this inquiry is that neither Senator McCarthy nor Roy Cohn, the committee counsel, nor anyone else knew just which of Mr. Wechsler's four books were involved. This is curious, because, while two of the books were written while Mr. Wechsler was a communist, two were written after he had broken from the communists and had begun his present career as an effective anti-communist writer. Since the books did not play a very great role in the five hours of hearings, anyway, we must look further to see just why Mr. McCarthy so assiduously attempted to show—without the slightest concrete evidence and in the face of Mr. Wechsler's entire mature career—that the editor of the *Post* is still "serving" the communists.

We have repeatedly said that the investigative function of congressional committees is an important and a desirable one. We believe it is the citizen's duty to respond fully and frankly to congressional investigators (as Mr. Wechsler did), just as it is the duty of the investigators scrupulously to observe the citizen's constitutional rights. We think that newspapermen are no more immune from investigation in respect to allegedly subversive or seditious activity than anyone else. The mere fact that a man works on or writes for a publication does not give him any special privilege if, as and when his loyalty comes under scrutiny.

But there is another basic American principle involved here, too, and that is the principle of freedom of the press. The real question is whether or not Mr. McCarthy was using his undoubted right of investigation as a cover for an attempt to harass and intimidate Mr. Wechsler as an editor who has bitterly and uncompromisingly opposed Mr. McCarthy. It is our opinion after reading the transcript that this is just exactly what Mr. McCarthy was doing.

The whole tenor of the questioning of this editor was to show that, inasmuch as he had never had a good word to say for the leadership of the various congressional committees investigating communism, he must thereby be serving the communist cause. The repeated references to the editorial policy of the New York *Post* revealed clearly what was in Mr. McCarthy's mind. The Senator has every right to attack the *Post* or any other newspaper if he wants to, but we think it gets very close to an infringement on one of America's basic freedoms if he uses his vast powers as chairman of an investigating committee of the United States Senate to accuse an editor of continued subservience to "the communist ideal" because that editor's writings are not to his liking.

The mere fact that Mr. Wechsler had fought communists in and out of the labor movement, had resigned from one newspaper (now defunct) because he thought it was being manipulated by communists, had participated in liberal and therefore bitterly anti-communist organizations, had written innumerable articles and editorials against communists and communism—all of this carried no weight with Mr. McCarthy. Mr. Wechsler's crime seems clearly to be that he has also fought Mr. McCarthy's methods, a fight in which this newspaper, too, has been proud to participate.

The rising threat of communist aggression is and has been for years a matter of the gravest concern to all of us in the free world. It is not only right but necessary that we take every possible defensive step to meet this real and growing danger. We have to build up our armaments, we have to support our allies in Europe and in Asia, we have to use force to resist aggression whether in Korea or in Greece, we have to develop our own political, social and economic strength as well as military. But in the process of alerting ourselves and our friends to the Russian imperial-communist menace—which "peace offensives" do not dissipate—some Americans have become frightened. Fear leads to panic, and panic can lead to the subversion of our most precious institutions. Americans have to be alert, strong and steady. But they do not have to be scared. It is contrary to the best interests of the country to capitalize on fear.

Much of the same thing was said by a large number of big and little newspapers in many parts of the country. For a long time I had felt rather lonely in this encounter; I did not feel that way any longer. I was even tempted to hope that the editorial support I received reflected an incipient revolt against McCarthy.

There were voices on the other side, notably Arthur Krock and David Lawrence. They did not hold that McCarthy had proved a case against me or even, indeed, that the hearings had been worthwhile; they simply argued that no issue of freedom of the press was involved since it was clear that I was continuing to exercise my freedom to criticize Senator McCarthy. This seemed somewhat like saying that a reckless driver should not be arrested until he kills someone. Or, as Elmer Davis remarked, it was equivalent to saying that attempted rape was no crime if the aggressor failed to pin down his victim.

Two other comments—one adverse and one friendly—seemed more interesting. The first was written by Dr. James Burnham, a one-time Marxist scholar, in that solemn organ of the intellectual Right known as the *Freeman*. In a lengthy evaluation of the record of the hearings Dr. Burnham absolved me of "subjective" treason: "The positive evidence gives no sufficient reason to regard Wechsler as still communist or pro-communist, as subjectively disloyal." Then Burnham went on:

> If Senator McCarthy had stuck to the political effect of Wechsler's conduct and left aside the question of subjective "loyalty" and motive, then his ground would have been firmer. It is not necessary to determine that Wechsler and his political associates are traitors in order to prove that they are mistaken in their convictions, false in their analyses, wrong in their advice and through the results of their actions injurious to the interests of the nation.

This was an echo of something I had heard long ago. In the time of the communist theory of "social-fascism" it was often said that it was irrelevant whether socialists were well-intentioned fellows; their deeds "objectively" abetted fascism; therefore they were social-fascists. Dr. Burnham's argument was comparable: I had erred; thereby I had damaged "the state"; therefore it was perfectly proper for McCarthy to go after me. Though I might not be a "conscious" traitor, I deserved to be hanged because of what Dr. Burnham decided were the grievous consequences of my acts.

More entertaining was a parody of the McCarthy hearings written by Malcolm Muggeridge, the brilliant and witty editor of

*Punch.* The hearing room was recreated and Senator McCarthy was the witness, being questioned about a series of suspicious circumstances.

CHAIRMAN. Well, Senator, picking up our questioning where we left off yesterday, you will admit, I take it, that when you defeated the late Senator Robert La Follette in the Wisconsin primaries in 1946, you had the support of the communist and fellow-traveler vote?

SENATOR MC CARTHY. What of it? As I said at the time, communists have votes, don't they?

CHAIRMAN. Please answer the question, Senator. Did you have the support of the communist and fellow-traveler vote against La Follette?

SENATOR MC CARTHY. I believe so.

CHAIRMAN. Right. Now would you also agree that La Follette, whom you defeated with the aid of this vote, though holding strong liberal views, was intensely anti-communist, long before you or most other professed anti-communists of today thought of taking up such a position?

SENATOR MC CARTHY. I'm not familiar with the late Senator's record.

CHAIRMAN. It's not within your knowledge, then, that he was one of the very few members of the Senate to see, in advance, the appalling dangers of the mood in which President Roosevelt approached the Yalta Conference, to the point that he actually went to see the President before he left for Yalta to plead with him to take a tougher and more realistic attitude towards the Russians?

SENATOR MC CARTHY. No, it's not.

CHAIRMAN. You see what I'm getting at, though, don't you, Senator—that the communists and fellow-travelers in Wisconsin had very good reasons for wanting to get La Follette out of the Senate and you in, and were delighted when you succeeded?

SENATOR MC CARTHY (banging the table, thereby stimulating

a new burst of energy on the part of the photographers). If that is so, they've had every reason subsequently to regret it.

CHAIRMAN. Are you so sure?

SENATOR MC CARTHY. I'd like to read into the record a resolution passed by the American Communist Party published in the *Daily Worker* to the effect that Senator Joseph McCarthy is one of the bitterest and most unrelenting foes of communism. . . .

CHAIRMAN. You can read anything you like into the record, Senator, but did you help to draft the resolution?

SENATOR MC CARTHY. Did I help . . . that's ridiculous. We're both grown up, aren't we?

CHAIRMAN. Answer the question.

SENATOR MC CARTHY. No, I didn't.

CHAIRMAN. Now another question. Have you got any present or former communists on your staff?

SENATOR MC CARTHY. I . . .

CHAIRMAN. The question, Senator.

SENATOR MC CARTHY. My staff has been carefully selected and screened . . .

CHAIRMAN. What we want to know is whether there are any present or former communists among them.

(A *pause*)

SENATOR MC CARTHY. Two former communists who . . .

CHAIRMAN. Good. For the record, the Senator employs two former communists. He was elected in Wisconsin with communist and fellow-traveler support. He denies being as of now a member of the Communist Party, but it is a matter of public knowledge that his activities since he became a Senator have greatly benefited the cause of communism here in the United States and abroad. Furthermore, it can be said with certainty that, if he were an under-cover party member, chosen for that reason to oust La Follette (particularly dangerous, from the communist point of view, because a Progressive himself, and bearing a name famous among Progressives, and at the same time intensely and knowledgeably anti-communist), everything he has done and said subsequently would support such an hypothesis.

(Senator McCarthy begins to expostulate violently, again lavishly photographed the while.)

CHAIRMAN. You'll have every opportunity, Senator, to rebut these grave charges. The session is now suspended.

I have thought about Krock's explanation that my two-day appearance before the McCarthy committee was inconsequential because I am still alive and functioning. Despite all I have written, it is not quite possible to communicate the quiet horror of examination by McCarthy. I have no wounds to exhibit; I write what I please about McCarthy. I bear every external resemblance to the person I was a moment before the telephone call from Washington. But I do not commend the experience to anyone else; I fear for those who may be called before him who do not happen to be editors of newspapers and cannot fight back. And I am saddened by those in responsible positions—in Government and the press—who keep inventing reasons for avoiding a quarrel with the man.

There are moments when each man is alone with himself; he knows his weaknesses and his failures, his vanities and his follies. But these are endurable discoveries; they are real, they have rational roots, they are explicable. But no moment can be much more hideous than that in which your own estimate of yourself is alleged to be a case of mistaken identity; when you are charged with harboring the doctrine that you long ago renounced; and, worst of all, when you know that the men who are making the charge do not believe what they are saying. To be catapulted into the realm of madness without losing one's own reason is a rough journey.

And most important of all is the return trip. For aberration is infectious. The crucial thing is to avoid succumbing to an irrationality as great as the one you have left. The communists say that McCarthyism is proof that there is no terrain where the liberal may still stand with dignity and honor. But this is as delusive as the notion that a man cannot combat communist tyranny without joining hands with the despots of the Right. There are no inevitabilities: no "locomotives of history," no "waves of the future."

Frightened men are forever telling us that the time for reflection is past. Senator McCarthy's followers assert that only the methods of the primitives can save us, and that it no longer matters how many cruel injustices are committed and how many falsehoods spoken if a single enemy is finally caught somehow somewhere some day. A few ritualistic liberals tell us with equal intensity that any form of resistance to communism must finally make us all prisoners of McCarthy, as though it were impossible for rational men to use their minds in defending their liberties. These are rival absurdities of the age of suspicion. Democracy cannot protect itself by losing either its soul or its sense. We did not become totalitarians in a world-wide war against fascist tyranny; no categorical imperative decrees that we must choose between madness and submission now. To combat the underground infiltration of communist saboteurs and espionage agents we primarily need effective counter-intelligence; to combat the fraudulent ideological thrust of world communism we need, it seems to me, cool human intelligence.

In the long run, only panic can defeat us. The panic of those who say that McCarthy's political vigilantism has rescued us is often matched by the terror which prompts others to say that McCarthy has already destroyed the republic. Neither proposition is valid. I should hardly be tempted to minimize the damage McCarthy has done, and perhaps what I fear most is the erosion of those values of fairness and mercy which we have so long treasured. The spread of know-nothingism is currently our gravest domestic threat. But the battle is far from over; it has, I think, just begun. And it will not be won by men who are so distracted by the McCarthy danger that they dismiss the external challenge of Soviet imperialism. This is, in essence, the parallel of the McCarthy hoax; for what he and like-minded men have done is to distort all reality by picturing the bedraggled American communists as far more menacing than the massive Soviet power, and by identifying with the communists all those who reject McCarthy's intolerant version of history.

The right to be wrong is an ancient democratic liberty; like the Soviet prosecutors, the McCarthyites would define as treason anything that they regard as error.

In any contest with despotism, freedom is ultimately our greatest strength. The vision of America as a refuge of liberty and justice has won us esteem in the world; men who despoil that vision may lose us the comradeship of millions who yearn for liberty.

Those who say it is too late for civilized men to confront complex problems thoughtfully are society's eternal undergraduates to whom all human conflict is a kind of wild football game. They always minimize democracy's resources and grow frantic when it fails to score the first touchdown or is penalized for taking too much time in the huddle. But at critical moments in the past the processes of freedom have survived all the counsels of desperation; there is no justification for a national loss of nerve now.

Morris Raphael Cohen, the beloved philosopher, wrote nearly twenty years ago:

> When the communists tell me that I must choose between their dictatorship and fascism, I feel that I am offered the choice between being shot and being hanged. It would be suicidal for liberal civilization to accept this as exhausting the field of human possibility. I prefer to hope that the present wave of irrationalism and of fanatical intolerance will recede and that the great human energy which manifests itself in free thought will not perish. Often before, it has emerged after being swamped by passionate superstitions. There is no reason to feel that it may not do so again.

Amen.

# Index

332

Roosevelt, Franklin D., Jr., **216**
Roosevelt, Theodore, 39
Rosenberg, Ethel, 258
Rosenberg, Julius, 258
Rosenwald, Marion, 161
Ross, Carl, 94
Ross, Don, 21, 22
Ross, Harold, 255, 256
Rovere, Richard, 131, 283
Rushmore, Howard, 251, 255, 258, 264, 266, 272, 280, 282, 305, 306, 307, 312

Sann, Paul, 243
Santayana, George, 48
Saulnier, Raymond J., 60
Schiff, Dorothy, 237, 239, 250, 253, 256, 257, 304
Schine, G. David, 7, 264, 266, 283
Schlesinger, Arthur, Jr., 204, 213, 243, 257, 260, 261
Scripps, E. W., 165
Scripps-Howard newspapers, 158, 165, 169, 175, 237
Seabury Committee, 41
Senate Finance Committee, 40
Senate Foreign Relations Committee, 261
Severing, Carl, 14
Shannon, William V., 265, 266
Sherman, Harry, 292
Shishkin, Boris, 213
Silone, Ignazio, 35
Sirkin, Abraham, 75
Smith Act, 67, 68, 149, 244
Socialist Party, 41, 42
*Social Justice*, 174
Sokolsky, George, 243
Southern Methodist, 85
*Soviet Russia Today*, 122
Spanish Republic, 234
Sparkman, John J., 262
*Spectator*, 4, 6, 21–26, 29, 31, 34, 40–42, 44, 49, 50, 52, 53, 60, 62, 63, 65–67, 73–77, 237
Stalin, Joseph, 16, 104, 115, 116, 118, 122, 123, 142, 143, 146, 148, 150, 205, 211, 218, 234, 245, 274
Starobin, Joseph, 105–108, 122, 149, 150, 223
Starobin, Norma, 105

State Department, 32, 90, 179, 197, 207, 237, 273, 310
Staunton Military Academy, 22
Stearns, Harold, 39
Steffens, Lincoln, 38, 39
Steinhardt, Laurence A., 222
Stevenson, Adlai, 238n., 256, 257, 260, 261, 270
Stewart, Maxwell, 138
Stimson, Henry L., 14
Stolberg, Benjamin, 4
Stone, Harlan F., 41
Stone, I. F., 140, 153
Strachey, John, 36, 37, 39, 44, 54, 60
Strack, Celeste, 85, 93, 95
Streit, Clarence K., 14
*Student Advocate*, The, 85, 86, 93, 94
Student League for Industrial Democracy, 84, 85
Surine, Don, 3, 4, 6, 266
Swarthmore College, 85
Symington, Stuart, 296, 303, 306–309, 313

Tammany Hall, 41, 42, 123
Tass, 122
Taylor, Glenn, 232, 233
Taylor, Horace, 48
Teachers Union, 212
Thackrey, Ted, 237–239
Thomas, J. Parnell, 273
Thomas, Norman, 4, 23, 40, 41, 74, 120
Thomas, R. J., 199
*Time* Magazine, 125, 157, 159, 256
Tito, Marshal, 150, 231
Townsend Harris High School, 17, 18
Transport Workers Union, 170, 171
Treasury Department, 190, 191, 193, 197, 198, 276
Trilling, Lionel, 20
Truman, Harry S., 6, 203, 206, 207, 227, 238, 239, 256, 270, 277
Tudor, Charles, 158
Tugman, William M., 301n.
Tugwell, Rexford, 44, 231
Tyler, Gus, 92

Un-American Activities Committee, 273, 274